New Media Language

'What is the relationship between the media we consume and the language we use? In this book, academics and media practitioners come together to offer their views. The result is a book that is hugely diverse, always thought-provoking, and very entertaining. It functions both as an accessible introduction to the study of sociolinguistics and the media, and makes a real contribution to the field.'

Caroline Bassett, University of Sussex, UK

New Media Language brings leading media figures and scholars together to debate the shifting relations between today's media and contemporary language.

From newspapers and television to email, the internet and text messaging, there are ever increasing media conduits for the news. This book investigates how developments in world media have affected, and been affected by, language. Exploring a wide range of topics, from the globalization of communication to the vocabulary of terrorism and the language used in the wake of 11 September, *New Media Language* looks at the important and wide-ranging implications of these changes. From Malcolm Gluck on wine writing to Naomi Baron on email, the authors provide authoritative and engaging insights into the ways in which language is changing and, in turn, changes us.

With a foreword by Simon Jenkins, *New Media Language* is essential reading for anyone with an interest in the language of today's complex and expanding media.

Contributors: Jean Aitchison, John Ayto, Naomi S. Baron, Allan Bell, Alexander Bergs, Douglas Biber, Deborah Cameron, John Carey, Martin Conboy, Catherine Evans Davies, Malcolm Gluck, David Hendy, Angela Kesseler, Robin Tolmach Lakoff, Diana M. Lewis, Nuria Lorenzo-Dus, Yibin Ni, Alan Partington, John Simpson, Raymond Snoddy, Jennifer M. Wei.

Jean Aitchison is Rupert Murdoch Professor of Language and Communication at the University of Oxford. Her publications include *Words in the Mind: An Introduction to the Mental Lexicon* (3rd edn, 2003), *Language Change: Progress or Decay?* (3rd edn, 2001) and *The Articulate Mammal* (Routledge, 4th edn, 1998). **Diana M. Lewis** is a research assistant in the Faculty of English Language and Literature at the University of Oxford. She has published research on language change and variation.

New Media Language

**Edited by Jean Aitchison and
Diana M. Lewis**

Routledge
Taylor & Francis Group

LONDON AND NEW YORK

First published 2003 by Routledge
11 New Fetter Lane, London EC4P 4EE

Simultaneously published in the USA and Canada by Routledge
29 West 35th Street, New York, NY 10001

Routledge is an imprint of the Taylor & Francis Group

© 2003 Jean Aitchison and Diana M. Lewis
Typeset in Perpetua by The Running Head Limited, www.therunninghead.com
Printed and bound in Great Britain by Biddles Ltd, Guildford and King's Lynn

British Library Cataloguing in Publication Data
A catalogue record for this book is available from the British Library

Library of Congress Cataloging in Publication Data
A catalogue record for this book has been requested

ISBN 0–415–28303–5 (hbk)
ISBN 0–415–28304–3 (pbk)

Contents

PART II Modes of the media

PART III Representations and models

Contributors

Jean Aitchison is Rupert Murdoch Professor of Language and Communication at the University of Oxford. She is the author of several books, including *Language Change: Progress or Decay?* (3rd edn, 2001) and *Words in the Mind: An Introduction to the Mental Lexicon* (3rd edn, 2003).

John Ayto is a lexicographer. He is the author of several books, including *The Oxford Dictionary of Slang* (1998) and *Twentieth Century Words* (1999).

Naomi S. Baron is a professor at American University, Washington, DC. She is the author of several books, including *Alphabet to Email: How Written English Evolved and Where it's Heading* (2000).

Allan Bell is Professor of Language and Communication at Auckland University of Technology. He was previously a journalist and he is the author of *The Language of News Media* (1991) and co-editor of *Approaches to Media Discourse* (1998).

Alexander Bergs is an assistant professor in the English Language and Linguistics Department at the Heinrich-Heine University, Düsseldorf. He is the author of *Modern Scots* (2001).

Douglas Biber is Regents' Professor in the Department of English at Northern Arizona University. He is the author of *Variation Across Speech and Writing* (1988) and co-author of *The Longman Grammar of Spoken and Written English* (1999).

Deborah Cameron is Professor of Languages and head of the School of Culture, Language and Communication at the Institute of Education, University of London. She is the author of several books, including *Good to Talk? Living and Working in a Communication Culture* (2000) and *Working with Spoken Discourse* (2001).

John Carey is Emeritus Merton Professor of English Literature at the University of Oxford. He is the chief book reviewer for *The Sunday Times*, author of *The Intellectuals and the Masses: Pride and Prejudice among the Literary Intelligentsia, 1880–1939* (1992) and editor of *The Faber Book of Reportage* (1987).

Martin Conboy is a lecturer at the Surrey Institute of Art and Design University College. He has published research in both media studies and film studies and is the author of *The Press and Popular Culture* (2002).

Catherine Evans Davies is an associate professor of linguistics in the Department of English at the University of Alabama. She has published research on cross-cultural communication and discourse and has research interests in media language.

Malcolm Gluck is wine correspondent of *The Guardian* newspaper. He has written twenty-three books on wine including the annual best-selling wine guide *Superplonk*.

David Hendy is a lecturer in the School of Media, Arts and Design at the University of Westminster. He is the author of *Radio in the Global Age* (2000) and is writing a social and cultural history of BBC Radio Four for Oxford University Press.

Angela Kesseler has lectured in the English Department at the Heinrich-Heine University, Düsseldorf, and currently teaches full time at a secondary school near Cologne while working on her PhD.

Robin Tolmach Lakoff is a professor at the University of California at Berkeley. Among her several books are *Talking Power: The Politics of Language in our Lives* (1990) and *The Language War* (2000).

Diana M. Lewis is a research assistant in the Faculty of English Language and Literature at the University of Oxford. She has published research on language change and variation.

Nuria Lorenzo-Dus is a lecturer at the University of Wales, Swansea. She has published research in language studies, including media discourse and intercultural communication.

Yibin Ni is a lecturer on the University Scholars Programme at the National University of Singapore. He has research interests in media language.

Alan Partington is an associate professor at the University of Camerino. He is the author of *The Linguistics of Political Argument: The Spin-Doctor and the Wolf-Pack at the White House* (2003).

John Simpson is a Fellow of Kellogg College, Oxford. He is Chief Editor of the *Oxford English Dictionary*, and co-author of *The Oxford Dictionary of Modern Slang* (1992).

Raymond Snoddy is Media Editor of *The Times* and author of *The Good, the Bad and the Unacceptable: The Hard News about the British Press* (1992).

Jennifer M. Wei is a professor at Soochow University, Taipei. She is the author of *Virtual Missiles: Metaphors and Allusions in Taiwanese Political Campaigns* (2001).

Acknowledgements

The editors are very grateful to the Faculty of English Language and Literature at the University of Oxford and News International for funding the conference on Language, the Media and International Communication which gave rise to this volume. The people who have helped with the conference and with this book are too numerous to list, but special thanks must go to Paul Burns, Kate Flint, Godfrey Hodgson and Gillian Reynolds.

The editors and publishers gratefully acknowledge permission to reproduce copyright material from the following: the BBC for permission to use documents from their Written Archives Centre (chapter 7); the Rowman and Little-field Publishing Group for permission to use material from *Virtual Missiles* (chapter 13).

'Waiting for *The Times*' by Benjamin Robert Haydon (1786–1846). Reproduced by permission of Times Newspapers Limited.

Foreword

Simon Jenkins

The media never rest. Their various modes are in perpetual circulation. Consulted, scanned and read in every country and on every continent, they are a vital means of communication in the modern world. Sometimes criticized or even abused, they are also refreshed and renewed as they accomplish multiple tasks.

Yes those who rely on the media should be aware of their changing character. They must learn to ride the tiger of these fascinating changes. More and more various modes emerge each year.

The essays in this book are a user's manual. They trace the evolution of modern media emerging in new places with new purposes. These essays span the world. They are in English, though, as some point out, English is not the inevitable language of the global future.

Yet reading these essays, I am left with a sense of awe. In this collection we read of the struggle to embrace both journalistic brevity and professional verbosity. We hear about the role of spin doctors, bureaucrats, chat-show hosts, emailers, wine writers, marriage counsellors and political cirumlocutors. We hear how people inform one another and talk to each other, via the media.

The media do more than nurture and guard diversity. They are guardians of tolerance itself.

Introduction

Jean Aitchison and Diana M. Lewis

In recent decades, the media have seen an unprecedented amount of change, in quantity, technology, and wider public participation. New media modes have come to the forefront: newspapers and radio have been joined by television and the internet. The speed of transmission has increased, and many more readers/viewers participate both passively, and actively.

A flood of publications has attempted to analyse the media in recent years. Some of these have explored underlying aims and attitudes: a recurring, and traditional, theme has been possible ways in which the media might be misleading its readers/viewers (e.g. Fowler *et al.* 1979; Fowler 1991). Relatively few have investigated the language of the media in any depth – surprisingly perhaps, since language is at the core of media communication. Even visual modes, such as television and billboards, are interwoven with speech, writing and sign.

But all this is changing. This book arose out of a conference at the University of Oxford on Language, the Media and International Communication (April 2001) and contains selected conference papers, together with other contributions. The contributors include both academics (the majority) and journalists – both analysts and practitioners need to be combined to achieve a balanced overview – and some contributors have a foot in both camps.

The overall aim is to explore current-day media language, and how it has changed, or is changing, and how this affects our view of the world. Also, to look at the reverse, at how the media may be affecting language. Of course, in all this, language is inevitably interwoven with broader trends and issues.

Four topics provide the cornerstones of the book, and these make up the four sections. Part I, 'Modern media discourse', contains chapters which outline and discuss how media communication has changed in recent years. Part II, 'Modes of the media', explores various ways in which media discourse is realized at the current time. Part III, 'Representations and models', focuses on the way the representation of particular topics can influence the perceptions of readers or the audience. Part IV, 'The effect of the media on language', looks at ways in which the needs of media might be affecting our speech or written records.

Each part therefore has a separate main theme. However, in another way, the sections overlap, in that certain key points recur. Above all, two paradoxes emerge – or perhaps contrasting trends may be a more accurate description, as opposing forces pull in different directions.

Globalization versus fragmentation may be the most noticeable two-way tug. News reports leap across the globe in seconds, and this has resulted in some similarities in media styles across widely separated geographical regions. In other cases, the reverse has happened, the immensity of the world has led to a tightening of small-scale networks, resulting in some fragmentation, as people try to maintain local ties and their own identity.

This trend is by no means new. Near the beginning of the twentieth century, the linguist Ferdinand de Saussure noted that parochialism and the desire to break away were contrary but pervasive tendencies in language: 'Dans toute masse humaine deux forces agissent sans cesse, simultanément et en sens con-traires: d'une part l'esprit particulariste, l'"esprit de clocher"; de l'autre, la force d'"intercourse", qui crée les communications entre les hommes'[1] (Saussure 1915/1968: 281). And global traumas have long been personalized by journal-ists. A major air crash, for example, is routinely reported as an event worthy of world-wide notice, while at the same time reporters try to make the tragedy vivid by highlighting the fate of innocent individuals: 'One little shoe is all that was left of flight 999' is a journalistic cliché. But the contrast between the global and the personal has become more pronounced in recent years, and so has a related tug between conformity and individualization.

Linguistic expansion versus language compression is a second prevalent con-tradiction. Extended reporting of major events is now the norm. Column inches have increased, and newspaper pages have multiplied. Numerous extra links are available on the web, so that multiple aspects of a story can be explored. Television reports can be accessed round the clock. Yet at the same time, compression of information is a major feature. Headlines summarize a whole event in a few words, and dense noun phrases pack a variety of descrip-tive facts into a small portion of a sentence.

These conflicting trends have become more noticeable recently, as revealed by the chapters in this volume, which together provide a fresh look at the directions in which media discourse is moving.

Note

1 'Among humans, two forces operate continuously, simultaneously, and in opposite directions: on one hand is localism, the "*esprit de clocher*"; on the other, the
pull of interaction, which builds communications among people.'

References

Fowler, R. (1991) *Language in the News: Discourse and Ideology in the Press*, London:
Routledge.
Fowler, R., Hodge, B., Kress, G. and Trew, T. (1979) *Language and Control*, London:
Routledge.
Saussure, F. de (1915/1968) *Cours de linguistique générale*, Paris: Payot.

Part I

Modern media discourse

This section contains chapters which outline and discuss how media communication has changed in recent years.

Bell shows how changes in technology have affected journalistic practice. He illustrates this by outlining media reports of two expeditions to the South Pole, almost a century apart: Captain Scott's in 1912 and Peter Hillary's in 1999. In each era, the remoteness of Antarctica created challenges for contemporary technologies. Over the years, the main medium changed, from newspapers to television, and the lapse of time between an event and its reporting shrank dramatically, from months to minutes – though the need for scoops and keeping to deadlines remained constant.

Cameron suggests that discourse styles have spread across different cultures, even when separate languages are used. An appearance of friendliness and informality seems to be a goal which transcends the languages concerned.

Lakoff discusses whether political and other types of public discourse have grown coarser and less civil. Concern has been expressed, particularly in America, over apparently deepening levels of bitterness between members of each political party and their adversaries. A growing number of issues are found in which one side feels that the other is unwilling to listen, and words felt to be vulgar are thought to be on the increase. Taking a hostile position is perceived to be smarter and more interesting than seeking out mutual agreement. When these concerns were examined, Lakoff found that hostile confrontations were by no means new, though the style in which these hostilities were expressed had shifted in recent years.

Snoddy examines a number of widespread beliefs about the media which turn out to be groundless myths. For example, he debunks the predictions that traditional newspapers are about to fade away, that English will become the dominant language of the internet, and that globalization will lead to sameness.

Conboy investigates the language of the tabloid press. He outlines the development of a vernacular idiom, and the compression of the world into oversimple conceptual and linguistic categories such as punks, nuts and perverts.

1 Poles apart

Globalization and the development of news discourse across the twentieth century[1]

Allan Bell

Introduction

In this chapter, I take the media reporting of two expeditions to the South Pole as a case study in the development of news discourse across the twentieth century. The expeditions are those under Robert Falcon Scott (1910–13) and Peter Hillary (1998–9). They are parallel stories of exploration and hardship from the beginning and end of the twentieth century. The ways in which their news reached the world illustrate three related issues in the globalization of international communication:

1 how technology changed the time and place dimensions of news delivery across the twentieth century (e.g. how fast the news is received, and through what medium)
2 the consequent and concomitant shifts in news presentation (e.g. written versus live televized coverage)
3 associated changes in how humans have understood time and place across the century – that is, the reorganization of time and place in late modernity (Giddens 1991; Bell 1999).

The remote location of Antarctica offers a specific advantage to these case studies: it stretches to the limits the technologies of communication and transport of the particular era, thus illustrating the boundaries of what is possible in news communication at the different periods.

The chapter's theme is the way in which time and place are being reconfigured in contemporary society, and the role played in that process by changing communications technology, journalistic practice and news language. *When* is a defining characteristic of the nature of news, a major compulsion in news-gathering procedures, and a determinant of the structure of news discourse (Bell 1995). News time is time in relation to place: what matters is the fastest news from the most distant – or most important – place (cf. Schudson 1987).

I will track the changes in technology and the reorganization of time/place across the twentieth century, using as timepoints the New Zealand coverage of the outcomes of these polar expeditions.

Captain Scott: 1912–13

The British expedition led by Captain Robert Falcon Scott reached the South Pole on 18 January 1912. They hauled their own sledges 1,000 miles across the world's severest environment from their base in McMurdo Sound on the edge of the Antarctic continent south of New Zealand. They found that the Norwegian, Roald Amundsen, had reached the Pole just a month before them.

On the return journey Scott and his party died well short of their base, the last of them on or after 29 March 1912. They were found eight months later by a search party sent out as soon as the passing of the Antarctic winter allowed travel. The relief party also found the detailed diary which Scott kept nearly to the last to tell the story of the calamitous journey.

News of their gaining the Pole and eventual fate did not reach the rest of the world until a year after it happened. In February 1913, the expedition's relief ship *Terra Nova* put in to a small New Zealand coastal town and telegraphed the news in secret to London. Local reporters pursuing the story were rebuffed. The news was then circulated from London and published in the world's newspapers on 12 February 1913, including in the *New Zealand Herald*, the country's largest daily. This became the archetypal late-imperial story of heroism for Britain and the Empire, which stood on the verge of the Great War that would signal the end of their pre-eminence.

The front page of the *Herald* on 12 February 1913 (Figure 1.1) carries the same masthead in the same type as is used today, but the rest of the page is totally different – eight columns of small-type classified advertisements. The advertisements carry through the first six pages of the paper.

News begins on page 7 and in this issue is dominated by the Scott story. There are some two pages of coverage, nearly half the news hole, split into a score of short pieces with headlines such as:

> HOW FIVE BRAVE EXPLORERS DIED
> HEROES LIE BURIED WHERE THEY DIED:
>   A TENT THEIR ONLY SHROUD
> CAPTAIN SCOTT'S LAST MESSAGE TO THE PUBLIC

The stories cover the search for Scott's party, reaction from other Antarctic explorers such as Amundsen, background on earlier expeditions and commentary on the fatalities. Two characteristics of the coverage appear here which are

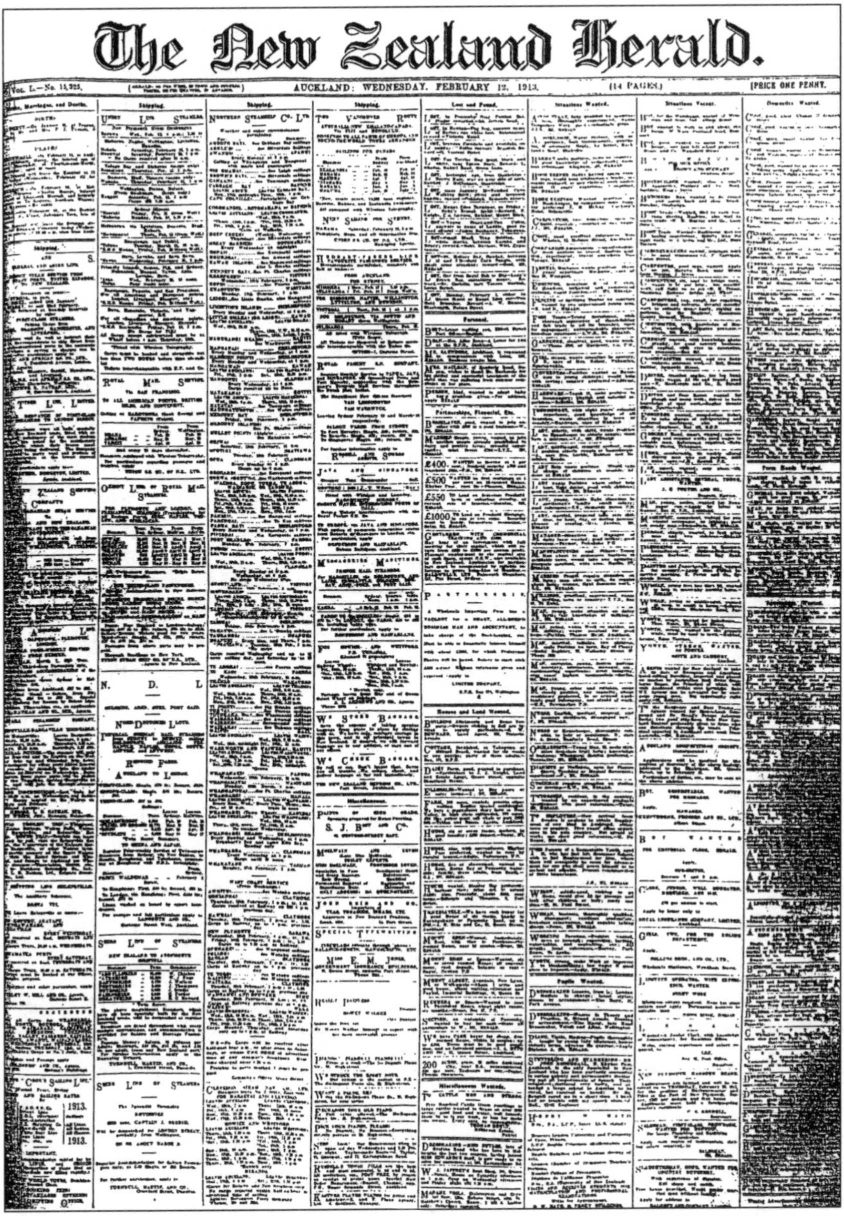
The New Zealand Herald.

VOL. L.—No. 15,325. AUCKLAND: WEDNESDAY, FEBRUARY 12, 1913. [14 PAGES.] [PRICE ONE PENNY.

Figure 1.1 *New Zealand Herald*, 12 February 1913, front page.

echoed again in the stories later in the century – first, nationalism as shown in the imperial geography of news. The information of Scott's demise was sent to London from New Zealand, released in London, and only then transmitted back for publication in the New Zealand press. Second is the motif of the waiting wife – on 12 February Kathleen Scott was on a ship between San Francisco and New Zealand, coming to meet her husband on his return. She did not receive the news of his death till a week after it was public, when the ship came close enough to one of the Pacific islands to receive telegraph transmissions.

So we have here a 'what-a-story' in Tuchman's terms (1978), dominating the news of the day – although not of course bumping the advertisements off the front page. In terms of the categories of news discourse which I use to analyse stories (see Bell 1991, 1998; cf. van Dijk 1988), all the central elements of time, place, actors, action and so forth are present.

The most obvious differences to a modern newspaper are visual – the absence of illustration, the small type even for headlines, the maintenance of column structure, and so on. What differs from later news discourse structure is that in 1913 the information was scattered among a myriad of short stories. Each sub-event has a separate story, which contemporary coverage in this kind of newspaper would now tend to incorporate into fewer, longer stories. All the information is there, and the categories of the discourse are the same, but the way they are realized and structured has shifted.

Turning from the general tenor of the paper and its coverage in 1913, we can focus on the specifics of the lead story, particularly its headlines (Figure 1.2). There are ten decks of headlines – not something one would see in a newspaper at the start of the twenty-first century. This is an extreme example because of the scale of the story, but five decks were not uncommon in the *Herald* at this period. The headlines are in fact telling the story. In some cases they refer to other, sidebar stories separate from the story above which they are placed. By contrast the modern headline usually derives entirely from the lead sentence of the story below it (Bell 1991), and certainly not from any information beyond the body copy of that story. That is, there is a qualitative shift in this aspect of news discourse structure across the century, from multiple decks of headlines outlining the story, to one to three headlines which are derivable from the lead sentence, with the story being told in the body copy.

The first striking thing in these headlines is an omission – they do not tell us that Scott reached the South Pole. No headline anywhere in the coverage in fact says that he reached his goal. The story is in the party's perishing – and it has remained so. Let us assume that a contemporary newspaper would run a ten-deck headline like this. How would today's headline writer edit these into contemporary style?

DEATH IN ANTARCTIC

The modern subeditor would have no problem with this: it could as easily be used today as a century ago.

DEATH IN ANTARCTIC

FATE OF CAPT. SCOTT AND PARTY

THRILLING OFFICIAL NARRATIVE.

MISFORTUNE FOLLOWS MISFORTUNE.

EVANS DIES FROM ACCIDENT.

OATES SEVERELY FROSTBITTEN.

DIES THAT OTHERS MIGHT PROCEED.

IN A BLIZZARD FOR NINE DAYS.

SHORTAGE OF FUEL AND FOOD.

A DEPOT ONLY ELEVEN MILES AWAY.

Figure 1.2 New Zealand Herald, 12 February 1913, p. 8.

FATE OF CAPT. SCOTT AND PARTY

The honorific *Capt.* would be deleted, especially in this archaic abbreviated form, and *party* in this sense falls into disuse during the century. The *Herald's* coverage of Peter Hillary's 1999 expedition refers to *the group* and Hillary's *team-mates*. It does use *party* but only in historical reference to Scott's expedition. There is thus an intertextuality here by which the press uses the vocabulary of reporting from Scott's own era when referring to Scott, rather than the labelling current a century later.

THRILLING OFFICIAL NARRATIVE

This is an impossible headline nowadays – lexically because *thrilling* and *narrative* (meaning 'news story') are both words of an earlier era, but more strikingly because of a shift in media and public consciousness. A century later *thrilling* and *official* can only be heard as mutually contradictory or ironical. Perhaps more tellingly, the concept of *official narrative* has shifted its significance. In 1913 it self-presents as the authoritative account of what really happened. The many stories about the Scott expedition published by the *Herald* on this day are sourced as 'copyrighted official accounts', the description clearly intended to reinforce their authority. In the twenty-first century such a labelling characterizes one voice – the official – among others. After a century of growing media and public scepticism towards official accounts, the undertone is that the 'official line or story' is to be regarded with suspicion. There has been a sea-change here in public and media attitudes towards authority and news sources.

MISFORTUNE FOLLOWS MISFORTUNE

Too 'soft' a headline for the press nowadays. It lacks hard facts, the repetition of *misfortune* wastes words, and the word is in any case too long. Linguistically it is the antithesis of modern headlining.

EVANS DIES FROM ACCIDENT

This would be made more specific, the multisyllabic word would again be rejected, and the temporal conjunction replace the resultative, because the temporal sequence is now taken to imply the causation – 'Evans dies after fall'.

OATES SEVERELY FROSTBITTEN

Severely would be deleted as unnecessary detail.

DIES THAT OTHERS MIGHT PROCEED

This sentence would become rather 'dies to save others'. The complementizer *that* plus subjunctive is archaic, giving way to the infinitive as a purpose clausal structure. *Proceed* again is nineteenth-century lexicon – 'continue' or 'keep going' would be preferred.

IN A BLIZZARD FOR NINE DAYS

Modern headlines do not start with a preposition, and this one would need a verb – 'stranded' perhaps. The rather static *in* would be replaced with more of an indication of agency – 'by'. The article goes, and the preposition in the time adverbial is not required. The end result would be no shorter, but much more action-oriented and dramatic – 'stranded nine days by blizzard'.

SHORTAGE OF FUEL AND FOOD

As a headline, this is too wordy to be contemporary. *Fuel and food* would be combined as 'supplies'.

A DEPOT ONLY ELEVEN MILES AWAY

Again, the article would go (even though in this case there is some semantic loss – the zero article could be reconstructed as definite not indefinite: '*the* depot'). Perhaps a verb would be introduced, and the order might be flipped to keep the locational focus on Scott rather than the depot – '(stranded) just 11 miles from depot'.

Looking at the changes our mythical modern headline editor would have made, we can see both linguistic and social shifts:

(a) The ideological frame has changed – there is no longer just *the* 'official narrative', but the official becomes one account among others.
(b) The discourse structure has moved from multiple-decked headlines which almost tell the story, to single, short, telegraphic headlines which summarize the lead sentence.
(c) The lexicon has moved on. Some words strike as archaic less than 100 years later, for others length makes them out of place in a headline and they are replaced by shorter, punchier items.
(d) The syntax also has tightened. Function words drop out, there is a shift to emphasize action and agency through 'by' and the introduction of verbs. An entire clausal structure ('that' + subjunctive) has become obsolete.

Journalistically speaking, then, the news has become harder, the language tighter.

Peter Hillary: 1998–1999

Nearly a century later, on 26 January 1999, the three-person Iridium Ice Trek arrived at the South Pole. They took eighty-four days to pull their sleds nearly 1,500 km from Scott Base in McMurdo Sound. Their explicit aim was to re-create Scott's man-hauled journey to the Pole, and to complete the trek back. Their leader was Peter Hillary, son of Sir Edmund Hillary whose expedition reached the Pole in 1958, and a significant mountaineer and adventurer in his own right.

The 1999 polar expedition was named for its sponsor, the ill-fated communications company Iridium. The team recorded a video diary of the journey as they went, and Peter Hillary commentated the daily progress of the expedition by satellite phone to the media. Their arrival at the Pole was videoed by Americans living at the polar station. The next day they flew back to Scott Base, having already decided to abandon the return journey on foot because of hardship and the lateness of the season.

The expedition arrived at the Pole at 5.17 p.m., and the world heard of their arrival within minutes. An hour after they got there, Peter Hillary was sitting on a sledge at the South Pole doing a live audio-interview on television and talking to his wife back home in New Zealand.

The main television evening news programmes in New Zealand go to air at 6 p.m. Early in this night's programme, *One Network News* (on the channel which has most of the New Zealand audience) announced that Hillary was about to arrive at the Pole and carried an interview with their reporter at Scott Base. At 6.20 p.m., a third of the way into the hour-long programme, news of the arrival was confirmed and Judy Bailey, one of the two news-anchors, conducted a live telephone interview with Hillary:

Bailey	And joining us now live by phone from the South Pole is Peter Hillary: Peter, congratulations to you all. Has it been worth it?
Hillary	Oh look it's – I must say having got here – ah – to the South Pole – everything seems worth it, Judy. I'm sitting on my sled at exactly ninety degrees south, it's nearly thirty degrees below zero, but I wouldn't – I wouldn't want to be anywhere else. It's just fantastic.
Bailey	Peter, how are you going to celebrate this wonderful achievement down there?
Hillary	Well I must say I think under different circumstances it could be very difficult but the Americans at the South Pole station have been most hospitable. About a hundred of them came out and

cheered us as we arrived at the Pole and they've given us a wonderful meal. They're making us feel very very much at home.
Look it's um – I don't think it's going to be any difficulty whatso-
ever. It's just wonderful to be here.

Bailey   Wonderful.

Here we are in a different era. Hillary is sitting at the Pole talking live to New
Zealand. The coverage gives the impression that the timing of the expedition's
arrival may even have been orchestrated for television, or at least that Hillary
was urged to get there in time so this could be carried live, because by the
next night the story would be dead.

Nationalism runs strong in the story. The anchor enthuses over Hillary's
achievement, lets her hands fall to the desk in delighted emphasis, and exhausts
the lexicon of ingroup self-congratulation (she and Hillary produce *wonderful*
four times in the last few lines of the transcript).

The Pole – one of the most hostile environments on earth – is also domesticated in this coverage. This is encapsulated in Peter Hillary's phrasing about
the hospitality of the Americans at the station – *They're making us feel very very
much at home.* The domestication deepens later in the news programme when
the other news-anchor, John Hawkesby, does a live interview with both Peter
Hillary at the Pole (by phone) and his wife, Yvonne Oomen, live on camera at
home in New Zealand. This is an extreme example of the private mingling
with the public (cf. Giddens 1991):

Hawkesby Peter's able to listen to you at the moment. Would you like – do
          you mind us eavesdropping if you just like to say to him –
Oomen   Oh no, that's fine. Darling, congratulations, I'm so proud of
          you. It's just wonderful.
Hillary   Oh look, I'm delighted to be here and I'm – I'm – ah – just glad
          to be talking to you – in fact I've – I partially did it for you too
          darling.
Oomen   I know, I know.

Publicly-oriented clichés – *delighted to be here* echoes Hillary's repeated phras-
ings throughout the interview – mix with the very private: *I partially did it for
you too darling – I know, I know.* There are catches in the couple's voices as they
address each other direct. The sense of voyeurism becomes acute, and during
the interview Hawkesby himself refers three times to this embarrassment.

The interviews are a different kind of coverage, largely lacking in informational content. They abound in clichés, focusing on the phatic and affective.

Yvonne Oomen is cast in the waiting wife role, just as was Kathleen Scott at the beginning of the century. It is a role she is clearly prepared to play, while it is equally evident from her on-air performance that she is a capable and independent woman (as was Kathleen Scott, according to the biographies).

Conclusion

These two cases are revealing about change and continuity in time and place, and their relationship across the twentieth century. News values are the same at a macro level while different at the micro level. Nationalism for example is obtrusive in both cases, but its object shifts from the self-assured, late-imperial character of the British Empire at the start of the twentieth century, to the rather brashly media-driven celebration of a local New Zealand hero at the end of the twentieth century. The waiting wife is part of both scenarios, showing that the underlying domestic construction of such undertakings changed little over the century.

However, the way in which the person of the waiting wife has to behave has changed, along with the positioning of the audience, as part of the social impact of the reorganization of time and space. For the newsworthy, exposure is now closer and more real – Yvonne Oomen is much more under scrutiny than Kathleen Scott was. For the audience, we are more voyeuristic, intruding on private lives in real time, not with the distancing of interview and the timelapse until publication. We are close up, but still of course at a distance. The hostile environment is presented as domesticated, and domestic life is introduced into the life of the expedition.

News practice also shows a mix of change and continuity. The deadline and the scoop drive the news in both periods, but the scooping medium changes from press to television. There is time compression, with the lapse between an event and its reporting shrinking exponentially from months to minutes. The immediacy of the coverage grows in another sense, with the move from the arm's-length character of print reporting, to television's display of events 'as if you were there'. True live coverage is still not quite achieved in 1999 – the arrival at the Pole could not be telecast in real time. And there is a shift from the official handout to the live interview as the basis of news, and from trust in the official handout to reliance on directly media-sourced information.

Accompanying these shifts is a change in news presentation, discourse and language. Newspaper design changes radically, most notably from the placement of classified advertisements to news on the front page. Cross-column headlines and text have increased (in part with the technological shift from letterpress to offset), and photographs have become the norm. The type size has increased. Story structure is reconfigured with the shift from multiple head-lines. There is linguistic compression, especially in the headlines, with function words dropped and the option for shorter, sharper lexical items. Some vocabulary is left behind as archaic. Thus the drive to linguistic compression which has characterized the development of news discourse for more than a century continues to be a major force in changing news language.

Note

1   This chapter is a revision of a plenary lecture presented to the Conference on Language, the Media and International Communication, Oxford, April 2001. An earlier, longer version appeared as Bell (2002) and also covered Sir Edmund Hillary's 1958 expedition. Acknowledgement is made to the *New Zealand Herald* for kind permission to reproduce the excerpts used in the chapter.

References

Bell, A. (1991) *The Language of News Media*, Oxford: Blackwell.
— (1995) 'News time', *Time & Society* 4(3) (special issue on 'Time, culture and representation', ed. S. Allan), London: Sage, 305–28.
— (1998) 'The discourse structure of news stories', in A. Bell and P. Garrett (eds) *Approaches to Media Discourse*, Oxford: Blackwell, 64–104.
— (1999) 'Media language and representations of identity', *Thema's en Trends in de Sociolinguistiek* 3 (*Toegepaste Taalwetenschap in Artikelen* [*Papers in Applied Linguistics*] 62/2), 57–71.
— (2002) 'Dateline, deadline: journalism, language and the reshaping of time and place in the millennial world', in J. E. Alatis, H. E. Hamilton and A.-H. Tan (eds) *Georgetown University Round Table on Languages and Linguistics 2000 – Linguistics, Language, and the Professions: Education, Journalism, Law, Medicine, and Technology*, Washington, DC: Georgetown University Press.
Giddens, A. (1991) *Modernity and Self-identity: Self and Society in the Late Modern Age*, Cambridge: Polity Press.
Schudson, M. (1987) 'When? Deadlines, datelines and history', in R. K. Manoff and M. Schudson (eds) *Reading the News*, New York: Pantheon, 79–108.
Tuchman, G. (1978) *Making News: A Study in the Construction of Reality*, New York: Free Press.
van Dijk, T. A. (1988) *News as Discourse*, Hillsdale, NJ: Lawrence Erlbaum Associates.

2 Modern media myths

Raymond Snoddy

Introduction

The more I think about modern media myths, the more a number of turning points in the media crystallize in my mind, as well as a realization of just how many false predictions there have been, and how many misunderstandings. I take it as an agreed starting point that the modern mass media is the single most important, or at least one of the most important, instruments of language change. Where then is the mass media heading, at what pace, and with what effect on communication and society?

It is very easy to sketch the outlines of an endgame in the world of communications. Technology will one day be so pervasive and so inexpensive that everyone, in the developed world at least, will have the ability to call up on the move every image and fact to a portable device that will combine the characteristics of a computer, television set and telephone. This will of course amount to The Death of Distance.

It seems too harsh to call such an oft-repeated vision of the future, which also carries overtones of The End of History,[1] a media myth. Yet such a prediction might as well be a myth for all it tells us about how quickly we will move to such a reality, or indeed whether we ever will get there at all in such an extreme form. All history suggests that things will not be as linear as that, although there is no question about just how rapidly communications and the media are changing.

Fast growers: digital TV and mobile phones

Two areas changing with unprecedented speed in the United Kingdom, for example, are digital television and mobile phones.

There were, in 2001, more than eight million digital televisions in Britain out of twenty-three million homes, the highest penetration of digital television in the world. With it comes not only more than 200 channels of television, but also access to the internet, home shopping and other forms of interactivity. It is, however, early days in understanding how people use multi-channel television and the new hard-disk-based personal video recorders, and what effect they will have on established channels.

If anything, the march of the mobile phone in the UK – matched in many places – has been even more dramatic, rising from 5.7 million subscribers in 1996 to more than forty million in 2001. But what no one predicted – and this should warn us against making simplistic forecasts – is the importance of short text messaging, particularly for the youth market. Absolutely no one forecast the rise of SMSs (short text messages) to 750 million in December 2000.[2]

The cultural significance should not be underestimated. Who would have thought that 37 per cent of the messages told someone they loved them (see Kesseler and Bergs, this volume), or that 13 per cent told someone they had been dumped. On Valentine's Day 2001, more than 400 people used the Vodafone network to propose marriage. Unfortunately, we do not know how the recipients responded to such a romantic approach or, more puzzling, how Vodafone knew in the first place.

We will probably have to learn to cope with even faster cycles of technological change. But not everything has always been as it seems, and we need to remind ourselves of this before we and some cherished institutions are swept away in a tide of technological determinism.

Survivors: radio and newspapers

One of the fastest growing media remains radio, because it is flexible and personal. For example, the BBC (British Broadcasting Corporation) World Service, which was supposed to be fading away a decade after the end of the Cold War, announced new record listening figures in 2001 of 153 million. For good measure, another expanding area of the media is 'outdoor' (posters/billboards). To the extent that the television audience is fragmenting, so the slack is being taken up by difficult-to-miss media – the vast back-lit poster site in front of your nose as you sit in a traffic jam.

My favourite media myth, though – and for very personal reasons – is the utter failure of newspapers to collapse and disappear as they were supposed to. The long-range forecasts were very precise: newspapers would be gone by the year 2000. Over the years, the potential assassins were seen as first radio, later television and later still the internet.

There was also a less apocalyptic version of this pessimistic forecast from no less a newspaperman than Rupert Murdoch. He believed that by the start of the new century there would be only three national newspapers in the UK. With a slight nod in the direction of self-interest, Murdoch believed there would be a popular daily that looked a lot like *The Sun*, a broadsheet that looked more than a little like *The Times*, and a mid-market paper that would have to be the *Daily Mail*. Amalgamations and consolidation would take care of the rest.

The reality is happily very different. There are still ten national newspapers in the UK, one more – *The Independent* – than there were twenty years ago when Rupert Murdoch made his forecast. In those two decades, circulations have indeed fallen from around sixteen million copies a day to more than thirteen million in 2001 – with most of the drop being suffered by the tabloids. That is quite an achievement, given the scale of the electronic competition. And, of course, paginations have greatly increased with the creation of more supplements than most of us want.

Indeed, broadsheet circulations have actually increased to around 2.8 million, with *The Times* increasing its sales to 720,000, helped by cover price cuts and a wider agenda, and the *Financial Times* close to 500,000, thanks to an ambitious international expansion. The *Financial Times* has also made a massive investment in FT.com (their online venture), including jobs for 100 journalists. The effect so far has been to reinforce the brand of the traditional newspaper, rather than undermine it.

There were a number of related newspaper myths, all of which predicted the end of the traditional newspaper. The first was the Tablet, a portable screen-based device produced in the US. You plugged it into your computer overnight, and the entire contents of your newspaper were downloaded. The Tablet never caught on, although it has its modern counterparts in palm-top computers. Then there was the *Daily Me* from the Media Lab of the Massachusetts Institute of Technology: your own personal newspaper downloaded overnight with your personal preoccupations there on the front page. Computer databases can clearly do that already, but the attraction of newspapers seems to be broader than just the provision of essential information we think we want to know.

Then there is the myth – which actually has more than a touch of reality about it – that young people don't read newspapers. What started out as a defensive experiment and has rapidly turned into a potentially successful business suggests that this need not be an inevitable progress. Every day on the commuting routes of the UK's major cities, you can see thousands of young people who are not readers of conventional newspapers picking up copies of *Metro*, the free daily newspaper. More than 900,000 copies were distributed every weekday in 2001. It amounts to the creation of virtually a new print-based national medium, and just maybe some of those young people on their way to school will graduate to grown-up newspapers.

The biggest myth of all was that the internet would inevitably kill off newspapers and it was only a matter of time. Worried newspaper executives rushed to set up electronic defences as journalists went off to become dot.com millionaires. An occasional one even made it, such as the founder of Moreover.com, a website which gathers together news from publications all over the world. Most have had to come looking for their old jobs back. It is early days yet, but I feel more and more confident in my original suspicion that the internet is not an immediate and obvious substitute for the mass media, however wonderful it may be for telescoping distance and uniting communities of interest around the world, and even for producing a new hybrid language half-way between the informality of speech and the formality of writing (see Baron, this volume).

The future

So far I have been on the relatively safe ground of things that were supposed to happen to the traditional media and have not, at least not yet. Now for the more dangerous stuff – the future.

The extent to which the mass media will be completely mobile in future may also amount to a partial myth, at least compared with the sums of money being invested and the high expectations of those involved.

It is easy to predict the useful bits. News headlines, share prices, football scores, with perhaps clips of the goals, plus fast internet access and easy email use will certainly take off. But will we really choose to watch whole television programmes or movies on handheld communication devices? As always, there is a cross-over between need, convenience and cost.

The main effect so far of the billions spent on third-generation mobile telecommunications licences – £22.5 billion in the UK alone – has been to plunge those who bought them into serious debt and even managerial crisis. And that is before either the networks or the receiving equipment have been created. People may find uses for such sophisticated technology that we have not yet imagined, but it has all still to be proved.

However, if a week is a long time in politics, then a year can be an eternity in communications. Howkins (2001) tells the story of how, in 1999, Telecom, the world's biggest communications fair held in Geneva every four years, was so oversubscribed that the Swiss Tourist Board had to open the city's nuclear shelters to provide sleeping accommodation. More than 190,000 people wanted to see the latest communications developments. It remains to be seen whether such enthusiasm can be sustained.

Another media myth, and a television one this time, is the idea that this is the decade when developed countries will finally leave the analogue world behind, and switch over entirely to digital. In the UK, where there are no fewer than four forms of digital distribution in operation – satellite, digital terrestrial, digital cable and ADSL (Asymmetric Digital Subscriber Line) phone lines – the government would like to switch off analogue between 2006 and 2010. In Ireland there is a fifth, the world's first digital microwave system. There is almost no chance of that switch-off deadline being met, failing massive government investment, and we are going to have to live with an untidy in-between world for much longer than that, perhaps twice as long.

There is no question that digital television is doing well in the UK, partly at least because the digital broadcasters are giving the equipment away for free. It is quite easy to see 50 per cent or even 60 per cent of the population signing up for digital multi-channel. It is not so easy to see what will impress the others with their multi-set analogue television homes, not to mention analogue video recorders, which would all be rendered useless by the switch-over to digital. Will politicians really want to tell millions of voters their television sets will no longer work unless they buy new equipment?

So far, what we have seen is remarkable stability for the main established channels, even in digital homes. Some of the new channels have been taking audience shares of 0.1 per cent. The Independent Television Commission (the regulatory body for commercial television) helpfully points out that in some cases there was an element of rounding up to get to that percentage. Independent Television (ITV), the main commercial channel, has fought back with event television – careful scheduling of large-scale popular and essentially classless programmes such as *Who Wants to Be a Millionaire?* and *Popstars*, the search for, and successful creation of, a chart-topping pop band. ITV has reversed the decline, at least in primetime, and in 2001 had a 38 per cent share.

With personal video systems (such as TiVos) there is the fear that channels will disappear as a concept, and that if everything is pre-recorded and no one watches the advertisements, the finances of commercial television will be completely undermined. I cannot prove it yet, but I suspect the advertising industry will be up to whatever challenge is thrown at it. Early US findings suggest that the ability to record automatically whatever you want tends to encourage viewing of the network channels and their high-profile programmes, and discourage aimless flicking among the endless choices available.

There is another myth that flows from the digital switch-off which could be potentially damaging in the UK and any other country facing similar challenges. The government is rushing ahead with new communications legislation, because naturally it believes its own propaganda that this change will happen this decade. Apart from the further deregulation of ownership rules, the Bill will have at its heart a new all-powerful but light-touch regulatory body – The Office of Communications (Ofcom).

Senior members of existing regulatory bodies have been bending over backwards to embrace the future. So it was in 2001 that the Independent Television Commission (ITC) produced an annual programme review markedly different from anything it had done before. The ITC merely 'noted' that the main current affairs programme on ITV, the leading commercial channel, had not covered some major foreign events and issues such as the Israel–Palestinian conflict or the fiasco of the US presidential elections. Current affairs have become 'problematic' on mainstream channels, according to one TV chief executive,[3] given the amount of television news and analysis already around elsewhere and the intensifying competition for audiences.

Funding

Another interesting issue is the true cost of having a public service broadcasting system in the UK. According to some estimates, the bill comes to as much as £4 billion a year, a figure that equates to a lot of hospitals. Viewers and listeners, as taxpayers, may well ask whether thay are getting the cultural return they have a right to expect. Such a question carries at least the possible implication that, in a multi-channel world of endless choice, the market can provide. Consequently, there may no longer be any need for public service organizations funded by a licence fee like the BBC.

This is another of my media myths – that the market can provide the complete range and diversity of high-quality programming for the entire population. Almost everything, so the argument goes, from arts channels to documentary channels, is available at a price. But for me there is as yet no substitute for public service broadcasting, when properly done, in providing a civilized national discourse, in a tone of voice that respects shared expectations and culture, and retains a core role in the democratic process, above all by having the freedom to produce 'problematic' programmes. This is a view supported by Graham (2000), who suggests that:

> Contrary to what is supposed by many, the case for public service broadcasters in the new world of globalisation and localisation is increased not decreased. In particular as the new technology generates new forms of

market power, the case for broadcasters with distinctly public purposes is enhanced. Moreover as national regulation via legislation becomes less effective, the case for influencing the market via direct provision also becomes stronger rather than weaker.

(Graham 2000: 12)

But even the BBC, with a total revenue of £2.3 billion, does not seem to be exempt from the pressures of competition.

The BBC flagship current affairs programme *Panorama* won a 2001 Broadcasting Press Guild award for a courageous edition called 'Who Bombed Omagh?' which revealed the names of the members of the Real IRA (an armed group based in Northern Ireland) who it says were responsible for those terrible murders. The Real IRA response was a car bomb outside the BBC Television Centre in West London. As far as *Panorama* was concerned, it was unfortunate that 'Who Bombed Omagh?' was the last edition of the programme to go out in its traditional Monday evening slot after more than thirty years. The programmes were shunted to a 10.15 p.m. slot on Sundays where, not surprisingly, the audience is considerably lower. The programme-makers hated it. The BBC executives claimed it was an act of kindness to protect the programme from the full rigours of weekday competition.

Current affairs programming, and its subject matter of how societies work and in whose interest, may indeed be 'problematic', but surely to keep it in mainstream channels at mainstream times is something worth fighting for. The danger is that otherwise, public service broadcasting might end up as another myth, something from a bygone age. Every year the gardening, cookery and makeover programmes seem to encroach further.

The globalization myth

Finally, here are a couple more myths – important myths if they should turn out to be true. One of the biggest myths of all when applied to the media is the globalization myth – that the big Hollywood players, such as Viacom and News Corporation, will dominate the world because they control vast engines of media production that start in Hollywood and ring the world with satellite channels, videos, advertising and merchandizing. In the process, almost casually, a global language, a bland global culture will be created and everything will be sameness.

Of course, channels such as MTV (Music Television) have carried western youth culture to the far corners of the globe, and in 2001 only parts of Greenland and Antarctica remain outside the reach of CNN (Cable Network News).

The interesting fact is that these channels have had to give up, if they ever had them, crude ambitions of global cultural domination. To have a business at all they have had to invest hundreds of millions of dollars creating regional and multi-language editions. Simplistic versions of globalization do not apply when it comes to the media (see Lewis, this volume). Surprising international consolidation certainly will continue, as in the case of Vivendi buying Universal Studios. But the cost of a lack of respect for language and culture can be very high.

Almost the final myth and another really big one – that English will be the dominant language on the internet and virtually everywhere else. Rather, as Cairncross (2001) suggests, English has emerged as 'the necessary standard': the default language, the linguistic equivalent of Windows or the GSM (Global System for Mobile communications) standard. The number of websites in languages other than English appears to be growing at an exponential rate, and although in 2000 half the people who used the internet were American, this proportion is dropping. It may also be in the business interests of the international media tycoons to recognize that there are world languages other than English. The world is moving towards four dominant language groups – Mandarin, English, Spanish and Hindi – it has been argued:

> These four languages have emerged as the leading forces in the world for the foreseeable future. If you are competing in the global media business these forces are irresistible and one ignores them at great peril.[4]

Claims that the world was moving towards a single, global Americanized culture, that would inevitably lead to a drop in standards, are not being borne out.

One final myth needs to be exploded. It is that we are heading for a simple, monochrome, homogenized, endlessly fragmented media that will lose much of its ability to carry and transmit culture. The reality is that increasingly people will be able to choose. They will choose to dip into international channels, and their love affair with Hollywood will not end, although it may be increasingly challenged. But they will also stay loyal to their own indigenous channels in their own languages.

They will use all the gadgets that technology can offer to choose individual programmes they want to watch now, not when some scheduler decides. They will also switch to channels because of brand values and assumptions of what that channel stands for and what kind of programmes are likely to be found there. There will still be big media events, and at least some contribution to the creation and sustaining of a national culture – the importance of the shared experience.

And when we all have multi-channel digital devices, I believe there will still be a need for public service broadcasting to ensure diversity and quality, although it may by then have to be funded in a different way. That's my myth and I intend to stick to it until I have very firm evidence to the contrary.

Notes

1   See Fukuyama (1992).
2   The telecoms figures are all those given by David Edmonds, director general of Oftel, the telecoms regulatory body, in a speech at the Royal Television Society, 20 February 2001.
3   Patricia Hodgson, chief executive of the ITC, speaking at a press briefing.
4   James Murdoch, speaking at the 2000 Edinburgh International Television Festival.

References

Cairncross, Frances (2001) *The Death of Distance 2.0: How the Communications Revolution will Change our Lives*, London: Texere.

Fukuyama, Francis (1992) *The End of History and the Last Man*, London: Hamish Hamilton.

Graham, Andrew (2000) *The Future of Communications: Public Service Broadcasting*, discussion document presented to the Department of Trade and Industry and the Department for Culture, Media and Sport, 3 July 2000, available at <http://www.culture.gov.uk/creative/dti-dcms_graham.PDF> (accessed June 2002)

Howkins, John (2001) *The Creative Economy: How People Make Money from Ideas*, London: Allen Lane.

3 Globalizing 'communication'

Deborah Cameron

Introduction: communication style

The contemporary obsession with regulating the way people talk to one another is discussed in Cameron (2000a). Some of the ways in which service-workers nowadays are required to use the English language to their customers – the scripted salutations, the simulated friendliness, the relentless positive politeness, the perky intonation – are discussed in Cameron (2000b). A Hungarian doctoral student suggested (personal communication) that the style of speech described had also permeated service encounters in Hungary since the fall of communism and the coming of western businesses. Returning to her Budapest home for a visit after a lengthy absence, the student had repeatedly had a curious experience. Transacting business on the phone with someone, or in a shop, the question would suddenly occur to her, 'Am I speaking Hungarian or am I speaking English?'

Of course, she was speaking Hungarian; but the new style of service involved a kind of discourse which radically changed the way Hungarian 'felt'. For instance, Hungarian is among the many languages which grammaticize the distinction between familiar and formal address, and for service encounters the unmarked choice had always been formality. But many organizations in Hungary have adopted the western preference for informal and friendly service, producing utterances which the student heard as violating the rules for using her native tongue.

When people talk about the spread of English, they usually mean one of two things. The first is the adoption of English as a second or additional language by an increasing number of speakers in various parts of the world. 'English' here means the whole language system, though of course it comes in many different varieties, and its global dissemination as a second language is an impetus to the development of new ones. The second thing that often gets discussed is the borrowing of English vocabulary into other languages, so that

English words become nativized, part of other linguistic systems. But what interests me is a third thing: the international diffusion of certain discourse norms from the English-speaking world, which may displace established local ways of interacting *without* displacing local languages as such. It is not a question of telling people 'you should stop speaking your own language and speak English instead'. Rather it is a question of saying, 'by all means use your own language, but according to the cultural norms of an English-speaking society'. The result is the sensation the Hungarian student described – that you are not so much speaking Hungarian with English words in it as the other way round, speaking English but with Hungarian words.

Kubota (2001) provides another example. In Japan, since the 1980s, politicians, businesspeople and pundits of all kinds have advocated change under the banner of *kokusaika*, 'internationalization'. Japanese are exhorted to become more outward-looking, which in this context tends to mean looking towards the west, and especially the USA. The project of internationalization has influenced language teaching. The teaching of English in Japan now places more emphasis on practical communication, and large numbers of English native speakers have been recruited to assist in classrooms. But Kubota reports that internationalization has also affected the teaching of *Japanese* in Japan. It has been argued that the ways of writing traditionally taught in Japanese schools are oblique and illogical compared to the western model. Japanese students should be taught to organize their writing according to the logic which American students learn. Similarly, spoken genres like 'debate' should be taught to Japanese students, in an effort to counteract the supposed Japanese tendency to be more concerned with collective consensus rather than the expression of individual opinions. Kubota points out that these recommendations draw on well-established local beliefs about the uniqueness of Japan, its people and its language. What is new is not the suggestion that Japan is significantly different from the west, it is the suggestion that in an age of global communication, Japanese people need to become more similar to westerners – not just when communicating with foreigners, but also when using Japanese among themselves.

Rules of speaking

What the Hungarian student and Kubota describe could be thought of as a form of prescriptive standardization, involving not grammar or pronunciation but discourse norms for interpersonal communication. The prescriptions focus not on rules of *language* but on what ethnographers of communication call rules of *speaking*, and especially those relating to the interpersonal functions of interaction – things like formality, directness, politeness, the expression of emotional and attitudinal states. The prescribers in this case are not grammarians, lexicographers and elocutionists, but self-described 'communication experts' whose background is usually in psychology or therapy.

One of these experts, Judith Kuriansky, was present when I was invited to discuss my research on communication on the BBC World Service in 1999. There is cross-cultural variation in, say, what degree of directness or level of formality is considered appropriate in a particular kind of talk, I pointed out. Kuriansky replied that this variation constituted an obstacle to effective communication which an increasingly globalized world could not afford. She went on:

> I think it's essential for us to be able – in this global community and as the global community becomes even smaller through the internet and through all kinds of electronics – that we *are* able to communicate . . . It is essential that there be a uniform way of talking, for the economy, for national communications, for exchange of politics and even on the level of individual couples being able to communicate . . . And there are rules for that.
>
> (Transcript of *Outlook,* BBC World Service, August 1999)

So what are the rules propagated by communication experts like Kuriansky? Where do they come from and how are they being disseminated? Some themes recur consistently in prescriptive materials by experts dealing with the subject of interpersonal communication – texts written for professionals like counsellors and social workers, workplace communication training materials for customer-service workers, course materials for accredited programmes of education such as the British National Vocational Qualification, and popular self-help books written for a general audience. Below is a composite picture drawn from all these sources – for what is striking is the *consistency* of the prescriptions addressed to language-users as diverse as caring professionals, supermarket checkout operators, students on vocational courses and readers of pop-psychology books about sex or parenting or marriage. Just as there is little variation in the underlying model of 'good English' we find in grammar and usage guides for different groups – professional writers, school or university students, learners of EFL – so there is little variation in the model of 'good communication' we find in texts devoted to that subject.

The first theme is simply that speech is preferable to silence. An effective or skilled communicator is articulate and fluent; reticence is construed as lack of openness to other people.

The second theme is a preference for directness over indirectness. Effective communication, as the experts define it, does not depend on either the hearer or the context to do the work of producing meaning. Speakers must take responsibility for communicating clearly by performing speech acts on record and directly.

The third theme is a preference for a way of speaking that signals egalitarian social relationships. Even where the participants in an interaction are positioned asymmetrically, as in a job interview or an adult–child interaction, the recommendation is to minimize hierarchy and social distance, by choosing discourse strategies and stylistic markers from the more informal end of the repertoire, and maximizing attention to your interlocutor's positive face (that is, positive self-image, including the desire to be appreciated and approved of; see Brown and Levinson 1987).

The fourth theme is related to this: an emphasis on co-operative as opposed to competitive or agonistic genres of speech. Modern communication experts are about as far as they could be from the old western tradition of rhetoric, in which arguing a case to win was a central and valued skill. Today's ideal communicator is skilled in the arts of negotiation and conflict resolution, and believes that conflict arises mainly from people misunderstanding one another – that is, from a failure of communication – rather than because people have deep-seated conflicts of interest and opinion, or indeed because in some circumstances people *enjoy* verbal conflict.

The fifth theme is the importance accorded by communication experts to verbal self-disclosure, often referred to in the literature as 'sharing'. Emphasis is placed on the ability to verbalize what one is feeling, and to convey emotions clearly using prosodic and paralinguistic resources. Experts stress the importance of sharing your feelings as a mark of your honesty and sincerity.

The prescriptions are very consistent, whether the expert is explaining how to communicate effectively with colleagues in a meeting, customers in a shop or loved ones in more intimate settings, as noted above. This in itself is peculiar: communicative competence as sociolinguists understand it (cf. Hymes 1972) precisely involves being able to *vary* your performance to suit different genres, settings, purposes and addressees. If we investigate patterns of verbal behaviour in any speech community, we typically find differences in the kind of discourse that will be used for playing with a small child, gossiping with friends, deciding on a course of action at a meeting, buying vegetables in a market and offering condolences after a funeral. Yet communication experts often say or imply that certain rules apply across all these different contexts and activity types. You might *say* different things at a market and a funeral, but your way of presenting yourself and relating to your interlocutor would conform to the same ideal: articulate, direct, egalitarian, co-operative, emotionally expressive, honest and sincere. This is presented not just as a linguistic ideal, but implicitly also as a definition of a morally admirable person. Gal (1995) has made the point that judgements on language-use very often have this moral dimension. Even misspelling a word or misplacing an apostrophe can attract moral censure: people may claim it shows the writer is too lazy or inconsiderate to get small details right. In the case of 'good communication', the moral dimension is very overt. In some texts the author says in so many words that silence or emotional inexpressiveness indicates a closed, ungenerous person; indirectness is manipulative; formality is indicative of authoritarian attitudes; arguing or disagreeing is aggressive.

The universality question

The ideal of good communication we find in expert literature, and the ideal of the good person which lies behind it, may be presented as universal, but on inspection it clearly is not. Ethnographic and sociolinguistic research has shown that discourse norms concerning silence, directness, formality, conflict and emotional expression are variable both within cultures and between them. We have plenty of evidence, for example, that in some speech communities, extended silences in conversation are not remarkable. Depending on context, they can signal respect, intimacy and other meanings quite different from the lack of openness communication experts associate with not talking. Indirectness is another very variable phenomenon. There are communities and contexts where a high level of indirectness is not merely tolerated but the norm (see Keenan 1976). There is a copious literature on the way language is used to mark varying social relationships across cultures, and it gives little support to the idea that formality and status-marking must always signal cold, distant and authoritarian attitudes. One context where communication experts stress the importance of constructing equality in discourse is relations between children and parents; but the literature on language socialization shows that child-centred parenting practices, and the associated treatment of children as equal conversational partners, are very far from universal (Schieffelin and Ochs 1986).

The culturally specific assumptions and values that inform expert definitions of good communication appear to have two main sources. In their detail, the norms recommended by many experts are clearly indebted to the practices of various kinds of therapy. The norm of directness, for example, comes from assertiveness training, which was developed by American behaviourist clinicians just after World War II to treat the extreme passivity of institutionalized psychiatric patients. The idea that talking is good for you and silence means resistance, that feelings should be verbalized and 'shared', and that people need continual positive reinforcement, can also be related to the practice of therapy in general.

But if therapy is the immediate source of many of these prescriptions, the deeper source is the culture where therapy has flourished most conspicuously over a long period: the mainstream culture of the USA. It is not difficult to relate the ideal conjured up in texts about good communication – honest, open, direct, co-operative and egalitarian – to the core values of American democracy. One analyst, Carbaugh (1988), has specifically related prevailing norms of good communication to three ideals which he claims are central to America's cultural self-image. They are egalitarian individualism, the belief that every individual is unique and each is of equal worth; freedom of expression, which is seen not only as giving the individual a right to express their opinions but also as placing on them a duty to do so; and what he calls 'righteous tolerance', the obligation to extend to others' freely-expressed opinions the same respect one wants for one's own.

Carbaugh argues that these ideals have been translated into cultural norms for interpersonal communication, basing his argument on a study of one year's output of a then-popular daytime television talk-show, *Donahue*. He observed that the host, Phil Donahue, consistently appealed to norms of individualism, free expression and righteous tolerance in conducting the discussions that took place on his show, and in judging particular contributions as more or less valid. Sometimes Donahue invoked the norms explicitly: if the audience failed to applaud someone who had expressed an opinion generally felt to be repulsive or insane, he would remind them of the individual speaker's right to free expression and the hearer's responsibility to give that individual credit for their 'honesty' and willingness to 'share'. At other times he referred to the norms more implicitly in his responses to what someone else had said. For instance, to a woman who suggested that it was never appropriate for adopted children to have contact with their natural parents, he said: 'no one is going to deny you your position, but the question is, why do you impose it on others?' (Carbaugh 1988: 30). The woman had violated the norm of righteous tolerance by insist-ing that her own view was more than just a personal opinion: it was correct and opposing views were wrong.

Neither I nor Carbaugh is claiming that the kind of talk observed on talk shows is representative or typical of Americans' talk in general. The argument here is not about the complicated empirical reality of people's communicative behaviour, it is about the metadiscourse that informs their ideas about how they should ideally behave. Carbaugh's point is that the norms that prevail on *Donahue* are quite markedly American norms. They appeal to notions of individualism, equality and free expression which are not necessarily shared, or valued in the same way, by all other cultures. Nevertheless, these norms are now being disseminated to many other parts of the world under the guise of promoting more 'effective' communication. The next questions I want to take up are about how and why this is happening.

Dissemination of discourse norms

Researchers who study the process of language standardization usually look for institutions that function, in a particular time and place, as 'focusing' agents. For instance, most historical accounts of the standardization of English would mention the influence of the chancery clerks and eventually the printing press in determining which variety of English would become the basis for a written national standard. It is also evident that since the inception of mass vernacular education, schools have played a key role in reproducing standard languages by teaching children to read and write them. In the case of the current focusing of discourse norms, however, the institutions which are most important are commercial institutions – businesses – and mass-media institutions.

As a result of the economic shifts of globalization, businesses are subject to increasing international competition. In addition, advanced economies are more and more dominated by the provision of services rather than the manufacture of goods. Customer service is what gives a modern company its edge over the competition, and this prompts companies to pay closer attention to how employees communicate, since the way language is used to customers contributes to their judgement of the quality of service. Many companies now require their employees to undergo communication training, and regulate their communicative behaviour on the job. Business communication training has thus become an important location for disseminating discourse norms. And when businesses move into new markets abroad, they take those norms along with them. A McDonald's restaurant in Budapest must serve its customers in Hungarian, but it will be Hungarian spoken according to the same norms of interaction which govern the company's service in Chicago. If the new style proves popular with local customers, some of its characteristics may be imitated by local businesses. Local entrepreneurs may seize the opportunity to set themselves up as consultants, offering advice to local companies which combines the ideas of global communication experts with the consultant's own local knowledge. This is one way in which certain ideologies and practices of communication spread.

Another way in which discourse norms are disseminated is through global mass media. Many of the best-selling English language self-help books in which a model of good communication is presented are either translated or imitated for markets overseas. The talk shows mentioned earlier are another good example. American talk shows are widely shown outside the US, and they often attract large audiences. This may prompt local media networks to develop their own home-grown imitations, with local participants using the local language, but with marked accommodation to the discourse style of the original. Montgomery (1999) has suggested that the norms of informality, emotional openness and sincerity, which increasingly apply to public as well as private discourse, may be reinforced by the dominance of television as a global communication medium (Montgomery's own analysis focuses on public tributes to the late Princess Diana). Television, as he points out, is an 'intimate' naturalistic medium: it allows the audience to see the performer's face in close-up and to hear every nuance of vocal performance. It therefore demands a 'sincere' and emotionally transparent performance style.

How should we evaluate the phenomenon I have been trying to describe here? I myself am critical of the contemporary ideology of communication, and of its global diffusion via the institutions of multinational capitalism. But my criticism is *not* based on a desire to preserve different cultures and their 'authentic' forms of discourse in hermetically sealed containers. Even if that were desirable, it would be an impossibility. The spread of generic and stylistic norms from one culture or language to another is not in itself a new phenomenon. Familiar examples from the western tradition include the widespread imitation of classical literary or rhetorical forms in western vernacular languages, and the influence of the styles in which the Bible was originally written on Christian religious discourse. Though they take different forms in different times and places, borrowing, imitation, syncretism and hybridization are all part of the history of languages.

Some commentators on globalization would say that we have entered a new era of history, one in which cultural contact takes a qualitatively different form and occurs in conditions of unprecedented asymmetry: the dominant position of the US in terms of economics, politics and media culture makes globalization synonymous with Americanization. Other commentators would contest these strong claims, and it may still be too soon to say whether they are justified; but one place to look for evidence is in changing ideologies and uses of language. When we consider the position of English in the world, its relationships with other languages and its impact on other cultures, this too should be part of our thinking.

References

Brown, P. and Levinson, S. C. (1987) *Politeness: Some Universals in Language Usage*, Cambridge: Cambridge University Press.

✳ Cameron, D. (2000a) *Good To Talk? Living and Working in a Communication Culture*, London: Sage.

—— (2000b) 'Styling the worker: gender and the commodification of language in the globalized service economy', *Journal of Sociolinguistics* 4: 323–47.

Carbaugh, D. (1988) *Talking American: Cultural Discourses on* Donahue, Norwood, NJ: Ablex.

✳ Gal, S. (1995) 'Language, gender and power: an anthropological review', in K. Hall and M. Bucholtz (eds) *Gender Articulated*, London: Routledge.

Hymes, D. (1972) 'On communicative competence', in J. B. Pride and J. Holmes (eds) *Sociolinguistics,* Harmondsworth: Penguin.

Keenan, E. O. (1976) 'The universality of conversational postulates', *Language in Society* 5: 67–80.

Kubota, R. (2001) 'The impact of globalization on language teaching in Japan', in D. Block and D. Cameron (eds) *Globalization and Language Teaching*, London: Routledge.

Montgomery, M. (1999) 'Speaking sincerely: public reactions to the death of Diana', *Language and Literature* 8(1): 5–33.

Schieffelin, B. and Ochs, E. (eds) (1986) *Language Socialization Across Cultures*, New York: Cambridge University Press.

4   The new incivility

Threat or promise?

Robin Tolmach Lakoff

Introduction

The last decade of the twentieth century saw a lot of public worrying in America about the growing incivility or 'coarsening' of political and other public discourse. This chapter examines some of these concerns.

Politeness and civility

Two words figure greatly in the current metadiscourse: *politeness* and *civility*. Politeness has been much discussed recently by linguists and other social scientists (Lakoff 1973; Leech 1983; Brown and Levinson 1987), who generally use the term to cover behaviour that allows participants to avoid hostile confrontation or (in Brown and Levinson's terminology) 'face threatening acts' or FTAs. The word in its scholarly sense thus includes both the popular usage, describing actions more or less synonymous with 'etiquette', and behaviour that is seen in its cultural milieu as 'friendly' or 'inclusive'.

Unlike *politeness*, *civility* has not (to my knowledge) been used as a term of art in the social sciences. In their common usage, the two words, while essentially synonymous, differ significantly as indicated by a Usage Note for *polite* in the *American Heritage Dictionary* (1992: 1401):

> *Polite* . . . impl[ies] consideration of others and the adherence to conventional social standards expected of a well-bred person . . . *Civil* suggests only the barest observance of accepted social usages; it often means neither polite nor rude.

What is 'coarsening'?

American pundits have had a great deal to say on the 'coarsening' of public discourse and behaviour. This public fascination with purportedly novel, allegedly bad behaviour raises three questions: is it really new, is it really bad, and is it serious enough to warrant the attention paid to it?

'Incivility' or 'coarsening' has been discussed under several headings:

1   What may be subsumed under 'the nerve of *those people!*': demands, or more accurately, requests, by groups who previously had no access to or influence over the form of public discourse, that the names by which they have been called be changed to eliminate negative attributions: 'black', and later, 'African American', for 'Negro'; 'woman' for 'girl' and 'lady'; 'Asian' for 'Oriental'; 'disabled' or 'challenged' for 'handicapped'; and many more.

2   The increasing use in public venues of language generally recognized as vulgar, especially by, or within the earshot of, those who had traditionally been protected from it. 'Ass' has become almost a commonplace on prime-time network television, and the censors even tolerate the occasional 'shit'. Also mentioned is the explicit sexuality in advertising, e.g. the 'nothing comes between me and my Calvins' Calvin Klein advertisements for under-pants; and daytime television talk shows in which literally almost every other word by the guests is bleeped, with (to prevent lip-reading) blue dots superimposed on their mouths.

3   The increasing public use, often by popular role models, of language both traditionally vulgar and contemporaneously 'politically incorrect': for example baseball star John Rocker's diatribes against 'faggots', 'niggers', foreigners, and just about everyone not like himself (Carroll 2000; Der-showitz 2000).

4   'Agonism', defined (in Tannen 1998) as 'an automatic warlike stance . . . A kind of programmed contentiousness . . . to accomplish goals that do not necessarily require it.' Agonism is not the use of explicitly offensive words *per se,* but the use of oppositional language in order to gain points in debate through polarization and ridicule of the opposition.

5   Road rage, air rage, and other 'rages' much discussed in the media: the allegedly increasing tendency, on the part of drivers, airplane passengers, and others, to behave in a hostile fashion to others in their environment. (We may note parenthetically that incidences of air rage have diminished to near-zero in the toughening up of air regulations in the wake of 11 September 2001.)

6   The use of emotionally explosive and vitriolic language in places of high *gravitas.* Congresspersons have become much less courteous toward one another, both in address and reference. In 1995, Newt Gingrich, then Speaker of the House of Representatives, was quoted by his mother in a television interview as calling first lady Hillary Rodham Clinton a 'bitch';

around the same time another Republican, Majority Leader Dick Armey, called his openly gay colleague Barney Frank 'Barney Fag'. Around the same time, the governor of California referred to the US Congress itself as a bunch of 'whores' (Sandalow 1995). In late 1995 Congressman James Moran, a Democrat, shoved a Republican off the floor of the House 'in a routine argument. Moran was first elected in 1990 in a race in which he said he'd like to rip his opponent's face off' (Levin and Roddy 1997).

This asperity in high places was especially shocking since Americans never adopted the British tradition of the genteelly-phrased barbed insult. Instead, American congressional discourse has in living memory confined itself to forced geniality: 'my friend from across the aisle', 'my worthy colleague', and so on.

Nor is the coarsening of public discourse restricted to government venues. Lawyers constitute an obvious resource. 'In law offices across the country, attorneys seem to be losing their manners – badgering witnesses, requiring needless depositions, missing meetings, and making themselves impossible to reach' (Sinton 1994). The same article notes that one Texas attorney 'claimed during a recent deposition that his opposing counsel could "gag a maggot off a meat wagon"'.

Political issues involving a high degree of emotion and dissension often provoke virulent rhetoric. A full-page ad in *The New York Times* (5 January 1995) accuses abortion foes of using inflammatory rhetoric to ignite a murder.

> Words of hate helped pull the trigger last Friday in Massachusetts. Two innocent women are dead today because leaders of the extreme religious right are heedlessly using a war of words to inspire killing. They call abortion providers 'baby killers'. They call hardworking, law-abiding citizens 'murderers and sinners'. They trivialize the Holocaust by equating it to abortion.

While the article points to the questionable rhetoric of the anti-abortion movements, its own could be called inflammatory and uncompromising as well.

Commentators blame the situation on different factors. Masks (1996) begins his plea for civility with a story about Michael Walcott playing his guitar in a class of sixth graders in Montgomery, Alabama.

> After finishing the song, Walcott asks the sixth graders, 'Would you behave more courteously in school if I promise to come back and play a concert for you?'
> 'No!' they exclaim in unison.

Masks continues:

> Walcott's song is an anthem out of season. It's a lonely plea for the virtue of respect in a time when schools use metal detectors to keep out guns and knives; when universities insist on speech and behaviour codes to stem the tide of hatred and disrespect; when legal cases become shouting matches; when the internet is littered with raunch; when political campaigns resemble food fights; when trash talk and head butts are the idiom of sports; and when popular culture tops itself from week to week with displays of violence, sex, foul language, and puerile confession.

It's hard to see the connection between the ten-year-olds' too-direct honesty and these much more serious problems.

An op-ed piece in the *New York Times* by Michael J. Sandel, a philosophy professor at Harvard, makes similar observations, but draws somewhat different conclusions:

> Meanness is out of season in American life, and calls for civility echo across the land. Fed up with attack ads, negative campaigns and partisan rancor, Americans are also distressed at the coarsening of everyday life – rudeness on the highways, violence and vulgarity in Hollywood movies and popular music, the brazenly confessional fare of daytime television, the baseball star who spits at an umpire . . .
>
> Americans are right to worry about the erosion of civility in everyday life. But it is a mistake to think that better manners and decorum can solve the fundamental problems of American democracy. In politics, civility is an overrated virtue . . .
>
> The cultural conservatives are right to worry about the coarsening effects of popular entertainment, which, taken together with the advertising that drives it, induces a passion for consumption and a passivity toward politics at odds with civic virtue. But they are wrong to ignore the most potent force of all – the corrosive power of an unfettered market economy.
>
> (Sandel 1996)

And finally, in the *Milwaukee Journal Sentinel*, Steven Greenhut views the same data but sees a different cause and cure:

> Today's civility peddlers are right to point their fingers at our coarsening public culture. Americans should be ashamed, if we still know what that

word means, of the rudeness, violence, and profanity that ooze out of every pore of our popular culture.

But these purveyors of politeness throw all 'incivility' into the same bag, lumping together outspoken politicians like Jesse Helms with abortion-clinic bombers and misogynistic rap stars. They also fail to recognize that, by turning America into a patchwork of competing victim groups, modern liberalism is at the root of the collapse of civic virtue.

(Greenhut 1997)

Incivility across history

Many critiques are apocalyptic in tone. Since Americans' knowledge of history is often weak, it is not surprising that many commentators speak and write as though this were the first time in history that such bad behaviour has been on public display. If this were true, then the fears might be rational: something new, something terrible, has happened to human interaction, something that poses a distinct threat to us as a social species. If, on the other hand, it has happened before, then the worries are overblown.

American fears of a new incivility reflect a persistent myth of a past golden age, a prelapsarian Eden where everyone was cordial to everyone. But such periods were the exception, not the rule.

It is true that for the half century ending in 1991, America was continually at war, hot or cold. There was always a *them*, an enemy at the gates, and *we* had to stick together to keep *them* at bay. So although there were many things Americans could and did disagree on during that period, ultimately the civility of our public discourse reflected our sense that we had to stick together, had to get along . . . or else.

Even then, consensus could be fragile. The Vietnam War of the 1960s and its epiphenomena (sex, drugs, rock and roll) occasioned serious breaches of public civility. The chants of the left were considered shockingly inappropriate: 'Hey, hey, LBJ, how many kids have you killed today?'

In 1991 the world changed. For the first time in the conscious memories of most Americans, there was no enemy, except those on the other side at home. So Americans turned on themselves. The open rancour felt new and disturbing.

Two centuries ago, the 'era of good feeling' during Washington's presidency (1789–97) promptly gave way to an 'era of bad feeling' under Adams (1797–1801) and Jefferson (1801–9), as parties were organized and their diatribes achieved a level of nastiness that far surpassed anything we can achieve today. In the mid-nineteenth century the quality of public debate declined still further. The United States was struggling with slavery: the north was increasingly abolitionist, but the south fought back under the banner of 'states' rights'. Because the south's orators in Congress were more powerful than their northern counterparts, they tended to win the rhetorical battles and succeeded in framing the public argument as about states' rights vs. federalism, rather than the morality of slavery. Because the sides could not explicitly debate the questions that really divided them, the rancour surfaced in particularly unpleasant ways. In the period leading up to the American Civil War, members of Congress increasingly came to physical blows in the course of debate. As Levin and Roddy note (1997):

> Rep. [Representative] Preston Brooks (D-S.C.) [Democrat-South Carolina] walked off the floor of the House and into the Senate in 1856 and used his walking stick to beat Sen. [Senator] Charles Sumner (R-Mass.) [Republican-Massachussetts], to a bloody pulp.

Nor was vitriolic public discourse an American invention. The ancient Romans, whom we often imagine as embodiments of public *gravitas* and *dignitas*, also developed abominable styles of public discourse, for rather similar reasons, as the Roman Republic came to its end. In his campaign for the consulate in 64 BCE, Cicero was encouraged by his brother to attack his opponent Catiline as a monster who

> isn't even afraid of the law . . . [H]e came into power during the civil war, starting his murder spree under its cover. How can I even bring myself to say this man is running for the consulship – someone who killed a man . . . beating him with a centurion's staff . . . driving him literally to his very grave . . . and while the man was still alive, cut off his head . . . A man of such gall, wickedness, and perversity that he practically seduces little boys in their parents' laps!
>
> (Cicero 64 BCE, 8–10)

For the Romans, as for us, incivility grew as differences developed between political factions, and as the previously disenfranchised gained political power.

Geniality and consensus tend to flourish in societies that are homogeneous and in which all members share common interests; or, failing that, where only one group, itself homogeneous, has the ability or right to control public discourse. That was the case in ancient Rome before the first century BCE, when the only people with a voice were patricians with shared political and economic goals who were connected through ties of marriage and family. Once that cohesion began to erode, so too did consensus and with it civility.

Incivility and 'political incorrectness'

For Americans, the last thirty-five years have been a period when those who had for so long unilaterally controlled the language of public discourse – because they were the only ones with automatic access to that discourse, namely white middle- to upper-class men – have been gradually forced to cede that unilateral right and begin sharing language control and meaning-making with others: blacks, women, members of other classes. The 'political correctness' critiques of the late 1980s represent their dismay at this change and their attempt to keep it in check. The extension of meaning-making power leads to what is perceived as 'coarsening' in a couple of ways:

First, many of these groups have different discourse styles from the genteel white middle class. To appreciate this, you have only to look at the talk shows reviled by a few of the commentators quoted above. Guests tell salacious stories of highly inappropriate sexual entanglements, tales of violence and brutality. They tell them in nonstandard dialects. Often they tell them proudly, or at least shamelessly. Often too these tales are so interlarded with obscenities that you can't follow them for the bleeps. A middle-class viewer wonders: what on earth could lead people to make such public spectacles of themselves? But they appear to be having fun, the nastier the better. One can only conclude (based on several indicia of infra-middle-class membership: dialect and dress, for instance) that a class difference is involved. So a lot of what passes for bad behaviour may simply be non-middle-class behaviour.

Moreover, many of the groups achieving discourse power have never had it before. There are centuries, if not millennia, of resentment, for being shut out and shut up: can anyone blame the newly voiced if they shout, if they aren't totally willing to let bygones be bygones? Until women, blacks, and others begin to feel that the public floor is really, permanently theirs, the heat will not subside, nor, I suggest, should it.

And finally, because so many new groups, with strikingly new interests ('special interests', as the Old Guard calls them) have come onstage, the debate will become more heated as it gets more complicated. There is more to debate – issues that were formerly not even raised because they were not what the Old Guard was interested in.

An article in *The New York Times Sunday Magazine* (Sullivan 2001) suggests that 'the culture wars are over'. The heat has toned down, he says. Nobody is paying attention to the controversies that consumed us over the last decade. 'While there are still plenty of inflammatory moments, and plenty of opportunity for dissent, the crackle of gunfire is now increasingly distant.' His example: provocative behaviour by the new Bush administration concerning gay and reproductive rights is receiving a decidedly muted response. Sullivan feels this is, overall, a good thing.

I disagree. I have certainly felt that public language sometimes reaches new lows of tastelessness and unimaginably high decibel levels. I long at times for that hypothetical golden age when Americans all shared each other's interests, or if they didn't, were demure about it. But if we understand that what is taken by many as a decline in civility actually represents an increase in democracy, and the enrichment of public discourse with radically new opinions, daringly expressed, perhaps we can feel better about it. Besides, the abrasiveness is in part the result of the novelty of language rights for many of us. Once everyone gets used to having a stall in the marketplace of ideas, they will feel less of a need to be belligerent about demanding it.

Then, too, recent events have underscored the value of uncensored public discourse, as long as it permits the free exchange of dangerous ideas. In the immediate aftermath of the attacks of 11 September 2001, there was a constriction in the US of the possibility of political disagreement. Democrats ceased, at least for a time, to be a party of opposition, and with good reason. When their leaders tried to question Republican decisions or actions, they were branded 'unpatriotic' or 'treasonous'. Academics too were branded with those epithets for any interpretations of events other than the official one (cf. Martin and Neal 2001).

The new civility and consensus, while widely praised, are more threatening to a democracy dependent on a thriving 'marketplace of ideas' than even the most virulent forms of incivility they (temporarily at least) displaced.

Conclusion

We live in difficult times, and our public discourse is the proof of that. It is obnoxious to be assailed by all kinds of virulent language. It is easy to sympathize with calls to clean it up, tone it down, and be nice. But much of our exuberance stems from positive social changes: the inclusion of new groups into the public political and cultural discourse. What many call 'incivility' or 'coarsening' is no more than the members of those groups trying on their new roles and new power. Even in those cases where the language is truly offensive, there is reason to hope that, once inclusion becomes accepted as the norm, our exuberance will naturally calm down.

References

Bayer, P. B. (1990) 'Dangers in crackdown on "hate speech"', *The San Francisco Chronicle*, 8 May 1990.

Brown, P. and Levinson, S. C. (1987) *Politeness: Some Universals of Language Use*, Cambridge: Cambridge University Press.

Carroll, J. (2000) 'On the matter of John Rocker', *The San Francisco Chronicle*, 2 February 2000.

Cicero, Q. Tullius (64 BCE/1972) *Commentariolum Petitionis*, ed. Dante Nardo, Milan: Mondadori.

Dershowitz, A. (2000) 'Baseball's speech police', *The New York Times*, 2 February 2000.

Greenhut, S. (1997) 'Can we learn to keep a civil tongue? "Civility" push just a plot by left to hush up right', *Milwaukee Journal Sentinel*, 23 March 1997.

Lakoff, R. (1973) 'The logic of politeness; or, minding your p's and q's', in Claudia Corum, T. Cedric Smith-Stark and Ann Weiser (eds) *Papers from the Ninth Regional Meeting of the Chicago Linguistic Society*, 1973, 292–305.

Leech, G. (1983) *Principles of Pragmatics*, London: Longman.

Levin, S. and Roddy, D. B. (1997) 'Rise in incivility, public fistfights sparks a backlash', *Pittsburgh Post-Gazette*, 12 October 1997.

Martin, J. L. and Neal, A. D. (2001) 'Defending civilization: how our universities are failing America and what can be done about it', American Council of Trustees and Alumni, Defense of Civilization Fund, November 2001, available at www.goacta.org

Masks, J. (1996) 'The American uncivil wars', *The Buffalo News*, 4 August 1996.

Sandalow, M. (1995) 'Latest rhetoric in Washington – enough to make a politician blush', *The San Francisco Chronicle*, 3 February 1995.

Sandel, M. J. (1996) 'Making nice is not the same as doing good', *The New York Times*, 29 December 1996.

Sinton, P. (1994) 'Taming Rambo-style lawyers', *San Francisco Chronicle*, 20 September 1994.

Sullivan, A. (2001) 'Life after wartime', *The New York Times Magazine*, 18 March 2001.

Tannen, D. (1998) *The Argument Culture*, New York: Random House.

5 Parochializing the global

Language and the British tabloid press

Martin Conboy

Introduction

This chapter sets out to investigate certain features of the language of the tabloid press and the political implications of that language as it moves into the twenty-first century. The continuing effectiveness of this language in commercial and political terms is dependent upon its genres and styles of language appropriated from vernacular and everyday culture. The tabloid press in Britain, despite its very contemporary appeal, retains a certain continuity in format, content and language with older forms of popular printed entertainment such as chapbook, ballad, almanac and broadside. This is evident from its reliance on heavy black type, outsize headlines and the dominance of illustration to its inclusion of gossip and sensationalism.

With the *Daily Mirror*, popular journalism in Britain in the mid-twentieth century came to mean, as never before, a combination of style (including layout), mass circulation and address (rhetoric/content). According to Smith (1975), the *Mirror* had developed a distinctive style of demotic speech. Yet he criticized its subsequent development in the following terms:

> starting from an authentic populism in 1945, [it] has stylised working class language into parody . . . ever unbridling the radical conscience that, once, had helped its readers to recognise and accept their own political responsibility.
>
> (Smith 1975: 238)

It is that shift to parody and the willingness of readers to participate in it as a more playful form of identification, perhaps as a retreat from the homogeneity of class identities, which fuels the next great convulsion of language in the popular press in Britain (see Conboy 2002). The contemporary *Sun* is the most prolific exponent of this language of a post-class vulgarianism.

With the development of on-line news media and archival retrieval for quality newspapers, the traditions of the tabloid press, particularly in Britain where it has such a robust market position, will enable it to continue for a specific readership. The language of *The Sun* is the fundamental element of its commercial and popular success (Bromley and Tumber 1997).

The continuing vigour of the tabloid press and its dependence on vernacular and colloquial language raise questions about the ability of local, even parochial media languages to flourish within the broader discourses of globalization, and indeed within the political economy of the global corporations which produce them (Featherstone 1993; Conboy 1999). It is achieved by engaging with the ambiguities of a community of readers which is constructed, both materially as a market and in an imaginary fashion, in the style of a particular voice.

Linguistic strategies

One significant feature of *The Sun*'s language is its use of poetics in public language as an enactor of community. Such word play draws the individual reader into an enjoyment of language as part of a larger community of readership, the better to construct and educate that community. This forms part of what, in relation to advertising, Cook refers to as a 'need for display and repetition' (Cook 1992: 228). This communal identification in a textual community is assisted by what Billig calls 'the syntax of hegemony' (Billig 1995: 99). It is added to by phone-ins, telephone polls, letters pages and branded readers' offers on holidays and special offers.

Fowler writes of the complex attraction of this playful language:

> Interestingly, *The Sun* indulges in 'poetic' structures in places where it is being at its most outrageous about politics or sex. Cues are foregrounded to the point of self-parody. Deplorable values are openly displayed, pointedly highlighted; even a critical reader can be disarmed by pleasure in the awfulness of the discourse.
>
> (Fowler 1991: 45)

The compressed nominal phrase (see Biber, Ni, this volume) is the predominant tabloid agenda-setting instrument and, in its influence on sound-bite political campaigning, this linguistic device has profound implications for the public sphere. It acts to destabilize deference for the political process, as well as the politicians personally involved, thus fulfilling, after a fashion, the newspaper's traditional role as watchdog, but with a more populist, irreverent agenda.

Under the headline 'The pompous Lord Irvine should abolish himself', *The Sun*'s political editor writes:

> His best friends say he is 'brilliant, hardworking and loyal'. They also admit he is arrogant and abrasive . . . As another minister puts it: 'Derry has got a brain the size of a melon and a nous the size of a gnat.' Lord Irvine, lover of fine wines and good living will not resign. Nor will he be sacked.
>
> (*The Sun*, 26 February 1998)

This is reinforced in the leader that day in a phrase pulled most explicitly from spoken discourse: 'His Lordship is suffering from a severe dose of TGBH. Too Grand By Half.'

When coupled with the vernacular voice in editorials, this compressed form of cultural allusion – partly stylistic, partly functional – indicates the collapse of complex arguments into a one-liner point of view. If the public sphere was envisaged as a domain in which access to good accounts of knowledge could be debated using rationality, then the tabloids, in their compression of the world into categories and single utterance perspectives, are acting to simplify these areas of knowledge. The echoes of popular language they use to achieve this seem to be making political and social news available for the average reader, and actively constructing that community of readership as they proceed. Populist categories which effect this include on a regular basis the following characters of the British popular press's lexicon: *hunks, fellas, the Beeb, shocker, pervert, plonker, stunna, beauty, fiend, groper, nut, love-cheat*.

However, this process also constitutes a narrowing of cultural and linguistic reference. It is a cultural compression, a set of allusions to the way the world works. One might say that in its compressed style of debate any rational political debate has imploded.

These linguistic strategies combine to assist in the creation of a vernacular idiom, in print. In the twenty-first century, the English language, in the tabloids, continues its evolution, recentred in a pseudo-democratization of the tabloid voice as the vernacular becomes increasingly foregrounded in the popular press.

An important feature of the tabloids' use of English is that it shifts language from reporting to an engaged and often enraged personalization of the political sphere. It is interesting to note that the idiom of the popular press in Britain mimics a voice of popular, carnival disrespect and irreverent jesting and flippancy but it is one which is often employed to serve the ends of powerful groups whose interests overlap with the frustrations and annoyance of a more excluded/marginal political class. Because of its insistence on the performative aspects of its representation, it is a language which quite literally claims a part in the activity of everyday life for its readers. This is a powerful instrument; its claim to be a part of the lives of its readers reinforces that relationship through a self-consciously deployed range of rhetorical devices.

The distinctiveness of the popular culture of the tabloids lies in its ability to combine commercial success with its rhetorical power to claim to speak in the people's name and with their voice.

The language of *The Sun* is positioned at a particularly productive intersection between the formation of an idiom of vernacular English and the politics of the popular, problematically located in the language of a new public sphere between entertainment and information, between media institution and the carnival crowd in its mimicry of the popular.

Claims to popular representation have been woven into traditional genres chosen to most effectively incorporate the popular voice. At the site of struggle over the signification of the popular, the language of the tabloid press is evidence of the ability of a specific media discourse, at a distinct historical moment and at a particular location, to articulate a culture as speaking for the people in a rhetoric which is able to claim an element of authenticity with the 'residual orality' (Ong 1982) of folk culture. Another feature which supports the popular press's claims to authenticity is that of local specificity. The consequent restriction of such a culture means that popular traditions have often been profoundly conservative in themselves while continuing to be representative of the beliefs of ordinary people (Burke 1978; Sparks 1988).

The asylum debate

In *The Sun*, this can be illustrated by the ways in which the recent asylum debate was covered. Pressures on existing legal and political processes within Britain at a time of increased mobility of refugees and asylum-seekers across the European Union had reached a point, by early 2000, where they had become a key issue for the government to deal with, as well as an easy target for hostile coverage in *The Sun*. Within this single issue, the paper was able to combine hostility to foreigners, antipathy towards the European Union and opposition to the Labour government. Exploiting the demotic style of appeal to its readers and its populist political rhetoric, its language drew on the narrow appeal of parochialism and even xenophobia to set a disturbingly simplistic agenda for a complex global issue.

The technique of informal address can be applied to exclude from as well as include into community, as illustrated when Prime Minister Tony Blair is pictured on a walkabout in South Wales eight months previously, with an asylum-seeker who turns out, according to *The Sun*, to be an illegal immigrant:

NICE TRY ALI
But your 'mate' Tony can't give you political asylum
(*The Sun*, 28 February 2000)

There is a clear implication that Blair can be cosied up to on a personal level, fitting into broader accusations that he is too soft on immigration. It is reactionary and inflammatory material, inciting distrust of the outsider but dressed up in a tone of familiarity and jest. Ali is depicted as cunningly attempting to exploit Blair's weakness. The familiarity is portrayed as contemptuous. Politics dissolve into matters of personal interest and relationships, not providing a softer focus to public-sphere debate but distracting attention from the political insinuations of the personal address and the light tone of reporting.

In a direct exhortation to its readers to make their concerns vocal, *The Sun* sets itself up as the champion of unexpressed views. This fits within the tradition of the repressed public of the carnival and the anarchic whose voice is submerged by formal politics and the concerns of the powerful. This silent majority is mobilized textually here in ways which contribute to a generalized fear of foreigners at the same time as the newspaper can parade its credentials as a very vocal, populist watchdog, keeping an eye on potentially slack politicians on behalf of its readers. William Hague, *The Sun* readers and the electorate are collapsed into one nexus of concern and the effect is highlighted by the late shift to addressing the Leader of the Opposition by his first name:

Speak out
Have you noticed something odd about the Tories' campaign against beggars and fake asylum seekers?

There isn't one.

The silence from Hague and his men is deafening.

Why? When *The Sun* said last week that Britain has had enough, we were spot-on.

Your calls and letters prove how strong public opinion is . . .

Don't be timid, William. This is a real issue that enrages voters.

For goodness sake, ask Tony Blair some difficult questions about it today.

(*The Sun*, 15 March 2000)

The strategies of this colloquial tone are extended into commands, written as if emanating from the people themselves. This is the popular as performative. In their use of commands, newspapers present themselves as having an immediate, performative potential (Halliday 1978, Fowler 1991) which they can deploy in the name of the people and their tastes and sensibilities.

The major popular newspapers are owned by and serve the financial interests of some of the wealthiest men in the world. Their readers in Britain include a fair proportion of the country's least well-off and most politically marginalized. Through a skilful employment of a rhetoric of the popular, at least this branch of the mass media can legitimate itself in terms of the meritocratic, consumerist imperatives which it claims are at its heart. The vernacular voice is part of the dyadic attraction of the popular press, drawing the reader into a dialogue conducted in a familiar tone, but it takes its part in a much broader appeal by being integrated into a community which stretches beyond dialogues and into nation. This part of the popular, its ability to close down perspectives to a narrow, national focus, becomes part of a global strategy to legitimate certain news media practices at a local level.

One performative function of the popular press is the confirmation of the existence of a national space and indeed a national identity. The vernacular rhetoric of the popular press can be employed to construct a popular view of community defined from the perspective of the threat of the outsider. This is a specific illustration of what McGuigan writes of in terms of *The Sun*:

> *The Sun* is, arguably, symptomatic of and contributory to a political culture in which popular pleasure is routinely articulated through oppressive ideologies that operate in fertile chauvinistic ground. It is populist in the worst sense.
>
> (McGuigan 1993: 184)

A single-theme version of the editorial column '*Sun* Says' on 9 March 2000 strikes up the terms of one recent controversial and characteristic debate:

Britain has had enough
SCROUNGERS, illegal immigrants and criminals are sucking this country dry.

The cost of this multi-billion pound racket is staggering.

And it is hard-working taxpayers who are footing this bill . . .

They used to say the streets of London were paved with gold.

Today they are paved with East European women and children harassing passers-by for money – and robbing them when they say N O.

But our courts must ALSO hand out maximum sentences to the local crooks here who are cashing in across the country.

The crooked landlords fiddling millions in housing benefit.

The bent employers escaping tax by hiring workers for cash, no questions asked.

BRITAIN HAS HAD ENOUGH

(The Sun, 9 March 2000)

The headline becomes a slogan for a series of campaigning features over the next weeks which orchestrate the popular newspaper's armoury of devices to involve its readership with an agenda the newspaper itself is setting and then selling to the readers as the popular voice. The series of growl words sets the tone of the debate: these people are illegal, immigrant and criminal. The nation is appellated as hard-working and once again in terms of its own economic integration through its taxes. Citizens are articulated commercially as primarily tax-paying contributors to the nation articulated here as an imagined economic community. There is a familiar echo of an old folk-story in the allusion to Dick Whittington's London, paved with gold. The second part of the piece works an old rhetoric of the corruption of crooked landlords and sets them against the foregoing version of upright tax-payers – the ordinary people – but the rhetoric omits any consideration of the contemporary globalized flows of capital and people which trigger such crises as economic migration. There is therefore no attempt to move beyond the surfaces of populist prejudice here, simply a demonstration of the effectiveness of remaining rhetorically on the surface and using the popular newspaper as a forum for populist protest. The capitalization stresses the key terms of the debate and orchestrates in the final slogan the readers, the tax-payers and the nation into one bloc of implicit support.

The Sun's series of stories featuring asylum-seekers to Britain entitled BRITAIN HAS HAD ENOUGH is full of devices intended to add to the impression that the popular newspaper is following the impetus of popular reaction and simply attempting to enhance it. The rhetoric of dialogue and the strategies aimed at building an effect of nationalism through the paper are reinforced by the use of interactive feedback from the readers. This promises a kind of popular democratic feedback but it remains one compromised by its agenda having emanated from the press not the people. It remains what Hoggart termed, in a previous era, 'callow democratic egalitarianism' (Hoggart 1958: 178).

One device is the phone-in, which promises not only to take opinions but also to call readers back to discuss the issue and canvass opinion.

YOU TELL US
We want to know what you think about the way refugees are treated in Britain. Call us on this number, we'll ring back.

This interactive democratic hotline serves to enhance the performative power of the newspaper when it calls in direct and colloquial questioning of the government of the day:

Today we demand of the Government: What the hell are you going to DO?
(*The Sun*, 13 March 2000)

On the same day there is a sinister version of this interactivity with a *Sun* journalist being sent to Romania to beg, in a cynical comparison which deliberately obscures the motivation and desperation of such economic migration.

BRITAIN HAS HAD ENOUGH
Sun girl begs in Romania and is given just 1p

I TRIED begging in Romania yesterday and discovered why its gipsy scroungers are heading for Britain.
     The answer was right there in my begging bowl – 'earnings' of ONE PENNY.
     While the grasping nomads of Eastern Europe can wheedle £20 an hour out of soft Londoners, my reward for two hours of humiliating pleading was a worthless two notes.
(*The Sun*, 13 March 2000)

As the interactive campaign gathers pace as part of its engagement with its own construction of the popular, *The Sun* is able to demonstrate its effectiveness and thereby the legitimacy of its claims as public watchdog on behalf of the people.

Time to kick the scroungers out
Angry *Sun* readers jammed our phone lines yesterday demanding: 'Kick the scroungers out.'
(*The Sun*, 15 March 2000)

The following sequence from this particular week indicates the intensification of the campaign, the simplification of a complex issue through the tabloid techniques of mnemonics and phone democracy, and the reliance on an angry rhetoric which claims to include the voice of the people. Indicating the effectiveness of these populist speech acts, the Home Secretary is obliged to respond to the paper's concerns:

STRAW ANSWERS OUR TEN QUESTIONS
YOU THE JURY
IS Jack Straw doing enough to solve the refugee crisis?
If you think yes phone . . .
If you think no phone . . .

(*The Sun*, 15 March 2000)

BRITAIN HAS HAD ENOUGH
17,539 *Sun* readers lash Straw
17 extracts from phone calls to YOU THE JURY

(*The Sun*, 16 March 2000)

BRITAIN HAS HAD ENOUGH
35,441 READERS LAY INTO STRAW
. . . An amazing 98 per cent of votes . . .

(*The Sun*, 17 March 2000)

ASYLUM-SEEKERS' CIG SCAM BUSTED BY SUN
Smoked out . . . Polish immigrant sells bootleg ciggies to customer at Hackney market and (right) offers pack to *Sun*'s Emily Smith.

THE *Sun* today exposes a bootleg cigarette scam fronted by asylum-seekers – which is robbing Britain of 32.5 BILLION a year . . .

That means huge losses in duty – money the government could use to build hospitals and schools.

(*The Sun*, 21 March 2000)

Another picture features the caption 'Having a laugh at Britain's expense . . . Polish woman flogs cigs to queue'.

The use of slang appears to endorse the impression that the outrage expressed by The Sun is spontaneous and in keeping with the mood of a public whose language it claims to share. Immigration is a complex issue but it is one which *The Sun* seeks to close down through a variety of rhetorical and generic devices to a simple range of targets which can be exploited for maximum effectiveness in appealing to populist sentiments.

Conclusion

Perhaps the tabloids' call to nation are more rooted in desperation. A predominantly white, male and patriotic nation hostile to Europe and sensitive to its past glories stands in for a nation which has ceased to exist – the community represented as a simulacrum to stand in for the loss of nationhood which would spell the end for the popular newspaper in Britain as we know it and its commercial ambitions. The popular press has a vested interest in the survival of at least a rhetorical version of the nation or its simulacrum. The application of this rhetoric of the vernacular is a formative aspect of the nation/community in the popular newspaper. It is doubly effective in being able to combine its readers and the members of the nation as one community to legitimate its own claims that it is writing/talking on behalf of a homogeneous community and therefore an identifiable and profitable market.

This brief examination of the language of the popular press has demonstrated some of the ways language can be used to draw the popular into highly reactionary positions, narrowing down the reader's ability to interpret the world and bringing into dramatic contrast international communication and parochial representation.

References

Billig, M. (1995) *Banal Nationalism*, London: Sage.

Bromley, M. and Tumber, H. (1997) 'From Fleet Street to cyberspace: the British "popular" press in the late twentieth century', *European Journal of Communication Studies* 22(3): 365–78.

Burke, P. (1978) *Popular Culture in Early Modern Europe*, Oxford: Oxford University Press.

Conboy, M. (1999) 'The ethnic origins of readerships' in *The New Europe at the Crossroads*, New York: Peter Lang.

—— (2002) *The Press and Popular Culture*, London: Sage.

Cook, G. (1992) *The Discourse of Advertising*, London: Routledge.

Featherstone, M. (ed.) (1993) *Global Culture: Nationalism, Globalization and Modernity*, London: Sage.

Fowler, R. (1991) *Language in the News*, London: Routledge.

Halliday, M. A. K. (1978) *Language as Social Semiotic*, London: Arnold.

Hoggart, R. (1958) *The Uses of Literacy*, Harmondsworth: Penguin.

McGuigan, J. (1993) *Cultural Populism*, London: Routledge.

Ong, W. (1982) *Orality and Literacy: The Technologizing of the Word*, London: Methuen.

Smith, A. D. (1975) *Paper Voices*, London: Chatto and Windus.

Sparks, C. (1988) 'The popular press and political democracy', *Media, Culture and Society* 10: 209–23.

Part II

Modes of the media

This section looks at various ways in which media discourse is realized at the current time.

Carey explores similarities and differences between newspaper reporting, general reportage and literature. He argues that reportage can be viewed as a natural successor to religion.

Hendy looks at Britain's BBC Radio Four, and illustrates the difficulties of achieving a 'middlebrow' voice on radio. He goes on to show that the BBC now recognizes that the gulf between an 'elite' voice and a 'popular' voice is not always bridgeable.

Kesseler and Bergs examine love letters sent via text-messages, and deny that they consitute a threat to literacy.

Baron looks at e-style (email style) and shows how it overlaps with and differs from existing discourse modes.

Lewis argues that the digital mode of communication is shaping a new discourse of news reporting.

6 Reportage, literature and willed credulity

John Carey

Introduction: reportage vs. literature

Reportage and literature have had an uncomfortable relationship. They have often been thought of as mutually exclusive. Literature, as represented in university courses, has traditionally consisted of fiction, poetry and drama. Its binding characteristic is held to be that it is 'imaginative' – that is, not true. There are some exceptions to this rule. Boswell's *Life of Johnson*, for example, and the diaries of Pepys and Evelyn, though works of reportage, have been granted literary rank. But generally speaking reportage, in the sense of eye-witness reporting, has been associated with the rise of the news media, dating from the late nineteenth century, and allocated an inferior cultural status.

It is, however, a much older genre than such a view assumes, and its relationship to 'literature' is more complex. The indications are that it is as old as fiction, if not older. Examples from ancient Greece include Thucydides's description of the plague in Athens in 430 BC and the Greek general Xenophon telling how he led his band of mercenaries through the wilds of Persia. From then on every historical period yields examples: Caesar's invasion of Britain, the siege of Jerusalem by the Romans in AD 70, the eruption of Vesuvius that destroyed Pompeii. In the medieval and early modern period, outstanding examples of eye-witness reporting are the murder of Thomas à Becket, described by a monk who was standing beside him, the Crusades, described by participants on both sides, and the Spanish atrocities in America – the first recorded example of genocide in the modern world. From the end of the eighteenth century reportage mushrooms. The French Revolution, Trafalgar, Waterloo, and the wars and natural catastrophes of the nineteenth and twentieth centuries all feed enormous amounts of eye-witness experience into the culture. These and other examples are found in Carey (1987).

Reportage has an ancient pedigree, but it was radically altered by the advent of modern communications. The assumption that, in its contemporary phase, it is integrally linked to the news media is perfectly correct. What changed was not the genre but its recipients and the means of delivering it. Crucial innovations were the Education Acts of the late nineteenth century in England, which entitled every child to elementary education, and the electric telegraph, which was first used by American reporters during the Civil War. When they came to Europe to cover the Franco-Prussian War, they telegraphed the battle stories to their papers back home, and the British popular papers quickly followed suit (Knightley 1978).

Arguably, the advent of mass communications represents the greatest change in human consciousness that has taken place in recorded history. The development, within a few decades, from a situation where most of the inhabitants of the earth would have no knowledge about how most of the others were faring, to a situation where the ordinary person's mental space is filled with reports about the doings of complete strangers, represents a revolution in mental activity which is incalculable in its effects. If we ask what took the place of news reporting in pre-modern man's brain, the likeliest answer, I have argued elsewhere, is religion (Carey 1987: xxxv–xxxvi). It supplied a permanent backdrop to pre-modern man's existence as news does for his modern counterpart. The sense of a larger world beyond the personal, a world with its own meanings, stories and conflicts, and the awareness of this as a universal context that dwarfs the merely individual – these things were the province of religion and have become the province of news. Also, one function of religion is to give an assurance of personal immortality, and arguably news offers the same service, though the recipient is generally unconscious of it. Because news persistently presents the individual with accounts of the deaths of other people, it places him continuously in the position of survivor. By showing that we have escaped the violent and terrible ends that have overtaken others, it sustains, as did religion, our eager wish to believe that we will not die.

In order to discuss reportage as a genre we must first determine how it is to be recognized, and this presents an unexpected but, it seems, insoluble difficulty. We might take the familiar modern theoretical position that all texts are self-referential. They do not, it is alleged, relate to a world outside themselves, but operate intertextually. Derrida's dictum '*There is nothing outside of the text*' is often quoted. On this view, the notion of a non-textual reality that precedes and generates the text and can be accessed through it is an illusion. 'There has never been anything but writing', Derrida insists (Derrida 1976: 158). The noted student of his work, Barbara Johnson, glossing this, affirms: 'Nothing, indeed, can be said to be *not* a text' (Derrida 1981: xiv. The italics are in the originals.) This position obviously threatens the very existence of reportage, since reportage relates by definition to a reality outside the text.

Without this relation, there would be no distinction between reportage and fiction.

Graebe's testimony

To remind us of what is at stake in this theoretical issue we might take a piece of reportage from World War II – an account by a construction worker, Hermann Graebe, of the massacre of Jews by Nazis in the Ukraine in October 1942. This is Graebe's testimony.

> On 5th October 1942, when I visited the building office at Dubno, my foreman told me that in the vicinity of the site Jews from Dubno had been shot in three large pits, each about thirty metres long and three metres deep. About 1500 persons had been killed daily. All of the 5,000 Jews who had still been living in Dubno before the pogrom were to be liquidated. As the shooting had taken place in his presence, he was still much upset. Thereupon I drove to the site, accompanied by my foreman, and saw near it great mounds of earth, each thirty metres long and two metres high. Several trucks stood in front of the mounds. Armed Ukrainian militia drove the people off the trucks under the supervision of an SS man. The militia men acted as guards on the trucks and drove them to and from the pit. All the people had the regulation yellow patches on the front and back of their clothes and thus could be recognized as Jews. My foreman and I went directly to the pits. Nobody bothered us. Now I heard rifle shots in quick succession from behind one of the earth mounds. The people who had got off the trucks – men, women and children of all ages – had to undress upon the orders of an SS man, who carried a riding or dog whip. They had to put down their clothes in fixed places, sorted according to shoes, top clothing and underclothing. I saw a heap of shoes of about 800 to 1,000 pairs, great piles of underlinen and clothing. Without screaming or weeping these people undressed, stood around in family groups, kissed each other, said farewells, and waited for a sign from another SS man, who stood near the pit, also with a whip in his hand. During the fifteen minutes that I stood near I heard no complaint or plea for mercy. I watched a family of about eight persons, a man and a woman, both about fifty, with their children aged about one, eight and ten, and two grown up daughters of about twenty to twenty-four. An old woman with snow-white hair was holding the one-year-old child in her arms and singing to it and tickling it. The child was cooing with delight. The couple were looking on with tears in their eyes. The father was holding the hand of a boy about ten years old

and speaking to him softly, the boy was fighting his tears. The father pointed to the sky, stroked his head, and seemed to explain something to him. At that moment the SS man at the pit shouted something to his comrade. The latter counted about twenty persons and instructed them to go behind the earth mound. Among them was the family which I have mentioned. I well remember a girl, slim, and with black hair, who as she passed close to me, pointed to herself and said 'Twenty-three'.

(International Military Tribunal 1949, reprinted in Carey 1987: 569–71)

Graebe goes on to describe the pits full of dead and dying, the soldiers who are doing the shooting, and so on. My point in citing this passage is simply that authenticity is vital to what it is and what it does to us. If it were fiction, we might find it affecting, or we might think it impertinent that fiction should presume to capitalize on such suffering. Either way, our reaction would be different. If we discovered that it was a false story, that Hermann Graebe had made it up, it would radically alter its impact on us.

Yet in fact we have no way of telling whether Graebe's account is true. The situation is paradoxical. The power the piece has over us depends on its being factual, but we do not know that it is factual, and have absolutely no means of authenticating it. We recognize in ourselves a wish to believe – a willed credulity. This seems to be a factor in the reception of all reportage, not just the Graebe piece. Reportage arouses a will to believe, an act of faith. It is a trait that it has in common with no other literary genre, but which reinforces the affinity with religion that I touched on earlier.

The reasons for our anxiety to believe reportage are no doubt complicated and variable, but they seem to group themselves under two headings. The first is our desire for a stable reality. Scepticism about the validity of reportage threatens this, leaving us uncertain and disturbed. The second seems to be an impulse to react emotionally in a way that would be inappropriate if the stimulus were merely fiction. This comes into play most, of course, with samples of reportage that are potentially deeply moving, like the Graebe piece. Having been moved, we wish to believe, it seems, that our emotions have a basis in something that actually happened.

Reporter-novelists: Orwell and Waugh

A test-case that illustrates this reaction is George Orwell's 'A Hanging', an account of an execution in Burma during British rule (see Orwell 1970: 66–70). Whether Orwell, in the normal course of duty, would have been present on such an occasion has been questioned (see Crick 1980: 85). But the piece is so powerful that the general critical reaction has been to claim that, even if not factual in every detail, it is based on Orwell's real experience of such events. Unwillingness to concede that it might be fiction seems directly related to the horror and indignation that it arouses. The emotion strengthens or validates the belief, and is at the same time created by the belief. The situation is circular.

The tendency of this argument, if it is accepted, is to make the boundary between reportage and fiction both more and less permeable than it might have seemed. It is less permeable, indeed, completely impermeable, in that reportage is an account of external reality and fiction is not. It is more permeable in that we are unable, in practice, to distinguish between fiction and reportage. This permeability has allowed for easy transference between reportage and the novel. The novel is, generically, fictitious reporting, and early examples of the novel, such as Defoe's *Journal of the Plague Year*, passed themselves off as authentic reporting – though Defoe's book was not authentic, it was imaginative recreation derived from survivors' reports and hearsay. With the rise of popular newspapers and magazines, novelists who were also reporters became more common. Dickens and Graham Greene are outstanding English examples, and the often close relationship between their reporting and their fiction has been traced by critics and biographers (Sherry 1989–1994; Slater 1994–2000).

Evelyn Waugh is another reporter-novelist who provides rich opportunities for studying the transitions between journalism and literature.

An opportunity to observe how reportage and fiction inter-relate in Waugh's writing is provided by an episode in his novel *Men at Arms* (1952). In book 3, chapter 5, Waugh's hero Guy Crouchback leads a landing party at Dakar, a port near Freetown in West Africa. They get ashore and carry out a successful reconnaissance, and Crouchback behaves with great personal courage, ordering his men back to the boat for safety and staying behind alone to face the enemy's fire till the last man has returned to the beach. This last man is the savage veteran Colonel Ritchie Hook, whom Guy agreed to take along only as a favour, and who has brought back a souvenir. He has been saying that he wants to collect 'a coconut', and now he lays in Guy's lap 'the wet, curly head of a Negro' – one of the African auxiliaries serving with the Vichy French who were in control of Dakar.

This disturbing episode, spiked with racism and barbarity, grew out of two episodes in Waugh's own military career that are worth examining. A keen patriot, he enlisted in December 1939 and was commissioned in the Royal Marines. From the start he was extremely unpopular with fellow officers and other ranks – pompous, authoritarian, insubordinate. At the same time he was undoubtedly courageous, and more intelligent than his comrades, which did not make for popularity. In August 1940 his Marine unit sailed to Dakar, as part of the support force for a landing by Free French troops. The port was thought to be weakly defended. In the event, the expedition proved a fiasco. The allied fleet arrived off Dakar on 23 September to find that the Vichy garrison, far from being prepared to surrender, was resolute and much stronger than had been supposed. A Free French delegation, sent to discuss terms, was arrested and imprisoned. A second delegation was fired on. It seemed likely that Waugh's Marine unit would be sent into action. They even got as far as manning the boats and setting off, but were recalled. Then their troopship headed out into the Atlantic. The mission had been cancelled.

There is no doubt that Waugh felt angry and humiliated by the episode. He was already tired of the Marines, and they of him, and on his return to base he applied successfully for transfer to the commandos, despite the fact that he was thirty-seven and not very fit. The commandos were a crack force, intended for rapid raids behind enemy lines. Critics called them Mr Churchill's murder gangs. Waugh joined 8 Commando and after assault training on Arran and Holy Island his unit sailed for Egypt. From there, in April 1941, he took part in his first and only commando raid.

The objective chosen for attack was a small town behind enemy lines on the Libyan coast called Bardia. The commandos' job was to destroy the stores and defences. According to Waugh, allied intelligence reported that 2,000 enemy troops were stationed there, guarding a transport centre. In the event, this information proved false. The town was deserted; the only vehicles were abandoned trucks. In November 1941 Waugh published the story of the raid in *Life* magazine (reprinted in Waugh 1983: 263–8). It was the first public account of a commando raid and, for propaganda reasons, it had to present the facts to the best advantage. Waugh emphasizes the exceptional toughness, enterprise and fighting spirit of the commandos, which, given that he is one of their number, risks seeming self-congratulatory, and is not much improved by the modest disclaimer that 'There was nothing peculiar about our men. They were simply the best types of the regiments from which they came.' That the commandos, completely unopposed, were able to blow up a tyre dump and a small bridge is applauded as a dashing military triumph. The only German troops they encountered were a couple of motorcyclists who drove straight through two commando detachments and escaped ('Everyone near had a shot at them with Tommy guns and grenades but they somehow got through'). Waugh puts the best face possible on this incompetence. It effected 'exactly what British higher command wanted', because it ensured that news of the landing got back to the

Germans, who 'sent a strong detachment of tanks and armoured cars to repel the imagined invasion', thus weakening their frontline. Waugh writes as if he were in command of the operation, foreshadowing Crouchback's prominence in the Dakar raid in *Men at Arms*. During the voyage out, he recounts, comrades detailed to remain on board came to him and pleaded to be allowed to go ashore. He 'managed to fit most of them in'. When the landing parties are held up by an anti-tank ditch, it appears to be his responsibility to sort out the problem ('Something is wrong up front . . . I go forward to find what it is'). As battalion Intelligence Officer he had, in fact, a junior role. Acting as time-keeper, he remained close to the beach with battalion HQ, and watched the commando detachments make off into the darkness. His account of the action was second-hand, derived from participants.

In Waugh's personal diary the raid appears very differently (Waugh 1976: 495–6). It is scathingly recorded as a series of blunders. Though the commandos had been practising night-time landings of this kind for months, inefficiency and confusion were apparent from the start. One boat failed to get into the water; and another went to the wrong beach. Even though they encountered no opposition, the commandos were able to do considerable damage to themselves. One of the four detachments shot and killed their officer by mistake. The *Life* magazine account credits the commandos with blowing up a coastal defence battery, but the diary concedes that the guns had been destroyed some weeks before, when allied troops evacuated the town.

Comparing the two accounts in his biography of Waugh, Martin Stannard concludes that the *Life* magazine version provides 'an amusing example of how self-aggrandizement and propaganda can twist dull fact into heroic fantasy' (Stannard 1992: 28–30). This may be right. But Stannard's verdict is based on an acceptance of the diary account as factual. It emanates, that is to say, from the willed credulity that we have noted as a persistent factor in the reception of reportage. The disasters revealed in the diary account, and the apparent cover-up in the *Life* account, make the former an exceptionally powerful object of willed credulity.

However, neither Stannard nor any of Waugh's other biographers produces any evidence to corroborate the diary account. Waugh's diaries, splenetic and provocative, impose their own farcical template on reality, and can scarcely be treated as sober fact. In other words the diary account, like the *Life* account, lands us in a familiar dilemma. We have no means of judging its truth, though truth is the only thing that qualifies it as reportage and distinguishes it from fiction.

There is a temptation when confronting this difficulty simply to abandon the distinction between reportage and fiction, to concede that all reportage is fictional in the last resort, that all viewpoints are subjective, and that observation always alters what it observes. The danger of such a position is immediately obvious, however, if we recall Hermann Graebe's testimony about the massacre of Jews in the Ukraine. To suggest that his account should be read as fictional in any sense would, we would all agree, be monstrous. Yet, unless we have searched for and found corroboratory evidence, that agreement is only another way of voicing the willed credulity that, as we have observed, is an enabling condition of reportage, and that correlates with its quasi-religious function in our culture – though in religious contexts we call willed credulity 'faith'. We are left with a paradox: reportage depends for its impact on authenticity, and has no means of validating it.

References

Carey, J. (1987) *The Faber Book of Reportage*, London: Faber and Faber.
Crick, B. (1980) *George Orwell: A Life*, London: Secker and Warburg.
Derrida, J. (1976) *Of Grammatology*, trans. G. C. Spivak, Baltimore, MD: Johns Hopkins University Press.
—— (1981) *Dissemination*, trans. B. Johnson, London: Athlone Press.
International Military Tribunal (1949) *The Trial of German Major War Criminals. Proceedings of the International Military Tribunal Sitting at Nuremberg Germany 1945–1946*, part 19: 16 July 1946–27 July 1946, London: HMSO.
Knightley, P. (1978) *The First Casualty: from the Crimea to Vietnam: The War-Correspondent As Hero, Propagandist and Myth-Maker*, London: Quartet Books.
Orwell, G. (1970) *The Collected Essays, Journalism and Letters of George Orwell*, vol. 1, edited by S. Orwell and I. Angus, Harmondsworth: Penguin.
Sherry, N. (1989–1994) *The Life of Graham Greene*, vols 1 and 2, London: Cape.
Slater, M. (ed.) (1994–2000) *The Dent Uniform Edition of Dickens' Journalism*, vols 1–4, London: Dent.
Stannard, M. (1992) *Evelyn Waugh: No Abiding City, 1939–1966*, London: Dent.
Waugh, E. (1976) *The Diaries of Evelyn Waugh*, edited by M. Davie, London: Weidenfeld and Nicolson.
—— (1983) *The Essays, Articles and Reviews of Evelyn Waugh*, edited by D. Gallagher, London: Methuen.

7 Speaking to Middle England

Radio Four and its listeners

David Hendy

Introduction

Nation shall speak peace unto nation

BBC motto

The BBC's motto, with 'nation' speaking 'unto nation', pitches language into the heart of the broadcasting mission. It gives a nod to the spirit of 'common culture', though not necessarily, for the BBC at least, a culture in which every voice and every achievement is equal. Indeed, in Lord Reith's day the only voices on air were those with 'a claim to be heard above their fellows' (Scannell and Cardiff 1991: 316). Under his leadership the Corporation claimed guardianship of the nation's standards of spoken English. But the BBC has also shown, if sometimes belatedly and grudgingly, a 'tendency to adjust' (McKibben 1998: 469). In time, it has found itself having to accommodate a wider range of voices, not all of them as 'well-spoken' as the earliest BBC announcers.

By the 1980s, the writer Jonathan Raban was confident enough to argue that radio, in particular, was hospitable to many *different* kinds of language:

> As an idle radio listener, twiddling between stations, one drifts from the most elaborate and carefully scripted language through every shade and tone to the most unofficial and unrehearsed grunts and squawks. On radio there is no median register, no particular way of speaking that could be said to represent the medium in neutral gear . . . Radio is by turns gossipy, authoritative, preachy, natural, artificial, confidential, loudly public, and not infrequently wordless. Its languages bleed into one another.
>
> (Raban 1981: 86–7)

But in truth we are not as promiscuous as Raban with the dial on our radio sets. We tend to live nowadays in 'mutually exclusive auditory niches' (Douglas

1999: 348–9). No radio station can command the undivided attention of the best part of a whole nation enjoyed by the BBC's pioneering National Programme. For most broadcasting enterprises this is a perfectly acceptable limitation – a liberation even – for there is something rather comforting to the broadcaster about being able to concentrate on, say, *either* the mature and educated classical music lover *or* the young urban clubber: there is no sense here of different languages 'bleeding' into one another, because one can somehow find roughly the 'right' language, a *particular* language, to speak to such neatly defined audiences.

Upper-middlebrow seriousness

For Radio Four, though, the task of finding the right language has been particularly fraught. As heir to the Reithian Home Service, and before that the National Programme itself, it is regarded by many in broadcasting as the rock upon which all else was founded. But it occupies slippery and treacherous terrain. It is listened to by the country's political elite – its *Today* programme is a 'sort of organ of our constitution' according to one former Cabinet Minister (Donovan 1997: ix); the novelist Sebastian Faulks recently proclaimed that 'its fidelity to a kind of humane, upper-middlebrow seriousness has done more both to define British society and to hold it together than any political or artistic movement of the last 100 years' (BBC Online 2001).

But mention 'middlebrow', and we open up a Pandora's box of other connotations too. 'Middlebrow', writes Humble, 'has always been a dirty word', embodying culture that is 'too easy, too insular, too smug' (2001: 1). For intellectuals, it always betrays a whiff of ugly mass culture and suburban small-mindedness about it (see Carey 1992). We are in 'Middle England' – not a geographical or even a sociological middle, but an essentially rhetorical terrain 'at once comforting and vague' (Cannadine 1998: 183). It was precisely here that the Home Service positioned itself in 1965, just two years before it turned into Radio Four, as being for 'the broad middle section of the community' – a 'middle section' that became broader still when Radio Four inherited speech programmes from both the Third *and* the Light after 1970. Was occupying such a broad middle ground asking for trouble, especially at a moment of British life characterized by historians as marking the 'breakdown of consensus' in politics and culture? Could the centre hold? Or, to put the question specifically in terms of language, has Radio Four been able to find the right 'voice' with which to speak to such an ill-defined but fissiparous community of listeners?

Our first response might be a tentative 'yes'. As early as the 1930s, broadcasters gradually recognized that a medium listened to in the setting of home and family needed to adopt a style of address that, if not quite like everyday conversation, was at least more intimate and colloquial than formal, literary ways of communicating. Fairclough has observed further changes on Radio Four in the 1980s and 1990s: the decline of received pronunciation, the use by presenters of *you* as the indefinite pronoun of choice rather than the more middle-class *one*, and the projection of expressive personality by presenters. It all amounts to what he describes as a less abstract and a more experiential discourse, with presenters typically 'talking to "us" about "them"', extending their implicitly claimed co-membership of the "lifeworld" to a claim to represent the audience point of view in commenting on the experts' (Fairclough 1995: 128–49).

This would suggest a workable accommodation to changing times – that 'tendency to adjust' – without falling into the excess of homeliness that Richard Hoggart had warned against in 1957 in his *The Uses of Literacy*. It was, perhaps, the balancing act that the Minister of Education Sir David Eccles had in mind when he hoped that broadcasting in the 1960s and after would somehow close the gap between experts and 'plain men' and help build a 'general common culture' (Briggs 1995: 465). Yet the BBC's own archives betray a more agonized trajectory – one in which Radio Four's place in British middle-class life has posed its own firm limits on change. The network's search for an appropriate voice has been constrained, I would like to argue here, because it has had to contend more than any other British radio station with the unrealistic – and often contradictory – expectations placed on it by an unholy trinity of listeners, press critics and the BBC's own staff.

Take, to begin with, the listeners. In 1972, just under half are described by the BBC as 'middle/upper-class'. By 1989, when Radio Four had lost many listeners to the rival attractions of local radio and daytime television, over two-thirds of the remaining audience is classed as ABC1 (compared with 39 per cent of the British population as a whole). By 1997, the figure rises to three-quarters (compared with about 45 per cent of the population as a whole). Radio Four has always had a higher *share* of middle- and upper-class listeners than of working-class listeners, but the imbalance appears to have become steadily more marked. A 1987 audience survey asked listeners to characterize each BBC radio station as a person. Radio Four emerged as modestly successful, well-informed, interesting, humorous, reliable, professional, perhaps a little 'plump' and living in a '3-bed semi with garage' (BBC R9, 1987). The essence, we might say, of middle-aged, middle-class, Middle England.

Listeners' complaints

What is even more striking in this survey, though, is the recurring assertion by devotees that Radio Four's main appeal lay in being 'familiar, almost comforting', and that a network controller would change it 'at his peril'. It was these possessive characteristics that drove one senior producer to describe the Radio Four listener as 'acid' and 'complaining' (Smethurst 1997: 129). He was right, too, if the BBC's own records are anything to go by. The log of letters and phone-calls from the public received by the BBC in 1970, for example, shows that out of the 227,167 received that year, some 57 per cent were about radio, rather than television, and of these the overwhelming majority were about Radio Four. Complaints varied hugely: some about too much background noise, a few about poor delivery, a facetious tone, language in plays being 'too difficult', others attacking standards of grammar and pronunciation; larger numbers, perhaps some 40 or so letters or phone-calls a month, complained of 'bad language', particularly language regarded as 'obscene' or 'blasphemous', or complained of general immorality in plays 'obsessed' with sex or, in one memorable case, 'live frog-swallowing' on the *Today* programme (BBC R41, 1970).

What impact did these unending complaints have? Summaries of the correspondence were circulated among senior managers each week, and fears were regularly expressed by programme-makers that they gave the impression that no one liked any of the programmes. The Director of Programmes replied reassuringly that it was appreciated that complaints in general were 'indicative of the letter-writing temperament rather than the public mood as a whole' (BBC Weekly Programme Review Board (WPRB) 19 May 1971, 1 March 1972). There is, indeed, plenty of evidence that many of the complaints from listeners about language were systematically, and quite properly, discounted within the BBC as misrepresentative. 'There may well be', one BBC policy document says, 'a tendency to condemn changes in the use of words less for the changes themselves than for other changes in society which they may reflect'. The thinking of the public was summarized thus: 'if only the rude words would go away, then society would be different, that is, better' (BBC R101, 1971).

All this chimes with much of the listeners' own discourse, which has as an underlying theme, the need for Radio Four to act as a safe haven in the stormy sea of social change. Lord Stradbroke, writing to complain of the satirical tone of Radio Four's Sunday lunchtime current-affairs programme *The World This Weekend*, argued that,

The more the times appear in revolt, the greater is the need for people of firm character who recognize the possibilities for good, to resist all evil and serve as a model for others.

(BBC R34, 1968)

It was indeed an era in which television in particular seemed to be pushing the boundaries of taste, through programmes like the *Wednesday Play*, *Monty Python*, and characters like Alf Garnett. The letter-writing Radio Four listeners were quick to argue that they did not expect similar lapses on their network. 'It was utterly revolting', wrote one listener of a *Midweek Theatre*. 'We don't want the standard of radio plays to sink to those of TV's' (BBC R41, 1970). The Director of Programmes concluded that 'laxer standards in television programmes made the audience much more sensitive to examples of even mild departures from more traditional standards on radio' (BBC WPRB, 1971). There is also a subtext of revulsion at the wave of 'gloomy' news coverage of industrial unrest, drugs busts and student protests. Countless letters complained of 'dull, dreary' news programmes, and argued that 'intolerably morbid and depressing' plays offered little relief (BBC R34, 1968). Programmes on Radio Four were also making more and more use of 'actuality inserts' in which the detached tones of BBC announcers were now accompanied by soundbites of interviews with the *participants* of news events – people whose voices and words were inevitably partial, opinionated and sometimes incoherent. Complaint, Radio Four's Controller Tony Whitby observed, was often a reaction against 'the appearance on air of non-professionals', whose opinions and voices were taken to be representative of the BBC itself; sometimes, too, the whole obsession with language by some listeners was simply 'an excuse for ventilating their marked bias' against any programmes featuring the working classes (BBC WPRB, 1971).

Loyalty to listeners

The constant flow of listeners' complaints may have been met with a healthy dose of scepticism, but it could not fail to have some chastening effect. It was gradually acknowledged that more programmes in the 'middle area' were needed to 'give predictable pleasure to traditional Home Service listeners'. Over time, indeed, more care appeared to be taken over securing the loyalty of *existing* Radio Four listeners than in attracting new ones. When power-cuts forced an earlier nightly closedown on television in 1974, the evening radio audience suddenly quadrupled, though it was noticed that very few were turning to Radio Four. Why? The Head of Light Entertainment thought it might be the rather stolid arts and business programmes on offer at that time of day. The Director of Programmes replied that:

> Keeping faith with our regular listeners is important. They will be with us long after TV has reverted to its original hours . . . I am more concerned with the quality of the audience it attracts rather than its quantity.
>
> (BBC R34, 1974)

Indeed, despite periodic talk of boosting programmes in the 'middle area', the trend appears, if anything, to have been towards consolidating the audience of 'opinion-formers', even if that meant losing some of the easy-going ways of the old Home Service:

> It is beyond dispute that by lightening Radio 4 we could increase its audience. We believe, however, that this would be a betrayal of everything we have set out to do . . . Far from watering down serious Radio, we believe we should seek ways of making it more authoritative.
>
> (Managing Director of Radio, Ian Trethowan, in BBC R78, 1973)

Radio Four, Trethowan had declared, was 'the one part of the Radio output which is heard regularly by leading people in public life', and it was here that the standing of BBC Radio at large, its 'stature and authority' would be judged (BBC R101, 1972).

There were, then, firm limits to the extent to which Radio Four would pander to the preference of its listeners for 'unpretentious' and undemanding fare, for the views of influential critics and broadcasting professionals bore down even harder on decision-making. When, for example, Trethowan vetoed the broadcast of a four-letter word in May 1972, his reasoning was prosaically clear: 'it simply is not worth the inevitable row' (BBC R101, 1972). The BBC noted on more than one occasion that letters of complaint from listeners increased markedly after newspapers took up a particular issue. The newspapers – or at least the broadsheets – could not be ignored. Publicity for radio in a television age has been a scarce commodity, and the judgements of the radio critics – judgements that mostly concern Radio Four programmes – feed the wider nexus of critical 'opinion' by which the BBC's reputation as a whole has been judged.

A noble failure

Thus it was that the biggest publicity drive in BBC Radio history was launched in 1971 to alert critics to *The Long March of Everyman* – a twenty-six-part epic history of the British people. Its producers hoped to 'recapture' history from the elitists, to offer a programme where we heard the voices of 'Us' rather than 'Them'. It would also be an adventure in the use of sound itself, a 'montage' with human voices as the 'string section' in the 'Great Music of Audio' (*The Listener*, 18 November 1971: 683). Above all the series was a self-conscious attempt to do for radio what Kenneth Clark's *Civilization* had recently done for television: to garner critical applause for its scale and ambition. Unfortunately, when the series began, critics derided its lack of chronology and its failure to provide references. John Carey, for one, distrusted the whole enterprise:

> *The Long March* . . . should be seen as a contribution to the determined modern effort to discredit knowledge and replace it by pure sensation . . . The degradation of words is a needful element in this operation. Ideally, articulated sounds should issue from the larynx without involving the higher brain centres at all, as on Radios 1 and 2.
>
> (*The Listener*, 4 May 1972: 573–5)

Another reviewer commented that:

> The programmes have evidently been compiled with great enjoyment. Are *Them* enjoying it as much as *Uz*? There are, as we know, producers' productions and listeners' productions, and occasionally they don't coincide.
>
> (*The Listener*, 9 December 1971: 818–19)

This is a perceptive reading of the audience's tastes, for even in 1971 Radio Four's Controller recognized that montage techniques, with their lack of narrative signposting, probably demanded 'too much' of most listeners. Yet, radio producers were – and still are – drawn to elevating the medium to the status of 'sound cinema'. This is, suggests Raban, 'the desire to be *sui generis*, to be able to do something quite different from practitioners in any other literary or dramatic field' (1981: 84). But to believe that radio should in some way be *about* sound is, he argues, highly dangerous:

> The consequence of this assumption is that radio is threatened with a future equivalent to that of concrete poetry: a series of ever more ingenious experiments with what is really only the typography of radio, not its deep

structure . . . It suggests a future of sound effects, of radiophonic workshop toys, where words are an impure additive to the medium.

(Raban 1981: 81–2)

The Long March, then, brings us back to a central dilemma for Radio Four. BBC politics dictated that the network had to be seen to be stretching the audience, providing 'quality' and programmes of 'stature'. The tenor of British cultural life also made it difficult, the BBC itself admitted, to allow 'the middle-class drawing room of 1950 . . . to set the tone of broadcast speech' in the 1970s (BBC R101, 1971). But *how* could it move on to more adventurous territory without its notoriously conservative listeners losing patience? *The Long March* appears to have been a noble failure in getting its tone right. But across Radio Four as a whole, there is every sign of a sincere attempt to steer a middle course that might nudge the network forward at glacier-like speed.

Types of listener

There was, though, another longer-term strategy solidifying – a strategy based on recognizing different *types* of listening among the Radio Four audience. When Trethowan admitted, after hearing the first edition of *The Long March*, that 'he had had to concentrate very hard', Whitby's definition of the programme as one in which listeners would have to 'immerse' themselves proved accurate (BBC WPRB: 24 November 1971). But such dedicated listening was acknowledged to be very different indeed to the distracted background listening that has typified our experience of radio in the television age. We call radio a 'secondary' medium precisely because we get on with other things while listening. And that is why Whitby makes explicit a vital distinction, when he rejects the idea of giving a daytime repeat to *A Word in Edgeways* in place of *Any Questions*:

> *Any Questions* is fragmented: 10–12 questions in 45 minutes, 4–8 answers per question. It is therefore ideally suited for morning listening. *A Word in Edgeways* is essentially a piece of continuous thought and argument: to broadcast it at a time when most listeners could not give it the attention it deserves and demands would be a silliness.
>
> (BBC R34, 1973)

Another phrase which we find is the 'motivated' listener – someone the programme-maker can expect to be paying decent attention to what is being said – and who contrasts with the 'general' listener – someone unlikely to absorb anything too complex and 'continuous'. These are not necessarily different people, but probably the *same* people listening at *different times of the day*; for while television's evening watershed is based on a distinction between family and adult viewing, radio's watershed marks the boundary between mass listenership and a minority one, with the minority presumed to have opted deliberately for more demanding, perhaps more linguistically adventurous, programming.

So: did the centre hold? Not quite. Radio Four has indeed avoided the extremes of language – of Third Programme complexity and of pop-radio simplicity – in talking to its listeners. By default, and by design, it occupies a linguistic middle ground, talking to what it sees as an educated, curious lay audience. Even so, its manner of address is not quite uniform, for it recognizes, too, that the circumstances of listening vary, and that this allows for – indeed demands – a 'separating out' of programme styles wherever the competing demands of upper-middlebrow and lower-middlebrow modes of address cannot quite be bridged. In terms of today's Radio Four schedules, I think it fair to argue that an edition of Melvyn Bragg's *In Our Time* devoted to Greek philosophy is very different in its linguistic, aural and intellectual demands to, say, a slice of the *Today* programme that precedes it. Radio Four might not escape the 'middlebrow' label, but that tag now almost certainly encompasses a wider range of language than was once offered by the nostalgically remembered Home Service.

References

BBC documents from the Written Archives Centre, reproduced here by kind permission, are drawn from the following files: R9 (Audience Research), R34 (Policy), R41 (Programme Correspondence), R78 (Management Registry), R101 (Central Registry), and WPRB (Weekly Programme Review Board), available at <http://www.bbc.co.uk/thenandnow/wac_home.shtml> (accessed July 2002).

BBC Online (2001), available at <http://www.bbc.co.uk/radio4/four_you/myradfour/4you_myradio4_faulks16.shtml> (accessed April 2001).

Briggs, A. (1995) *The History of Broadcasting in the United Kingdom*, vol. 5, Oxford: Oxford University Press.

Cannadine, D. (1998) *Class in Britain*, New Haven, CT, and London: Yale University Press.

Carey, J. (1992) *The Intellectuals and the Masses*, London: Faber and Faber.

Donovan, P. (1997) *All Our Todays*, London: Jonathan Cape.

Douglas, S. (1999) *Listening In: Radio and the American Imagination*, New York: Random House.

Fairclough, N. (1995) *Media Discourse*, London: Arnold.

Hoggart, R. (1957) *The Uses of Literacy: Aspects of Working-Class Life, with Special References to Publications and Entertainments*, London: Chatto and Windus.

Humble, N. (2001) *The Feminine Middlebrow Novel 1920s to 1950s*, Oxford: Oxford University Press.

McKibben, R. (1998) *Classes and Cultures: England 1918–1951*, Oxford: Oxford University Press.

Raban, J. (1981) 'Icon or symbol: the writer and the "medium"', in P. Lewis (ed.) *Radio Drama*, London: Longman.

Scannell, P. and Cardiff, D. (1991) *A Social History of British Broadcasting*, Oxford: Blackwell.

Smethurst, W. (1997) *The Archers*, London: Michael O'Mara Books.

8 Literacy and the new media

Vita brevis, lingua brevis

Angela Kesseler and Alexander Bergs

Introduction

In 2000, for the first time ever, the tradition of Valentine's cards came under serious threat. Short text messages (known as SMS, originally coined from 'short message service') in telegraph style on mobile phones – 'I LUV U' – have, reportedly, outnumbered twenty-three million hand-written traditional Valentine's cards (VirginMobile 2000). While phone companies rejoiced at the news and declared a new age of virtual romance to have begun, conservative forces saw culture and literacy at bay. One question to be pursued in this chapter is whether these new means of communication really harm literacy and the development of communicative competence or whether media like email and SMS trigger or foster new ways of communication.

The first SMS was sent from a personal computer to a mobile phone on the Vodafone Network in 1992. Within less than a decade the new medium experienced such an increase that the number of SMS in the GSM (Global System for Mobile Communications) network reached one billion per month in April 1999 and has amounted to about thirty billion in December 2001 (Figure 8.1).

Although there has always been a dialectic or symbiotic relationship between economic and media development, the introduction of new media uses has always been a cause of concern for the public and the self-styled guardians of language and tradition (see Milroy and Milroy 1999; Baron 2000: 44–5; Thimm 2000: 9–10). Despite their wide usage, new message types like SMS and emails still appear unnatural or odd at least to parts of the public. Email has been frequently accused of ruining letter-style writing and grammar in particular, while short messaging is sometimes portrayed as a prime menace to communicative skills. Not only does it ruin the linguistic abilities of its mostly underage users, but it hinders the development of communicative competence in general: 'It could restrict people's ability to communicate. The quantity is increasing but the quality is rapidly decreasing' (Ken Lodge, cited in Allison 2001).

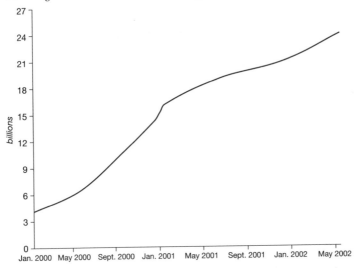

Figure 8.1 Increase in SMS traffic, 2000–2 (source: GSM Association, 2002).

In order to assess the advantages and disadvantages of the new media, one particularly marked genre has been selected: love letters.[1] What makes these a marked genre is their prototypical content. Speaking about love and romance or wooing a partner implicitly forbids brevity, clarity and directness. On the contrary, it should call for 'beautiful words' and metaphorical language, in short: an elaborate style. Working on the assumption of *vita brevis, lingua brevis*, the modern media should have profound effects on this particular type of text. Thus, it is a key question whether modern means of communication have changed the content and quality of love letters. The medium may not only be the message, it may also determine its shape.

Love letters as a genre

The genre 'letter' is not new to sociolinguistic research and has been subject to frequent discussions from a text-type theoretical, sociopsychological and technical perspective (e.g. Nickisch 1991; Barton and Hall 2000). 'Love letters', however, despite their huge popularity, have rarely surfaced in such research. This may be due to two facts. First, the topic is somewhat delicate and research material is difficult to obtain. Who would want to submit their personal, most intimate letters to (socio-) linguistic research? Second, research in love letters as such does not have the same practical applicability as that in business letters or job applications. However, there is no reason to assume that love letters do not constitute a sub-genre that is of equal linguistic interest to any other type of letter. They constitute both '[A] *message type that recurs regularly in a community* (in terms of semantic content, participants, occasions of use . . .)' (Ferguson 1994: 21; emphasis original) and 'a class of communicative events, the members of which share some set of communicative purposes' (Swales 1990: 58). Their purpose is, quite simply, to express amorous feelings and woo a partner. The question, however, remains, if, and in what ways, their identifying genre internal structure has changed over time.

Despite the fact that many people prefer not to talk about them, most have probably written or received love letters in their lives. Moreover, there seems to be a common perennial idea of what love letters should look like and how they should be composed. As regards materiality, the prototypical love letter (in most European societies) is hand-written on high-quality paper and may be decorated with certain attachments like sealing wax or ribbons, perfume, etc. As regards language, it should be written in a careful, elevated style; erotic maybe, but not overtly loaded with blunt sexuality. The imagery is conventionally limited; nevertheless writers should try to be as original as possible. Orthography, grammar, etc. should be flawless; corrections should be kept to a minimum. As regards content, it should flatter the recipient and describe the desire or longing of the author to be with the addressee. All these images and ideas seem to stem from a somewhat romanticized ideal depicted in literature and the cinema (e.g. Rostand's *Cyrano de Bergerac*). Collections like those by Lovric (1991) further promote this widespread prototype.

But does this prototype correspond to reality, present or past? As it turns out, this romantic, idealized notion is largely misconceived. Most of the (historical) love letters available today were written by important public figures. There are Ovid's love letters, one of Henry VIII to Anne Boleyn, the letters of Napoleon to Josephine and those of Simon de Beauvoir and Jean-Paul Sartre, to name only a few. The following excerpt illustrates this prototypical form:

> Take a little tender witchcraft of Love, and add it to the generous, the honourable sentiment of manly Friendship, and I know but one more delightful morsel, which few, few in rank ever taste. Such a composition is like adding cream to strawberries: it not only gives the fruit a more elegant richness, but has a peculiar deliciousness of its own.
>
> (Robert Burns to Agnes MacLehose, 21 December 1787)

The reason these letters were retained was their authors' renown – in some cases, the writers were even aware of this. Thus, the researcher faces the so-called observer's paradox, as described by Labov and others for present-day sociolinguistics (see Wardaugh 1998: 17–18): people talk differently when they know they are being observed or recorded. Moreover, this type of love letter was composed by highly literate authors. Therefore, it may be argued that it does not reflect actual language use of common people. This, in turn, means that the present-day cliché is based on one particular type of letter which today rarely, if ever, occurs. The historical data available mostly captures the upper end of the stylistic 'literacy' spectrum, while statements about literacy today mostly refer to the lower end of the spectrum. What this leads to, eventually, is comparing apples and pears.

One of the few sources of private lower-class language available today is the nineteenth-century London Foundling Hospital letters. The Hospital was a refuge for so-called 'fallen girls':

> those daughters of the people who applied to the Foundling Hospital did possess notes and love letters, which they attached carefully to their admission forms by way of evidence. Snippets of sentimental conversation, fragments of vanquished exchanges, faint echoing half-phrases in overlapping male and female voices, are thus retrieved from the depths of time.
>
> (Barret-Ducrocq 1991: 114)

These documents probably show much more accurately what the 'average' historical love letter looked liked. These letters were written with emotion, at the spur of the moment, by people who surely did not think their writings would be kept for future use of any kind. One striking feature, for instance, as Barret-Ducrocq notes (ibid.), is that this 'rare and precious material' shows a 'variety of tone, content and cultural level'. Contrary to what may be commonly assumed, only very few of these documents are devoted exclusively to the expression of amorous sentiments. Most of them were written for everyday purposes like making, altering or cancelling appointments. Also, authors were forced by convention to circumscribe their physical desires. Many examples show somebody swearing eternal love in the first lines of the letter, followed by a description of a job they had to carry out. Hardly any letter matched the prototypical letters described above:

> You will think it very unkind of me for not writing to you before but you will not when I tell you the reason I have been to Hastings with my master for a week and I enjoyed it very much indeed I should very much like for you to have been there with me indeed as Hastings is a very nice place . . .

I wish that you were living there with me . . . Your affectionate lover, John J.
XXXXXXXXX

My dearest Eliza, I just received your welcome letter and was verry pleased
to Receive it i was rather Disappointed as i hurried home for you but i
know it cant be helped at all times . . .

I accept the kisses you sent in your note with pleasure and will return
with interests on Friday night althou I would rather had them from your
lips than your hands . . .

Frequently we find the graphic symbolization of kisses as X. Also, as will be
shown in the following section, the use of images and metaphors is very much
the same as those in present-day emails and SMS.

Modern media: *vita brevis, lingua brevis?*

Globalization and medialization processes have led to an increase in communication efficiency and speed. The aim was to facilitate communication, to make it
faster and less costly. Whereas most media were originally designed for business
purposes only (i.e. to be used by a limited number of people for certain desig-
nated purposes), they have clearly lost that status by now. These technical means
are used just as much, if not even more, for private communication. This may be
called the exaptation of these means of communication, meaning that a medium
originally designed for a specific purpose is transposed to another context (e.g.
the private sphere). With the expansion of these new media, patterns of communication have also undergone great changes. An SMS dialogue like the following appears to be quite 'normal' today, at least among the younger
generation:

Hi How r u?	Hi! How are you?
Hi Gr8 thkz	Hi. Great. Thanks.
ILUVU Wubmv? ;-)	I love you. Would you be my Valentine?
ROFL	Rolling on the floor laughing.
:'-(	Crying
oxoxoLUWAM<3 >->-	Hugs and Kisses, I love you with all my heart. Roses.
IU2LUVUBIAON	I used to love you but it's all over now.
DROP 8-#	Drop dead.

SMS are messages of up to 160 characters, including spaces, which are sent and received via mobile phones (and special services on the internet). Because of the limited number of characters available, SMS writers have started to use and conventionalize certain complex iconic and symbolic signs. Adolescents in particular have begun to use their computers and mobile phones very creatively. Thus, the medium (itself) has become an essential part of the message and determines its shape. However, from what has been said so far it appears as if mobile phones cannot be the ideal way of communicating sentimental and romantic feelings. Technical requirements force writers to use a rather plain and direct style. Nevertheless, it appears that many people do use SMS (and email) as a medium for their love messages. VirginMobile reported that half of Britain's mobile users, i.e. twelve million people in 1999, *expected* a Valentine's text message from their lovers. In 2001, about 25 per cent of all weekly SMS in the UK, i.e. seventy-one million, contained flirtatious or romantic text (Garcia-Robles 2001). Also, it can be observed that more and more people are willing to publish the results of their romantic creativity on internet websites. Why has a rapidly growing number of people started using email and SMS for communicating their intimate feelings? Why are very many of them eager to present their messages on the internet? And do these new means of communication displace the old love letter?

Interviews show that the specific qualities of SMS and email make up a major part of their attraction. First, many people appreciate the local and temporal distance, especially when transmitting intimate messages. Thus, most of them feel more comfortable speaking openly about feelings, desires and conflicts. 'It seems these new forms of communication have filled a gap, offering something that face to face conversation does not' (Gaines 2001). Second, both email and SMS offer very comfortable, quick and easy ways of sending messages without forcing authors to sit down with pen and paper and write a letter to their loved ones, which they then have to take to the post office and pay for. 'The fact that email and text messaging are both short and quick is a big part of the attraction. Many people find them more informal than making a phone call or writing a letter, and so simpler to use' (Gaines 2001). In addition, for some contributors, the public declaration on the internet seems to have a greater value or is somehow modern, frank and bold: 'will u please announce to the nation that susan loves peter. ta. ;@)' (SMS posted on a website). The results confirmed what sociopsychologists have suspected for a long time. Email, SMS and internet chat reduce the factor of 'embarrassment' and 'inhibitiveness' to a minimum (see Döring 1999, 2000). There are full communicative possibilities without the hassle of interpersonal eye-to-eye contact. The disappearance of former taboos seems to have opened up the floor to something comparable to a kind of emotional exhibitionism.

Although users of email and SMS tend to use a more 'simple style', many love mails still contain the same images, metaphors and codes as the pen-and-paper love letters of the nineteenth century:

> It might frighten you and make you less inclined to kiss me. And although I wouldn't blame you, I don't want that to happen. Your kisses don't come very often as it is (even in your messages I'm rationed to only two X's!), and I certainly don't want to make them even less frequent.
>
> [email]

> To my angel . . . you are my dream come true. My life is my heaven now with you in it . . . you are my angel . . . I love you. I love you. I love you. :-)
> ~*~Joe~*~
>
> [email]

> If friendship could be bought or sold, as if it was stocks and shares. Those wise enough to invest in you, would all be Millionaires Luv Mel :o)
>
> [SMS]

> i love my lovely honey bunny very muchly shes the bestest
>
> [SMS]

> som1 tell sugarlips I LOVE HER!!! babychops ;-) xxxxxxx
>
> [SMS]

> dont luv sum1 like a flower ——-;-<@ bcoz a flower dies in season. luv them like a river bcoz a river flows 4eva
>
> [SMS]

> Jon – u are the * in my life! I'll always be yours. <3 <3 <3 love Cath
>
> [SMS]

The metaphors and images still revolve around LOVE as a JOURNEY, as a UNITY, as INSANITY; the object of Love as (appetizing) food, as a valuable object or divine being; BEAUTY or LOVE as a (natural) FORCE, etc. (see Lakoff and Johnson 1980: 139–40; Kövecses 1988). We also note very few differences in syntax and style, and these certainly do correspond to the differences in spoken and written language at around 1900 (as, for instance, the double superlative *bestest*, the overgeneralization of the adverb marker -ly, or the omission of various apostrophes), and so these are not particular to love letters. What can be seen, however, is the frequent use of creative iconicity (e.g. >->- 'Roses', <3 'Heart') and phonetic spellings (*bcoz*, *luv*). But, again, the latter is not unusual in comparison to earlier lower-class letters. There may be some differences, however, in the content of these messages. In older letters we rarely find sexual allusions, which is probably due to men's fear of paternity suits. Although the reduced space in SMS does not *necessarily* lead to more explicitness, it adds one possibility in this respect. While most SMS describe fairly harmless 'puppy love', as one person put it, 18 per cent of all users in the 1999 Nokia survey reported they also used SMS for naughty messaging of some kind (see Middleton 2000; SiemensMobile 2002).

So what has changed is that there is now another level on which users can toy around with language. On one level we still find old-fashioned writing, but on another there are short forms such as IU2LUVUBIAON ('I used to love you, but it's all over now'), PLZ4GVME ('please forgive me'), or emoticons such as ;-) ('wink') or :-& ('tongue tied'). There is no general tendency to use short forms, though. Most SMS resemble ordinary written language, despite colloquialisms such as 'U' ('you'), 'R' ('are'), '2' ('too'), which are frequent in informal writing (like postcards) anyway. Apart from that, SMS have surprisingly similar traits to common letter-writing in the nineteenth century. People use it mostly for giving short reports, making appointments, sending regards, but also for declaring their feelings.

Conclusion

The results of this study are of four different kinds, two relating to historical letter-writing and two to modern media. First, it has been shown that the commonplace conception of traditional love letters is somewhat misguided. Second, we can see, also on the basis of these letters, that what is commonly described as normal letter-writing style is clearly more a myth than a fact (see Milroy 1998). Lower-class writers (at least) were no more literate than today. The letters from the London Foundling Hospital contain a wealth of shibboleths and 'mistakes' on all language levels. A third result relates to present-day data. Here it can be seen that emails and SMS do not necessarily lead to directness and frankness in expression (except in 'naughty messages'). Instead, we find recurring figures and metaphors across all centuries. Also, the employment of orthographic symbols and secret written codes seems to be a stable feature of love letters across centuries and media: the 'X' in the nineteenth-century letter finds its equivalent in twentieth-century SMS 'X', the hand-written heart-shaped 'i-dot' has become the typed '<3'. This leads to a fourth, last and most important result. It seems that emails and short messaging today do not endanger literacy in their users by any means. Instead it may be argued that these media trigger and foster a hitherto unknown linguistic creativity in their users. Writers have always made the best of the graphic and linguistic means available; today, this is no different. Language users develop new means of communication *in addition to already existing ones*. It may be argued that the verbal play of SMS requires just as high and complex literary skills as letter-writing. The objection that SMS incur social isolation and loss of verbal skills can also be discarded. A diversification of communicative means, maybe in a Darwinian sense, can be diagnosed. As new communicative and linguistic skills develop, the emergence of a new kind of mass (media) literacy and creativity need not oust existing skills but may be extremely useful for the development of both old and new capacities in young people, always depending on what they want to do with the media at hand.

Note

1   This chapter presents work in progress from a larger research project concerned with the evolution of late modern English text types, carried out at the Forschungs-zentrum für Kommunikation, Medien und Sprache, University of Düsseldorf.

References

Allison, R. (2001) 'Phone txt chat "harms literacy"', *The Guardian*, 22 January 2001.

Baron, N. (2000) *From Alphabet to Email*, London: Routledge.

Barret-Ducrocq, F. (1991) *Love in the Time of Victoria*, London: Penguin.

Barton, D. and Hall, N. (eds) (2000) *Letter Writing as a Social Practice*, Amsterdam and Philadelphia, PA: Benjamins.

Döring, N. (1999) *Sozialpsychologie des Internet*, Göttingen: Hogrefe.

— (2000) 'Romantische Beziehungen im Netz', in C. Thimm (ed.) *Soziales im Netz*, Opladen: Westdeutscher Verlag.

Ferguson, C. A. (1994) 'Dialect, register, and genre: working assumptions about conventionalization', in D. Biber and E. Finegan (eds) *Sociolinguistic Perspectives on Register*, Oxford: Oxford University Press, 15–30.

Gaines, S. (2001) 'Now we're getting the message', *The Guardian*, 15 February 2001.

Garcia-Robles, V. (2001) 'Romance boosts SMS phenomena', available at <http://www.europemedia.net/shownews.asp?ArticleID=4806> (accessed 11 March 2002).

GSM Association (2002) 'GSM world', available at <http://www.gsmworld.com/technology/sms/smsgraph.shtml> (accessed 15 July 2002).

Kövecses, Z. (1988) *The Language of Love*, Lewisburg, PA: Bucknell University Press.

Lakoff, G. and Johnson, M. (1980) *Metaphors We Live By*, Chicago: University of Chicago Press.

Lovric, M. (ed.) (1991) *Passionate Love Letters: An Anthology of Desire*, London: Weidenfeld and Nicolson.

Middleton, J. (2000) 'Mobile users become engaged in "text sex"', available at <http://www.vnunet.com/News/1115130> (accessed 11 March 2002).

Milroy, J. (1998) 'Children can't speak or write properly anymore', in L. Bauer and P. Trudgill (eds) *Language Myths*, London: Penguin, 58–65.

Milroy J. and Milroy, L. (1999) *Authority in Language: Investigating Standard English*, London: Routledge.

Nickisch, R. M. G. (1991) *Brief*, Stuttgart: J. B. Metzlersche Verlagsbuchhandlung.

SiemensMobile (2002) 'Love is . . . on the mobile', available at <http://www.nua.ie/surveys/index.cgi?f=VS&art_id=905357617&rel=true> (accessed 11 March 2002).

Swales, J. M. (1990) *Genre Analysis*, Cambridge: Cambridge University Press.

Thimm, C. (2000) 'Einführung: Soziales im Netz – (Neue) Kommunikationsstrukturen und gelebte Sozialität', in C. Thimm (ed.) *Soziales im Netz*, Opladen: Westdeutscher Verlag, 7–17.

VirginMobile (2000) 'WITH LOVE FROM? Mobile messaging: the new romance this Valentine's Day', available at <http://www.virginmobile.com/mobile/help/20000209.html> (accessed 11 March 2002).

Wardaugh, R. (1998) *An Introduction to Sociolinguistics*, Oxford: Blackwell.

9   Why email looks like speech

Proofreading, pedagogy and public face

Naomi S. Baron

> If you have good language skills, you will be respected and admired; whereas if you clearly have no clue about grammar or vocabulary, you could become president of the United States. The choice is yours!
>
> Dave Barry, 'Wit's End', *The Washington Post Magazine*, 4 March 2001, p. 32

Defining the beast

What kind of linguistic entity is email? Use of networked computing to exchange written messages has been with us for three decades (Abbate 1999: 106–11), but proliferation of email within the broader public arena only seriously began in the 1990s. Given email's stagewise evolution, it is hardly surprising that commonplace depictions of the linguistic character of email (such as 'everyone uses emoticons' or 'email inevitably leads to flaming') are not universally applicable to messages written today by grandmothers, job applicants, customers ordering on-line, or teenage girls chatting through instant messaging (see Crystal 2001).

Surveying the burgeoning literature on email, we find the medium depicted in a variety of ways:

- letters by phone (email as a form of writing)
- speech by other means (email as a form of speech)
- mix and match (email as a combination of written and spoken elements)
- e-style (email as a distinct language style)
- contact system (email as a still-evolving language style).

(It goes without saying that when we use the terms 'writing' and 'speech', our sense is paradigmatic, ignoring the abundant variation found in both written and spoken styles across users and usage contexts – see, e.g. Tannen 1982; Chafe and Danielewicz 1987; Chafe and Tannen 1987; Biber 1988, 1995.)

The first two approaches attempt to pigeon-hole email into the mould of existing modalities of communication: either email is essentially a written message conveyed by a new electronic medium – 'letters by phone' (Spitzer 1986: 19) or it is speech that happens to be written down for transmission purposes – 'speech by other means' (Baron 1998). These two models (especially the latter) predominated in the early days of email and continue to thrive among the general public.

Language and media specialists tend to offer more complex models. The 'mix and match' approach empirically tallies the speech-like qualities of email and those that look more like writing (e.g. Yates 1996; Crystal 2001: 42–3). An alternative tack speaks of 'e-style' (or a synonym) that is neither speech nor writing (e.g. Ferrara *et al.* 1991; Maynor 1994; Collot and Belmore 1996). Recently, David Crystal (2001) has mapped out the distinct linguistic properties of what he calls 'Netspeak', which he defines as the language of computer-mediated communication. Finally, the 'contact system' argument suggests that the unfolding of email is very much like the development of a pidgin or creole. While the system has an identifiable grammar, there is also broad variation across users and usages. Since the system is still undergoing considerable transformation, there is no certainty how it will end up. Seen through this model, it is too soon to tell if email will eventually look more speech-like, more like writing, or become a distinct genre (Baron 2000).

Characterizing the linguistics of email has become not only a timely scholarly endeavour but downright fashionable. Student research projects are sprouting like mushrooms after a rain, if the email enquiries I have been receiving from would-be authors are any indication. While most have been reasonably formal and polite, one query stands out for the way it exemplifies the phenomenon the author purports to be studying.

The sender was a graduate student preparing a master's thesis, which was due very soon. Apparently his library did not have many useful sources. After presenting me a long list of questions, he closed with, 'OK NAOMI . . . I really need your information as soon as possible'. I responded (politely and briefly), though 'OK NAOMI' seemed rather presumptuous from a person who was probably half my age and was, after all, seeking my help. Apparently, my correspondent felt I was withholding information. He wrote back: 'If you know something . . . tell me.'

To appreciate why email is so difficult to classify, consider how some of the linguistic attributes of email measure up against speech or writing. With regard to such parameters as language style, assumptions about recipient responses, identity of audience, and presuppositions about durability of message, email seems to be Janus-faced – at once resembling and not resembling face-to-face speech (see table 9.1).

Table 9.1 Selective comparison of email characteristics with characteristics of face-to-face speech.

Linguistic parameters	Characteristics generally shared with face-to-face speech	Characteristics not generally shared with face-to-face speech
Language style	informal: – often avoid salutations (or use 'Hi') – use contractions, slang	HOWEVER often more informal than face-to-face speech
Responses	fast response time assumed	HOWEVER often don't get acknowledgement for assistance rendered
Audience identity	intended for limited, specified audience	HOWEVER can be forwarded to others without original sender's knowledge
Durability assumptions	senders act as if ephemeral (and often don't edit)	HOWEVER can print out can edit can reply with history

Table 9.2 Examples of hard-to-classify attributes of email.

Candour	Mixed writing mode
– high level of author candour (encouraged by perceived or actual anonymity) – higher level than usually found in face-to-face speech or even in much traditional writing	– though overall email frame is that of a memorandum, body of message is some- times constructed like a formal letter – signature files often contain more informa- tion than normally found in letters, including not only phone and fax numbers but also quotations or visual displays

At the same time, some aspects of email remind us more of written language, but do not neatly fit into conventional writing moulds. Two such examples involve the level of candour and the physical components of an email message (see table 9.2).

This chapter focuses on three attributes of email that characterize a significant proportion of the messages sent today (especially by more experienced users), spanning the spectra of age, gender and education:

- informality of language style
- psychological assumption that medium is ephemeral
- high level of candour (stemming, in part, from treating email as an ephemeral medium).

Taken together, these attributes commonly make for messages that are more off-the-cuff than reflective, more opinionated than objective, more blunt than subtle. (Use of humour in email can be an exception.)

Our question is not so much *whether* these attributes are speech-like (largely they are) but *why* email has these traits and, derivatively, what the presence of these characteristics tells us about broader issues of community behaviour. While the analysis centres on email usage in the United States, the same issues resonate elsewhere.

The argument goes like this. Technology often enhances and reflects rather than precipitating linguistic and social change. The growing American tendency for all writing to become more informal, less edited, and more personal and candid largely derives from transformations in American education over the past 125 years, along with a decline, especially over the last half-century, in concern for 'public face' – that is, the ways we reveal to others who we are (or wish to be) through such avenues as dress, decorum and language. The heavily speech-like character of much contemporary American writing bears witness to these transformations.

Education in America

Three educational reform movements have strongly influenced contemporary American writing style:

- Harvard University's transformation of English composition instruction in the 1870s
- John Dewey's work on progressive education in the early twentieth century
- the emergence of a student-centred curriculum from the 1970s onwards.

We will look briefly, in turn, at each of these phenomena (see Baron 2000 for more detail).

Charles W. Eliot became president of Harvard in 1869. Soon thereafter, the institution reformed its English composition curriculum, responding to Eliot's concern that incoming students could not write acceptable English prose

(Crowley 1998). The remedy entailed replacing the earlier rhetoric require-ment, which had students tackling such lofty themes as 'Can the Immortality of the Soul Be Proven?', with a practical regimen designed to 'teach a young writer to recognize and grasp the individual nature of experience' (Myers 1996: 38, 49). This new emphasis on self-expression soon permeated writing curricula throughout American higher education.

Focusing on lower education, the American pragmatist John Dewey drew upon earlier European ideas about empowering children as learners to argue for a student-centred approach to education that fostered children's creativity. Some of Dewey's followers developed lower-school curricula that replaced traditional work in grammar, spelling, penmanship and literature with what we now call 'creative writing' (see, e.g. Mearns 1925).

Progressive education garnered attention in early twentieth-century America and then largely faded from view. However, in the years following the student tumult of the Vietnam era, student-centred curricula attracted new followers, favouring tangible 'relevance' and learner viewpoint over content-driven, teacher-centred classrooms. This new pedagogical mandate began at the college level, then made its way into the lower grades. In the world of composition pro-grammes, a 'process' (rather than 'product') orientation set in, along with emphasis on personal opinion ('I think') at the expense of objective argumenta-tion ('It can be argued that').

One consequence of these reforms has been a shift away from formal rhet-oric to informal writing, placing more value on what students want to express than on the actual language (including sentence mechanics) used to express it. As a result, writing is often taught as a form of conversational social interaction (see, e.g. Bruffee 1984: 641–2). Not surprisingly, some teachers of English composition counsel students to reject the punctuation rules laid out in gram-mar books in favour of using punctuation to indicate rhetorical pauses in speech (Dawkins 1995: 534). This approach has also garnered support from some lin-guists (Danielewicz and Chafe 1985: 225).

The decline of public face

The pedagogical shifts we have been looking at have not occurred in a vacuum. Especially in the last fifty years, they have dovetailed with other American social trends that have generally emphasized informality over formality. These same trends have led more recently to some paradoxical views about individual privacy.

Sociologists such as Erving Goffman (1959) have looked at the ways people 'present' themselves to other members of their community. Like actors on stages, we construct our outward appearance based upon how we want others to perceive us – as wealthy or in need, intelligent or clueless, ambitious or cautious, leader or follower. This 'public face' we display to others is shaped by individual bent as well as by contemporary community norms. High fashion of the 1920s is today relegated to period drama, and the Boston accent that sounded so prestigious in the Kennedy era now sounds, well, simply like a Boston accent.

How have mainstream American attitudes towards public face been changing since World War II? Three significant shifts have been

- reduced emphasis on social stratification and on overt attention to upward mobility
- notable disconnects between educational accomplishment and financial success
- strong emphasis on youth culture.

Each of these changes has contributed to more casual behaviour with respect to dress, affect and language, often resulting in diminished attention to how we appear to others. Obviously, many Americans still consciously work to shape and convey images of themselves to others. People wear funky hats, put on accents, or spuriously report having advanced degrees. Members of on-line communities are notorious for presenting themselves as they wish to be seen, not as they are 'in real life' (see, e.g. Donath 1999). However, in the process of constructing public identities, contemporary Americans are generally less formal and less interested in self-construction for the purpose of social mobility than in times past.

How do these shifts play out in social practice? As Americans increasingly view themselves either as middle-class or as legally protected to be accepted 'as they are', there is less impetus to learn the fine points of etiquette or dress up for job interviews. When high-school or college drop-outs become multi-millionaire (or billionaire) rock stars, basketball players or CEOs of computer companies, the public's belief that higher education is necessary for financial success weakens. So, too, does public commitment to developing the sophisticated thought and language that higher education traditionally nurtures. As youth-driven entertainment (from Disney to Eminem) and adolescent lingo (think of the pandemic use of 'like') permeate the tastes of adults who once prided themselves on social and linguistic sophistication, the norms to which the nation's youth aspire are being dumbed down to match popular teenage practice (see Meyrowitz 1985 for an earlier discussion of these issues).

One recent manifestation of this move away from putting on a well-scrubbed public face is an emerging ambivalence about individual privacy. Yes, we are troubled when companies can track our buying habits, and we fight to limit access to personal medical records. Yet many respectable Americans do not think twice about undressing before curtainless windows, revealing intimate details of their lives on personal web logs (Branscum 2001; 'My Life as a Website' 2001) or appearing on 'reality' television programmes.

Such lack of social inhibition is also manifest in a lot of the email being sent ('OK NAOMI . . . if you know something . . . tell me'). Much as telephone callers have historically divulged more personal information and have often been more blunt with people they cannot see than with the same audience face-to-face, email is legendary for encouraging self-disclosure (e.g. Sproull and Kiesler 1991), often with a more incendiary tone than typically used in other forms of communication.

Sentence mechanics as social barometer

How does increased candour, coupled with growing disregard for the social and intellectual behaviours traditionally associated with upward mobility and education, relate to contemporary writing style? We said earlier that email (and contemporary prose more generally) tend to be characterized by informality of style, a psychological assumption that the medium is ephemeral, and a high level of candour. Let us consider how these characteristics, particularly the first two, manifest themselves in types of writing we have traditionally assumed needed to be carefully proofread before release for public consumption.

Some examples illustrate the point:

FOR EMERGENCY'S CALL

(sign on a locksmith shop in a Colorado ski village)

Go find a friend and tell them all about this fine book.

(book jacket puff by respected science writer)

Or consider:

Homer → home run
Albany → AlbaN.Y.
nothing → othing
M.D., Ph.D., F.A.C.S. → MD, PhD, F.A.C.S.

In recent years, not one but three venerable publishing houses have inexplicably mangled texts I submitted on computer disk. My 'Homer' (the archaic Greek poet) became 'home run' and 'Albany' morphed into 'AlbaN.Y'. In a recent issue of *History Today*, 'nothing' appeared as 'othing'. A costly magazine ad for a cosmetic surgeon informed readers that the good doctor was an 'MD, PhD., F.A.C.S.' (Fellow of the Academy of Cosmetic Surgeons), though obviously not a stickler for consistency in punctuation. Memory tells me that earlier in my adult career, the bar for printed text was set much higher. I am increasingly in accord with the thesis offered by a reviewer in the *Times Literary Supplement* that about ten years ago, all competent proofreaders must have been taken out and shot.

The real issue with 'E M E R G E N C Y ' S' or 'othing' isn't just proofreading. Rather, sloppiness in writing – even writing that purportedly has been edited – results from changing attitudes towards both privacy and public face. Are we intentionally flouting writing conventions? Probably not. Rather, we do not feel as driven as we once did to monitor what others see of us. Most of us have not forgotten how to proofread. Instead, we increasingly question the need to do so.

Email, rather than being a linguistic anomaly, is an example *par excellence* of this growing attitude towards writing as a medium that does not require attention to public face. In fact, some of the self-appointed gurus of email style blatantly scoff at the idea of subjecting email to editing – either by sender or receiver. Consider advice proffered by Hale and Scanlon (1999) in *Wired Style*:

> Think blunt bursts and sentence fragments . . . Spelling and punctuation are loose and playful. (No one reads email with red pen in hand.)
>
> (p. 3)

> Write the way people talk. Don't insist on 'standard' English.
>
> (p. 12)

> Play with grammar and syntax. Appreciate unruliness.
>
> (p. 15)

The shape of things to come

Email resembles speech because writing in general has become more speech-like, thanks in part to conscious pedagogical decisions and in part to changing social attitudes about how we present ourselves to others. But so what? Does it matter whether writing is formal or informal, edited or unedited, reflective or blurted out, reserved or candid?

Historians of English usage know that language communities go through normative and *laissez-faire* cycles, sometimes caring inordinately about such issues as dialect and prescriptive grammatical rules, other times revelling in the sheer inventiveness of a linguistically unconstrained citizenry (see e.g. Mencken 1919; Leonard 1929; Mugglestone 1995). Of late, some literary critics have cautioned that contemporary patterns of education and technology may be altering our earlier relationship with the written word (e.g. Steiner 1972; Birkerts 1994). Is email actually hastening the demise of traditional writing norms, especially in light of the galloping shift from hard-copy writing (and reading) to electronically mediated communication?

Perhaps like teenagers, we are going through an experimental phase that we will outgrow. Perhaps more normative (and contemplative) writing will return to fashion, in turn reshaping our notions of what email messages should look like. My own guess is that even if such a linguistic about-face does take place, it will not happen any time soon. For now, too many people are enjoying their linguistic recess.

References

Abbate, J. (1999) *Inventing the Internet*, Cambridge, MA: MIT Press.

Baron, N. (1998) 'Letters by phone or speech by other means: the linguistics of email', *Language and Communication* 18: 133–70.

—— (2000) *Alphabet to Email: How Written English Evolved and Where it's Heading*, London: Routledge.

Biber, D. (1988) *Variation across Speech and Writing*, Cambridge: Cambridge University Press.

—— (1995) *Dimensions of Register Variation*, Cambridge: Cambridge University Press.

Birkerts, S. (1994) *The Gutenberg Elegies: The Fate of Reading in an Electronic Age*, Boston, MA: Faber and Faber.

Branscum, D. (2001) 'Who's blogging now?' *Newsweek* 5 March, 62–3.

Bruffee, K. (1984) 'Collaborative learning and the "Conversation of Mankind"', *College Writing* 46: 635–52.

Chafe, W. and Danielewicz, J. (1987) 'Properties of spoken and written language', in R. Horowitz and S. J. Samuels (eds) *Comprehending Oral and Written Language*, San Diego, CA: Academic Press, 83–113.

Chafe, W. and Tannen, D. (1987) 'The relationship between written and spoken language', *Annual Review of Anthropology* 16: 383–407.

Collot, M. and Belmore, N. (1996) 'Electronic language: a new variety of English', in S. Herring (ed.) *Computer Mediated Communication: Linguistic, Social, and Cross-Cultural Perspectives*, Philadelphia, PA: John Benjamins, 13–28.

Crowley, S. (1998) *Composition in the University*, Pittsburgh, PA: University of Pittsburgh Press.

Crystal, D. (2001) *Language and the Internet*, Cambridge: Cambridge University Press.

Danielewicz, J. and Chafe, W. (1985) 'How "normal" speaking leads to "erroneous" punctuation', in S. Freedman (ed.) *The Acquisition of Written Language*, Norwood, NJ: Ablex, 213–25.

Dawkins, J. (1995) 'Teaching punctuation as a rhetorical tool', *College Composition and Communication* 46: 533–48.

Donath, J. (1999) 'Identity and deception in the virtual community', in P. Kollock and M. A. Smith (eds) *Communities in Cyberspace*, London: Routledge, 31–59.

Ferrara, K., Brunner, H. and Whittemore, G. (1991) 'Interactive written discourse as an emergent register', *Written Communication* 8(1): 8–34.

Goffman, E. (1959) *The Presentation of Self in Everyday Life*, Garden City, NY: Doubleday.

Hale, C. and Scanlon, J. (1999) *Wired Style: Principles of English Usage in the Digital Age*, New York: Broadway Books.

Herring, S. (ed.) (1996) *Computer Mediated Communication: Linguistic, Social, and Cross-Cultural Perspectives*, Philadelphia, PA: John Benjamins.

Leonard, Sterling (1929) *The Doctrine of Correctness in English Usage, 1700–1800*, New York: Russell and Russell.

Maynor, N. (1994) 'The language of electronic mail: written speech', in G. D. Little and M. Montgomery (eds) *Centennial Usage Studies*, Tuscaloosa, AL: University of Alabama Press, 48–54.

Mearns, H. (1925) *Creative Youth: How a School Environment Set Free the Creative Spirit*, Garden City, NY: Doubleday.

Mencken, H. L. (1919) *The American Language*, New York: Alfred Knopf.

Meyrowitz, J. (1985) *No Sense of Place: The Impact of Electronic Media on Social Behavior*, New York: Oxford University Press.

Mugglestone, L. (1995) *'Talking Proper': The Rise of Accent as Social Symbol*, Oxford: Clarendon Press.

'My Life as a Website' (2001) *Newsweek*, 12 March, p. 62.

Myers, D. G. (1996) *The Elephants Teach: Creative Writing since 1880*, Englewood Cliffs, NJ: Prentice-Hall.

Spitzer, M. (1986) 'Writing style in computer conferences', *IEEE Transactions on Professional Communication*, PC–29(11): 19–22.

Sproull, L. and Kiesler, S. (1991) *Connections: New Ways of Working in a Networked Organization*, Cambridge, MA: MIT Press.

Steiner, G. (1972) 'After the book?', *Visible Language* 6: 197–210.

Tannen, D. (1982) 'The oral/literate continuum in discourse', in D. Tannen (ed.) *Spoken and Written Language: Exploring Orality and Literacy*, Norwood, NJ: Ablex, 1–16.

Yates, S. (1996) 'Oral and written linguistic aspects of computer conferencing', in S. Herring (ed.) *Computer Mediated Communication: Linguistic, Social, and Cross-Cultural Perspectives*, Philadelphia, PA: John Benjamins, 29–46.

10 Online news

A new genre?

Diana M. Lewis

Introduction

'Nothing but a newspaper', wrote de Tocqueville, 'can drop the same thought into a thousand minds at the same moment' (1840/1946: 381). The heyday of the mass distribution of news was yet to arrive when these words were written. But by the mid-twentieth century, many national newspaper circulations were in the millions rather than the thousands. The advent of broadcast radio and television carried this mass audience trend still further. Yet at the start of the twenty-first century, it seems that mass communication is giving ground to a many-to-many model of communication, implemented via the internet, which rolls together the point-to-point model of the telephone with the one-to-many model of print and broadcast.

The word 'media' has come to mean both the technologies of communication and the public and private corporations that use them. These two senses are melded in Leitner's definition of 'media' as 'communication domains with specific communicative structures which are the cause of . . . content becoming *public*' (1997: 189, original emphasis). Owing to the low cost of electronic communication, the way content becomes public is changing. Where previously news was dependent on publishing/broadcasting companies for making its way from source to audience, it can now take a direct route. The rationale disappears for the bundling in the product of a single vendor of different information types – hard news, service information, social comment, advertisements, sport, etc. These diverse information types can spin free. News sources are changing, and so are news audiences. Moreover, what counts as news may be changing.

In September 1998, the Starr report of the investigation into US President Clinton was made available online to journalists and the public simultaneously. Within two days almost twenty-five million people had accessed it (Shaw *et al.* 2000: 73). The following year saw what has been described as 'the first internet war': the conflict in Kosovo (Taylor 2000). CNN.com's website during the crisis showed a tenfold increase in traffic from the Balkans (Pavlik 2001: 34). But it was not only regular journalists who reported on Kosovo: governmental agencies, international organizations, local witnesses, freelance journalists, news agencies, academics and interested others all used the internet to publish news, background and comment on the crisis. Cases like these reflect a changing model of news production and dissemination. And they reveal a more active reader approach to news.

Four characteristics of electronic communication are especially relevant to news dissemination. First, a single coding mechanism integrates writing, sound, image and video. Second, an unlimited amount of diverse information objects can be accumulated in a single textual space: electronic transmission favours bite-sized chunks of information in unbounded quantity. Third, the new means of communication results in different patterns of interaction, among changing sets of interlocutors. Fourth, a different medium has different connotations. The word 'news' can mean both 'important or interesting recent happenings' and 'information about such events, as in the mass media'.[1] News in this second sense is a social institution, largely defined by the form and distribution of traditional print and broadcast (as in 'be in the news', 'read/watch the news'). Changes in form and distribution therefore change our concept of news.

The discourse of online news

News genres

A text belongs to a particular genre to the extent that it displays the content, the form (physical and linguistic) and the distribution conventionally associated with some socially established task. Meaning is inferred from the form and the distribution; indeed, 'efficient communication relies not on how much can be said, but on how much can be left unsaid' (Brown and Duguid 2000: 205). An abrupt and obvious change in distribution therefore creates a sense of insecurity and opacity: a sense that part of the meaning is missing. Early online news design has built on conventions developed in print and broadcast, using continuity in form and content to provide a bridge to new genres.

The twenty-four-hour or weekly distribution cycle and the physical properties of newspaper have led to the 'news story' format, whereby a typical newsworthy event is turned into a narrative ordered by decreasing salience: the so-called 'inverted pyramid' of the newspaper article. Broadcast language, by contrast, is temporally constrained, which favours 'oral presentation' styles, conversational tone and soundbites. Online delivery is based on the combination of a small screen and a vast storage capacity. Presentation is therefore piecemeal, yet unbounded spatially or temporally. The tension between this atomization of information into small chunks and the gathering together of vast resources points to a database model: a relational information structure in which each news element can participate, at different levels of relevance, in a range of news structures.

The structure of online news

Online news design ideally achieves a balance between a focus on the minimalist data chunk and a view into the store beyond. Content is therefore layered, so that news is presented at several levels of detail. This layering weakens the concept of the 'news story' in two ways.

First, it removes the need for a 'basic level' of story. The traditional journalist (or subeditor) chooses a level of detail at which to build a news story depending on topic and perceived salience on the day. In newspapers, this story level is typically embodied by the news article, on which headlines, pictures, background, or comment are parasitic. In non-linear text, content is broken down into more finely grained textual and visual elements, each of which must be self-supporting, and none of which need correspond to the familiar 'news story'. However, a new 'basic level' of information unit may be emerging: in one manual, for example, would-be online journalists are invited to practise 'designing the perfect data chunk' (Bonime and Pohlmann 1998: 134–41).

Second, layering weakens the boundaries between stories. There is less pressure in hypertext to identify discrete news 'events'. News elements are embedded in and linked to wider content. A summary outline of one news item can simultaneously be a detail of another. A news topic is no longer developed in a series of static texts emitted at regular intervals with implicit links to other texts. It is developed as a cluster of dynamic, related, hierarchically-structured texts, like overlapping groups of concentric circles. The coverage by the BBC's online news service of the 2002 State of the Nation speech by US President Bush illustrates this model. A reader looking at an item about the speech might conceptualize the news cluster to which it belongs as something like the map in figure 10.1.

These news clusters reveal an emergent news genre differing from both print and broadcast: a theme-based group of news objects held together graphically, overlapping with other such groups, and undergoing progressive updating.

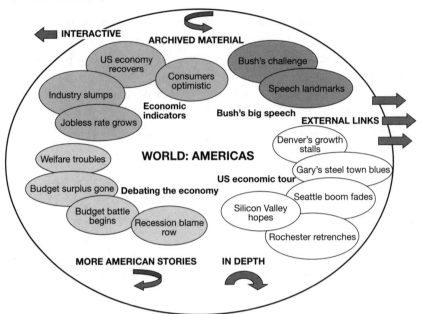

Figure 10.1 Schematic representation of a view of news from the Americas,
         BBC Online News, January 2002.

Contextualization

The fading of the traditional 'news story' does not mean that newsworthy happenings are no longer reported as narratives. Rather, the narratives are becoming shorter, and, more importantly, are seen to be parts of much larger and more complex narratives. This trend has been termed 'annotative journalism' (Paul 1995) or 'contextualized journalism' (Pavlik 2001).[2]

The award-winning CNN.com report on the conflict in Colombia[3] presents a collection of objects, including interactive maps, official and unofficial documents, statistics, articles from correspondents, experts' analyses, and links to off-site sources, as well as interaction with and among readers. Other news organizations are developing similar web-based special reports, unavailable in print. These reports cross many boundaries. They blend article with programme, by combining audio reports, written texts, video sequences, photographs and graphics. They blur the distinction between news and information, by linking up the past and the immediate: hot news that is added as it becomes known turns into background material for the interpretation of the latest events. And they mix journalistic output with material from a wide range of other published and unpublished sources, from government papers and legal documents to readers' comments. Their coherence is provided by a focus on a recognized topic: the conflict in Colombia, the conflict in the Middle East, the controversy over genetically modified plants, and so on. Such themes have often acquired their salience and coherence through the activities of the traditional agenda-setting mass media.

Despite the widespread fear that electronic text is ephemeral, electronic storage is not inherently less stable than paper storage. As with paper and other media, durability depends on management. Yesterday's electronic news text is potentially far more accessible to many more people than yesterday's print articles or broadcast bulletins. As Bierhoff *et al.* point out, 'important journalistic works do now not end up as fish wrap, but are a permanent resource for the audience' (1999: 71). Contextualized journalism is potentially an important and far-reaching development in news reporting

News style

Online news style is in a state of flux: clinging to the traditional news article genre while experimenting with hypertext. It is evolving in response to both new technological constraints and new audiences.

Electronic forms of news dissemination include multimedia 'webcasts', e-zines, news alert services, news tickers, e-journals and (we)blogs, newsgroups, personalized news trackers and email. Stylistic conventions are emerging for these various forms, but common trends can be discerned. Compression (see Biber, this volume) is carried even further online, driven by the tiny window on the vast information landscape. Paragraphs often consist of a single idea in a single sentence. Salient ideas may be expressed by bulleted lists of noun phrases rather than in clauses. Tables, charts and graphs are common. Captions to photographs tend not to name what is in the photograph, but to provide key pieces of news for readers who scan. Different modes of presentation suit different aspects of news reporting: audio, image, graphics, video and text are equally easy to present online, so that the visual expression of information (as opposed to illustrative visuals) is increasing (Horn 1998), as reliance on the word declines.

Language is above all tailored to audience, and the new configurations of audiences together with interactivity are leading to new styles of language. As noted by Castells (2000: 388), internet communication promotes the development of multiple 'weak ties' (Granovetter 1973): links that arise between people on the basis of their work, their interests or their specialisms, and result in (weak) peer-group communities. This type of link calls for neither public nor private discourse styles, but for a range of styles to bridge the published/ unpublished divide. What often appears to be informal and conversational language online, owing to its immediacy and to the shared knowledge and assumptions of participants, is at the same time less context-bound in other ways, since face-to-face contact is lacking. Most basic to audience design is choice of language. Most of the material on the world-wide web in 2002 was in English, although fewer than 50 per cent of internet users had English as their first language.[4] As new internet users come online, so languages other than English increase their share. News reports are increasingly bilingual (like the CNN report described above) or multilingual.

The future of news as a genre

Genres belong to particular discourse communities and therefore change when those communities change. With the spread of electronic communication, the discourse communities relevant to news are changing. As a result, the boundaries of what constitutes news, and of what constitutes journalism, are fading online. First, news values are changing. Hitherto, news has been thought of as events of common interest falling within particular time boundaries (recency) and space boundaries (proximity). Online, however, the absence of scheduling and geographical constraints means that the news values of recency and proximity are reinterpreted. And the sets of people defining the 'common' interest are regrouping or dissolving. Second, as the examples of the Starr report and the crisis in Kosovo illustrate, neither sources nor audiences are any longer technically dependent on journalistic intermediaries. Anyone with a story to tell or an axe to grind can purvey news at no more cost or effort than it takes to become an internet user. So will the journalist be bypassed? Will traditional journalism survive online?

Online journalism, according to one view, will need to focus more on providing an interpretation of the value and relevance of information accessed at source by the audience (e.g. Rheingold 2000). An important part of traditional journalism consists in the re-expression in a standardized, conventionalized format of an array of diversely-coded information. Even if everyone has access to press releases and original documents such as the Starr report, the argument goes, people will still want them abridged and interpreted by journalists.

Another view is that online journalism will adopt the model of 'civic journalism' as developed in the United States (e.g. Lapham 1995). This is journalism directed at a community defined by a small geographical area. It offers local news, fora for the discussion of local issues, and local information about what's on, timetables, public services and so on. It sees itself as a defence of local civil liberties against possible impingements, as a watchdog to ensure fair play.

A third view holds that the online medium is ideal for the development of communities of interest rather than geographical ones. Bell points out that 'mass communicators are interested in their peers not their public' (1991: 90). And indeed, most people are interested in their peers (see Odlyzko 2001; Kesseler and Bergs, this volume). Increasingly, the individual belongs to a range of different peer-group communities – social, professional, local, ideological, historical, hobbyist and so on. Focused news sites may thrive on audiences that it would be uneconomical to cater for in print.

So far it looks as though all these developments can prosper online.

Social prospects

But the role of traditional journalism has also been one of social control. Newspapers have been attributed a key role in nation building and maintenance (Anderson 1991). As de Tocqueville put it, 'newspapers . . . become more necessary in proportion as men become more equal, and individualism more to be feared' (1840/1946: 382). The most important role of traditional journalism has often been seen as that of agenda-setting. The journalist has been not only the gatekeeper who filters the floods of information into an orderly stream of news, but also the 'broker of social consensus' (Bardoel 1996: 297) who shapes a community's attitudes. If the mass media lose ground to electronic communication, journalism's role in community building and social control may weaken. Or will online journalism serve the same purpose?

Many deplore what Brown and Duguid describe as the 'blinkered euphoria of the infoenthusiast' (2000: 8). Proponents of electronic communication, it is suggested, place too much emphasis on the value of information and too little on the value of the social networks it binds. They are also said to undervalue the visibility of the media institutions that make news. But the social value of texts, as old and as enduring as text itself, is not in question. What is in question is the cohesion of mass audiences. With the exception of the telephone, the main communication technologies of the twentieth century – print and broadcast – have been centralizing. Mass-media organizations have tried to act as a brake on the natural tendency of large societies towards entropy (cf. Bailey 1990). But how firm is the particular social cohesion they promote? Will mass textual communities fragment, as a result of 'the miniaturization of community' in the information era (Fukuyama 1999: 87–91)?

The audiences of millions always were fragile groupings, far too heterogeneous for any notion of 'typical reader/viewer' to be of use (Bell 1991: 88–90). And there are signs that they are already fragmenting. In Europe and

North America, newspaper circulations are in steady decline[5] and advertising revenues are dwindling. American network television viewing has also been falling, especially for news.[6] Overall, Americans are sharing fewer media experiences than they used to: the mass-media audience is ageing and shrinking (Zukin 1997, ch. 6; Shaw *et al.* 2000: 75). The evidence suggests that news production and circulation will undergo further fragmentation within national borders and further extension across borders.

Conclusion

Electronic communication pulls in two directions. On one hand, its chief attraction for the individual has so far been its capacity to facilitate interpersonal communication. On the other hand, its instant global reach is unparalleled by any other communication vehicle: increasingly, news audiences are defined by much more than geography. There is thus a simultaneous individualization and globalization. These two tendencies are leading to a shift towards language and information design that is bound by different configurations of contextual factors. Online, boundaries blur between mass and personal communication, between the published and the unpublished, between news and information, and between geographically-defined communities and peer-defined communities.

The internet so far has been relatively open to access by individuals.[7] If it continues so, shifts in power are inevitable. For the world of journalism, this potentially involves a reduction in mass-media dominance over news creation and distribution. Dropping the thoughts of the few into the minds of the many becomes increasingly difficult as audiences become more fragmented and less passive.

Online news will not oust traditional news forms. But, as a growing part of the system of news production and circulation, it is redefining older news structures, and subtly changing the way we conceive of news.

Notes

1   *Collins Dictionary of the English Language* (1979).
2   On the paucity of contextualization in traditional news media, see Glasgow Media Group (2001).
3   'War Without End', available at <http://www.cnn.com/SPECIALS/2000/colombia/>, winner of the Enterprise Journalism (Affiliated) category, 2001 Online Journalism Awards.
4   In March 2002, around 82 per cent of web content worldwide was in English (source: Babel, <http://alis.isoc.org/palmares.html>), while around 43 per

cent of users had first language English (source: Global Reach, <http://www.glreach.com/globstats/>).

5   Source: 'Word press trends: on circulation'. Paris: World Association of Newspapers, 2001, available at <http://ww.wan-press.org/ce/previous/2001/congress.forum/wpt/circulation.html>.

6   US national network evening news viewing fell between 1965 and 1995 from around 83 per cent to around 42 per cent (Zukin 1997, ch. 6). See also Pew Research Center (1996).

7   In 2002, major issues of regulation (access, licensing, copyright and so on) had yet to be resolved.

References

Anderson, B. (1991) *Imagined Communities: Reflections on the Origin and Spread of Nationalism*, London: Verso.

Bailey, K. D. (1990) *Social Entropy Theory*, Albany, NY: State University of New York Press.

Bardoel. J. (1996) 'Beyond journalism: a profession between information society and civil society', *European Journal of Communication* 11(3): 283–302.

Bell, A. (1991) *The Language of News Media*, Oxford: Blackwell.

Biber, D. (this volume) 'Compressed noun-phrase structures in newspaper discourse: the competing demands of popularization vs. economy'.

Bierhoff, J., van Dusseldorp, M. and Scullion, R. (1999) *The Future of the Printed Press: Challenges in a Digital World*, Maastricht: European Journalism Centre.

Bonime, A. and Pohlmann, K. C. (1998) *Writing for New Media: The Essential Guide to Writing for Interactive Media, CD-ROMs, and the Web*, New York and Chichester: Wiley.

Brown, J. S. and Duguid, P. (2000) *The Social Life of Information*, Boston, MA: Harvard Business School Press.

Castells, M. (2000) *The Rise of the Network Society*, 2nd edn, Oxford: Blackwell.

Fukuyama, F. (1999) *The Great Disruption: Human Nature and the Reconstitution of Social Order*, London: Profile.

Gauntlett, D. (ed.) (2000) *Web.Studies: Rewiring Media Studies for the Digital Age*, London: Arnold.

Glasgow Media Group (2001) *Media Coverage of the Developing World: Audience Understanding and Interest*, Glasgow: University of Glasgow Mass Media Unit.

Granovetter, M. (1973) 'The strength of weak ties', *American Journal of Sociology* 78: 1360–80.

Horn, R. (1998) *Visual Language: Global Communications for the 21st Century*, Bainbridge Island, WA: MacroVu Inc.

Kesseler, A. and Bergs, A. (this volume) 'Literacy and the new media: *vita brevis, lingua brevis*'.

Lapham, C. (1995) 'The evolution of the newspaper of the future', *Computer-Mediated Communication Magazine* 2(7), available at <http://www.december.com/cmc/mag/1995/jul/lapham.htm> (accessed May 2002).

Leitner, G. (1997) 'The sociolinguistics of communication media', in F. Coulmas (ed.) *The Handbook of Sociolinguistics*, Oxford: Blackwell, 187–204.

Odlyzko, A. (2001) 'Content is not king', *First Monday* 6(2), available at <http://firstmonday.org> (accessed May 2002).

Paul, N. (1995) *Content: A Re-visioning. Production in the Electronic Products Newsroom*, St Petersburg, FL: The Poynter Institute.

Pavlik, J. V. (2001) *Journalism and New Media*, New York: Columbia University Press.

Pew Research Center (1996) *TV News Viewership Declines*, Washington, DC: The Pew Research Center for the People and the Press, available at <http://people-press.org/reports/> (accessed May 2002).

Rheingold, H. (2000) 'Community development in the cybersociety of the future', in D. Gauntlett (ed.) *Web.Studies: Rewiring Media Studies for the Digital Age*, London: Arnold, 170–8.

Shaw, D. L., Hamm, B. J. and Knott, D. L. (2000) 'Technological change, agenda challenge and social melding: mass media studies and the four ages of place, class, mass and space', *Journalism Studies* 1(1): 57–79.

Taylor, P. M. (2000) 'The World Wide Web goes to war, Kosovo 1999', in D. Gauntlett (ed.) *Web.Studies: Rewiring Media Studies for the Digital Age*, London: Arnold, 194–201.

de Tocqueville, A. (1840/1946) *Democracy in America*, trans. Henry Reeve, edited by H. S. Commager, London: Oxford University Press.

Zukin, C. (1997) *Generation X and the News*, Washington, DC: Radio and Television News Directors Association.

Part III

Representations and models

This section looks at how representation of particular topics has influenced the perception of readers or the audience, and affected their mental models.

Gluck examines wine descriptions. He divides them into two major types, experts showing off to other experts, and journalists who try to convey to the public the taste, feel and value of particular wines. He discusses the difficulty of doing this, and explores the role of metaphor.

Partington looks at briefings conducted at the Office of the White House Press Secretary. He outlines the often acrimonious rules of engagement between the 'spin-doctors' (spokespersons) and the 'wolf-pack' (the press). He explores the devices used and the relationship between 'truth' and 'spin'. He concludes that the latter is simply the 'art of rhetoric brought up to date'.

Wei describes the metaphors used in news coverage of recent Taiwanese elections. She finds that sets of metaphors such as marriage, financial transactions and colour terminology, are used to highlight certain ideas and hide others.

Lorenzo-Dus examines the notion of 'proper parenting' as exemplified in the BBC television talk show *Kilroy*. She shows how Kilroy, the talk monitor, controls the conversation and tries to ensure that traditional family and parenting values are promoted.

Davies analyses the *Martha Stewart Living* TV programme, which is presented in the USA, but is also syndicated throughout the world. She shows how viewers come to see Martha as representing a model of civility to aspire to, and explains how Martha promotes her desirable image.

11 Wine language

Useful idiom or idiot-speak?

Malcolm Gluck

The problem

We wine writers are the worst qualified of critical experts. This is largely, though not exclusively, because we are the most poorly equipped. The most important tool at our disposal is inadequate for the job. That tool is the English language.

How can language vividly convey what it is to experience the taste of a particular wine? We poor critics must conjure paragraphs from perfumes, and contrive fantasies from flavours. It is the unmentionable in full pursuit of the ineffable. Taste and smell, having no precise written language, are open to any interpretation.

The prose of wine writing, its struggle to depict abstract and highly personalized ideas, has given the world of wine writing two languages, or, more accurately, linguistic registers. The first is used to advertise the user's fluency with and command of his subject. Thus, a wine does not possess smell: it has a nose. A wine's flavour is its palate (further fragmented into mid-palate and back-palate). The alcohol which capillary action forces up (and then down) the sides of an agitated tasting glass is called 'the legs'. Backing this up is an exotic lexicon of more technical terms and phrases which add further lustre. Each denotes a perceived fault. Thus a wine can be 'corked', have 'VA', flaunt 'brett', be 'oxidized'; more grandly, a taster may announce 'the oak phenolics have stolen the fruit'. There is no need to explicate these in detail; it is sufficient that their exclusivity is recognized.

No lay person uses these terms for they are attempts, sometimes pretentious, to give the person who uses them the belief s/he is an expert. Crucially, the persons to whom such terms are addressed may also be convinced or conned into believing in the expertise of the user.

However, if we are to believe a psychotherapist, 'Special languages, like sexual techniques, are cover-ups' (Phillips 1995). What, then, are we wine writers trying to hide? Answer: our struggle to communicate.

Question: How many wine writers does it take to change a light bulb?
Answer: None. They work in the dark.

This old joke is not very funny. But working in the dark gives the wine scribe enormous powers. This is because the wine drinker is in the dark too, but imagines, sometimes believes, that the writer knows her way around. This belief is based solely upon language, but it is a different language from that cited above, which comprises pseudo-technical terms. The second language of wine description has fewer rules and less of a pedigree.

The language of this wine-speak has developed its own distinct credentials only in the last half century, specifically since the publication of Johnson's groundbreaking book *Wine* in 1966. Then it dawned on the 'wine journalist' – often whoever on the paper spoke passable French – that by manipulating words it was possible to acquire guru status, as well as the opportunity to taste some very nice wines. The very first paragraph of Johnson's book is as vibrant and evocative now as it was when written those decades ago:

> Think, for a moment, of an almost paper-white glass of liquid, just shot with greeny-gold, just tart on your tongue, full of wild-flower scents and spring-water freshness. And think of a burnt-amber liquid, as smooth as syrup in the glass, as fat as butter to smell and sea-deep with strange flavours. Both are wine.
>
> (Johnson 1966/1974: 9)

These definitions of Moselle and old Tokay (if I have inferred correctly) are surely not over-embroidered but perfectly and elegantly stitched descriptions of the nigh-indescribable. I swallow them both with delight and complete understanding.

This small but elegant pebble precipitated the avalanche of prose which wine language developed in the latter half of the twentieth century. This reached its apogee of expressiveness, and some say its preposterousness, when performers on television food and drink shows in the 1980s began to seem to lampoon wine, to treat it with metaphors of often barmy iconoclastic derision, entirely fitting for a liquid which was no longer the status symbol of the middle classes but the beverage of anyone who had merely enjoyed a week's holiday in Benidorm. Such language thumbed its nose at the traditions of wine; knocked it off its cobwebbed pedestal.

However, in spite of wine nowadays being a truly down-to-earth experience, enjoyed by over 70 per cent of Britons (whereas fifty years ago less than 4 per cent of the nation drank it), wine writers flourish and continue to develop impenetrable wine-speak. We continue to deal in the crepuscular and the shadowy, the indistinct and the elusive, and yet wine drinkers show no signs of being bored. We are still considered necessary sentries, providing the code words, those stimulating shibboleths, which show the shining path out of the dark.

How can I communicate exactly what it is I have tasted? Who knows anything about taste except the person who experiences it? Taste is individual; translation nigh impossible.

Top-Enders versus Bottom-Enders

This has led to an interesting development. Nowadays there are two kinds of wine writer, one more numerous than the other. Which kind of wine writer an individual is depends on which end of the bottle s/he starts at; the linguistic approach to both is different because the two viewpoints are dissimilar. In splendid Lilliputian fashion, it seems to me, wine writers are either Top-Enders or Bottom-Enders.

The Bottom-Enders begin on the lees, amongst the solid bits and bobs of the liquid left over from the winemaking. Such writers' focus is on the minutiae of the wine, the vineyard, the variety of the grapes, the philosophy of the wine grower. Such writers on wine are social animals before anything else: romantics, story-tellers, fabulists. They have a great many friends in the world of wine. Their language depends less on metaphor and more on imagery. It has great influence, mostly amongst wine snobs, wine merchants, serious collectors, and other wine writers. Writers who start at the bottom of the bottle maintain the myths of wine and are idealists; without them Bordeaux would never be able to claim a 'vintage of the century', for example. In consequence, purveyors of wine to the gentry applaud them and massage their egos.

The writer who starts from the business end of the bottle, the end the liquid flows from, has far fewer friends in the world of wine. It is harder, lonelier work being a wine critic rather than being a mere wine writer or commentator (Gluck 1999).

You pour out the wine. You regard its colour. You sniff around it. You agitate the glass to release the esters of the perfume and so better to appreciate the aromas, the nuances of the bouquet. You inhale these odoriferous pleasantries, or unpleasantries, through the chimney of the taste, the nostrils (the only access to the brain open to the air) and then you taste. You swill the liquid around the mouth and breath in air so that this liquid is aerated and experienced by up to ten thousand taste buds. The taste buds are arranged in sectors of differently orientated cohesion: one designed to recognize salinity, another alkalinity, another sweetness and so on. They connect with the brain which in turn provides the sensory data, memory based, to form the critic's view of what s/he is drinking. Some of the wine is permitted to contact the back of the throat, but only a small amount is allowed to proceed down the gullet, so that the finish of the wine can be studied. Then the wine is ejected and several seconds left to elapse whilst all these sensations are studied and written up as the impression the wine has left is mulled over.

As part of a working day, a critic like myself may taste over a hundred wines. I rarely think it wise to venture, critically, over 230 bottles in a single day, not because I find my taste buds flagging but because I dry up – linguistically. The brain tires long before the taste buds. Metaphors shrivel and become repetitive and the dark becomes truly oppressive and clammy. Perhaps recourse to a special language is indeed a cover-up.

The occasional linguistic academic attempts to make sense of the camouflage. Lehrer (1983) is a whole book devoted to the language of wine, and Aitchison (1997, 1999, 2003) also approaches the topic. She suggests wine language is rather inadequate to the task. The problems wine writers have in describing abstract ideas have particular poignance for any student of language, and Aitchison sees a direct parallel with the study of phonetics. She explains that around a hundred years ago, there was no hard and fast vocabulary to describe word sounds, so the writing on language smacked of the same undisciplined and inconsistent use of metaphors which we see in wine writing, making accurate assessment and like-for-like comparison almost impossible. The science of phonetics has now got its act together but, she suggests, wine language is still in the dark ages.

Metaphors and prototypes

How do we get out of the dark? We all grasp the easiest way out: the use of metaphors. The most common of these are fruit aromas and flavours because grapes do mimic many fruits, spices, vegetables and herbs as a result of the fermentation process: the more complex a wine, the more of these things it might exhibit (though chemical elements like the acids and the tannins are hugely contributive here). However, metaphors, according to linguists, have to share minor characteristics with the words they are describing and not major ones. To describe life as a flight on Concorde is a better metaphor than likening marmalade to jam.

This has led to an unfortunate development in my view: fruit metaphors and their precise detection and location in a wine bedevil the world of wine tutoring to the extent that far too many tutees consider themselves inadequate if they fail to unearth the exact fruits and/or vegetables and herbs the wine is said to possess. Texture is neglected, along with the finish in the throat; instead, a febrile, and often fruitless, mental game is played called 'Find the Fruits'. This becomes a point-scoring exercise and too many people in the wine trade, and those who go on wine courses, become convinced that this is the most important aspect of a wine. It is not. It has merely become received wisdom, and in some instances actually prevents the drinker enjoying the wine for what it is.

Bewildered readers of wine columns or viewers of TV wine shows must wonder whether the wines being described actually taste of damsons, loganberries or mangoes and so on. They must also marvel (which is the effect intended) at the wine tasters' brilliance at being so gifted as to find one or more of these things. The more alert viewer might muse over why the wine entertainer has not detected the aroma of grapes, which one might have thought rather more likely to appear than, say, ugli fruit. Even more odd, if the taster refers to the wine as 'grapey', this is to indicate something quite different and even, I suggest, ordinary – who wants a wine merely to taste of the berries it is made from? While many argue that the use of fruit analogies is extremely useful and gives drinkers a very clear picture of the wine, others believe the fruit idea is heavily over-used.

When a word is over-used it can frequently become 'bleached', to use the linguistic term. In short, it loses its meaning. 'Plummy' and 'blackcurrant' now have little impact as descriptors, because these flavours are attributed to wines so often – even though I use both terms when these words, to my palate, precisely describe the taste sensation. Eventually, words can cease to be metaphors and effectively become synonyms, or a shorthand which adds little descriptive substance. Aitchison once alleged that sauvignon blanc was so often described as 'gooseberry', that each had become almost to mean one and the same thing. She was, and is, right; but what am I to do when the very next New Zealand sauvignon blanc or Sancerre I taste recalls gooseberries? I have to record it as such, search as I might for other phrases to pin down the wine's sensation on the palate and nose.

In addition to its rather predictable use of fruit metaphors, wine language also appears to lack pairs of true opposites. Sweet and dry is the clearest example, but it is also one of the very few. What is more, it can only really be applied, most of the time, to white wines. When retailers introduce basic tasting codes for their wines, the whites can simply and clearly be clarified on a scale of sweet to dry, but the reds are harder to categorize. Most choose to classify them from full bodied to light bodied: these are not opposite words but merely comparatives.

Another linguistic device that could be employed far more often in wine writing is the 'prototype'. In language, descriptions can be built on prototypes which act as 'central points' about which to define related ideas and objects. Within linguistics you set up a prototype and see deviations from it, according to Aitchison (reported in Gluck 1996: 13). A bird can be said to have certain basic attributes such as a beak, feathers, thin stick-like legs, etc. With that in mind, one could establish a blackbird as a prototypical bird and describe other birds by simply relating to it. 'When people write about wine it would be very useful if they set up what would be their prototype,' she says. 'It would help to know what you regard as the centre point before you go on.'

Here at least the wine writer has some defence. Prototypes are used in wine writing, the most common relating to the established varietal character of a grape or the recognized style of a particularly well-known wine region. A pinot noir or chardonnay from the New World, for example, can be described as being Burgundian in style. Aitchison (1997: 93) quotes a tasting note from Clarke (1993) which provides an illustration: 'Wine of marvellous, minty, blackcurranty perfume with some of the cedar and cigar smoke spice of the great Médocs.' Here, Médoc serves as a prototype and Aitchison confesses that 'without the word Médoc there I would have been totally lost'.

One finds these allusions fairly frequently in wine reviews, and they can be effective, but only if the reader fully grasps the nature of the prototype. In order to be of maximum use from a linguistic standpoint, however, prototypes would have themselves to be defined somewhere – in a glossary or appendix – in order that they could function in the context of a write-up more or less as absolutes. Thus in defining them, one would unfortunately be back to square one; or would have to restrict one's writing to addressing wine specialists exclusively (a narrowing of focus which personally I would find unacceptable).

Another confusing factor is that the word Médoc works for anyone knowledgeable about Old-World wine. But in the past twenty-five years a new generation of wine drinkers, weaned on so-called New-World wines, has grown up, to whom Médoc may be, and in certain instances most decidedly is, an unknown quantity. In which case, the prototype is reader-selective and may not be appropriate. I myself use prototypes, but only when I feel confident that it serves an essential role in defining the wine. I am a frequent user of such prototypes when the wine under review has definite characteristics which make it comparable with wines costing a great deal more. 'Burgundian', for instance, has already lost some of its prototypicality because I use it to recall a style of burgundy of four or five decades ago, but younger writers, who have tasted only those burgundies from the 1970s vintages on, will have a different idea in mind when they say that a certain New Zealand pinot noir is burgundian in style. I would have to disagree with this writer's assessment and find the prototype otiose.

Therefore, using prototypes could never provide the whole answer because they are by definition literal. Describing a product such as wine, especially in the context of a newspaper or magazine, will always require impressionistic, figurative and metaphorical garnishing. Further, notes on a wine do not restrict themselves to how it looks, smells and tastes.

The conscientious critic will not only write up notes offering this analysis, but also perhaps rate the wine (points out of 100 or 20), and possibly provide ideas as to how each wine will perform with food – even those precise dishes for which each is best suited. This is, then, extremely concentrated analysis. It requires the taster rapidly to run through similarly performing wines at all price levels and arrive at a sensible value-for-money comparative judgement. It is often essential that metaphors and prototypes form part of the language of such a writer, and this must go beyond merely stating that all cabernet sauvignon tastes of blackcurrants and all chardonnay of under-ripe melon. It is this 'going beyond' that gives us Top-Enders the licence to say anything we please.

As a result, I have been taken to task more than once by Bottom-End critics for describing a wine as having the texture of 'crushed light bulbs', and for characterizing a wine for its 'sweaty richness' which, tongue firmly in cheek, inspired the further description that the wine was reminiscent 'of a sumo wrestler's jock-strap'.

Other, more mundane tastes, such as chocolate, pepper and toffee, are commonly found in wines and therefore also have obvious power as metaphors which can be further embroidered. Some have suggested (and count me in here) that fabrics make an extremely attractive metaphor system for wines. We already frequently hear wines described as silky and velvety, but what about corduroy? Sauvignon blanc can be likened to drip-dry cotton and Côtes-du-Rhône can justify the descriptor leathery. The human body – hairy, fat, fleshy, thin, etc. – can also provide an entry into an entire metaphorical system which is distanced from the product itself, yet useful in providing part of the true image of a wine.

This context can, however, produce knotty extremes which only the passionate linguistician would wish to unravel. One particularly pretentious wine critic, for example, once said of Palo Cortado that it was a 'strange hermaphroditic sherry', with the idea, I guess, that this would convey the feminine/masculine gender mix of this sherry style. But the descriptor 'hermaphroditic' is so extravagant, since it means to be possessed of both male and female sex organs, that the normal reader is surely left utterly confused instead of enlightened – and thus deterred from trying a genuinely delicious sherry.

The pressure to find more and more outlandish metaphors has been one of the defining factors in wine language. It becomes part of the individual wine writer's style and as long as the reader is left in no doubt of the writer's true opinion of the wine, then we can surely permit the indulgence.

But perhaps language needs to be supplemented by simple numbers: a rating system with points out of twenty. This gives the reader something which transcends the paucities and extravagancies of language. It offers an absolute, which language by itself cannot. Descriptions may be fun, rating is serious.

The delicious combination of pompous snobbery and specialized phraseology of the world of the wine buff makes it fertile ground for the lampooner. In Evelyn Waugh's *Brideshead Revisited* one of the many things Charles Ryder discovers through his relationship with Sebastian Flyte is a 'serious acquaintance' with wine.

> We warmed the glass slightly at a candle, filled it a third high, swirled the wine round, nursed it in our hands, held it to the light, breathed it, sipped it, filled our mouths with it, and rolled it over the tongue, ringing it on the palate like a coin on a counter, tilted our heads back and let it trickle down the throat . . .
>
>   . . . it is a little, shy wine like a gazelle.
>
> Like a leprechaun.
>
> Dappled, in a tapestry window.
>
> Like a flute by still water
>
>   . . . and this is a wise old wine.
>
> A prophet in a cave.
>
>   . . . And this is a necklace of pearls on a white neck.
>
> Like a swan.
>
> Like the last unicorn.

Rather than we wine critics shrinking from recognizing ourselves in this brilliant send-up, we would prefer to consider ourselves worthy of participation. Who would not like to be so Wildean as spontaneously to describe a young riesling as 'a necklace of pearls on a white neck'? Better yet, who would not like to taste such a wine?

References

Aitchison, J. (1997) *The Language Web: The Power and Problem of Words*, BBC Reith Lectures 1996, Cambridge: Cambridge University Press.

— (1999) 'Language of wine', in J. Robinson (ed.) *The Oxford Companion to Wine*, new edn, Oxford: Oxford University Press.

— (2003) *Words in the Mind: An Introduction to the Mental Lexicon*, 3rd edn, Oxford: Blackwell.

Clarke, O. (1993) *An Encyclopaedia of Wine*, London: Sainsbury.

Gluck, M. (1996) *Streetplonk 1997*, London: Hodder and Stoughton.

— (1999) *The Sensational Liquid: A Guide to Wine Tasting*, London: Hodder and Stoughton.

Johnson, H. (1966/1974) *Wine*, 2nd edn 1974, London: Mitchell Beazley.

Lehrer, A. (1983) *Wine and Conversation*, Bloomington, IN: Indiana University Press.

Phillips, A. (1995) *Terrors and Experts*, London: Faber and Faber.

12 Rhetoric, bluster and on-line gaffes

The tough life of a spin-doctor

Alan Partington

The spin-doctor and the wolf pack

Press briefings are 'a political chess game' (Reaves White 1999), in which 'both sides view everything the other side does as a mere tactic' (Kamiya 1998). Alternatively, they are 'rhetorical combat' (Kurtz 1998), a 'war zone' in which 'combatants with a multitude of agendas . . . prepared for battle' (Reaves White 1999). They are 'a wrestling match' and a duel or 'face-off' (ibid.) but also 'a weird formulaic dance' (Kamiya 1998). The podium is the 'spinmeister extraordinaire' (Kurtz 1998), eternally spinning the truth. The press are wild animals, the 'wolf pack' of my subheading, which 'fights over morsels' (Warren 1998).

Whatever the validity of these metaphors, what is beyond dispute is that the briefings held daily at the Office of the White House Press Secretary comprise a particularly fascinating genre of institutional talk in which the two parties involved have very different interests and aims in life. The podium wishes to project his political ideas and particular view of the world, the press wants to test that view – to destruction if necessary. The podium tries to give as little as possible away outside the official line. The press hope to uncover as much infor-mation as they can, especially any evidence of weakness, malpractice and inter-nal dissension. These differences become so severe at one point – during the Clinton–Monica Lewinsky affair and the near impeachment of the President – that communication between the two sides comes close to breaking down.

These briefings can be extremely important and highly delicate from a political perspective. Not only are the podium's words often treated by the press as White House policy, but they risk interpretation by non-American bodies as official US policy. And since they are broadcast both on television and on the internet, 'any misstep can be beamed instantaneously around the world' (CNN-allpolitics 1998) with disastrous political or diplomatic repercussions. All this exposure, of course, means fame: 'the chief White House spokesman's face is probably as well known as any cabinet member' (ibid.). Many of the journalists, too, are well-known television faces or newspaper by-lines.

In order to study the language and the rhetorical strategies of the two sides, I compiled a corpus of around fifty briefings (250,000 words) given over a period from 1996 to June 1999 by downloading the transcriptions from the web. This made them available for scrutiny using concordance technology (*MicroConcord* and *WordSmith*).

Rules of engagement

At the end of his last briefing, the press ask Mr McCurry about his feelings on retiring (my italics):

> Q: Do you have any words for the press? . . . for us?
>
> *Mr McCurry*: I am much too close to *the combat* that we've enjoyed here to make any profound comments. And I think that over time, I think I will reflect on the experiences I've had, but, look, this is *a contentious environment*, and it is, by design, *an adversarial relationship*. But what I've tried to do is make it a professional relationship and one in which we can still have *some measure of amicability* in the proceedings.

Note the descriptions 'combat', 'contentious environment', 'adversarial relationship'. As we have seen, the relationship between politicians and the press is generally perceived as highly adversarial. Note also however the mention of 'some measure of amicability'. The conflictuality is tempered in two ways: by the *familiarity* between the two sides, the fact they know each other so well, and by the co-operative presumption of journalistic *neutralism* (Clayman 1992), that is, is the convention that journalists are not held personally responsible for the accusations and criticisms contained in their questions. These are generally credited to others, especially other authorities (for example, other press agencies, politicians and so on) by the process of *attribution*:[1]

> Q: Mike, two publications today, the *Post* and the *Times*, both used the word 'paranoia' to describe the way the President feels . . .

The more damaging or dangerous the accusation, the more care has to be taken. Notice the number of attributing expressions in the following:

> Q: The New Zealand *Star Times* quoted General Schwarzkopf as saying in Auckland that the NATO bombing mistakes, as he termed them, in Yugoslavia, are, in his words, inexcusable.

Neutralism is of course entirely different from normal practice in conversation where speakers generally act under a 'with me or against me' assumption. Impartial responses and lack of positive feedback, not to mention aggressive or trick questioning (all typical of press interviews) would normally be taken as rejection or hostility (Clayman 1992: 198). Journalistic neutralism, then, is a formal practice particular to this type of institutional talk and its significance and use have to be learnt. As we shall see, there are moments of tension in these press briefings between the habits of conversation and the practices of institutional talk. In other words the neutrality of a question or a questioner can sometimes be in doubt.

An antagonistic press

The strategies employed by the press in the pursuit of an answer include: (1) simple belligerence, (2) negative and sarcastic reformulation, (3) devil's advocacy including the *agent provocateur* tactic, (4) embedding (hiding) the accusation, (5) dogged insistence. Examples of these follow.

The corpus contains several examples of *simple belligerence*, even outright rudeness:

> Q: Well, how is that an answer?
> Q: How could anybody really have believed that?

Questions are frequently spiced with sarcasm, for example, on delays in appointing officials:

> Q: I wonder, how long does it take to find out if Mr Foley paid Social Security for nannies?

Or on the administration's failure to keep a good enemy down:

> Q: You mentioned that Saddam Hussein has been in a box, a very tight box for quite a long time, but every six months or so he seems to act up. Is there any US plan to try to keep him more firmly in this box?

The sarcastic *reformulation* of a podium response is particularly noticeable:

> Q: Barry, the trip to California is still on next week?
> Mr Toiv: Oh, yes. There's a three-day trip to five states. The President's looking forward to visiting every one of them.

Q: He's looking forward to collecting money from every one of them
for the Democratic party. (Laughter)

The above example is light-hearted enough, but this doggedness and refusal to
be wooed can border on bloody-mindedness. The press see it as a vital part of
their job to present the other side of the rhetorical coin as aggressively as
circumstances allow. This entitles them, they feel, to act as *devil's advocate* and
to reformulate the podium's words in a negative, even cynical fashion, to see
how he responds. On the Kosovo crisis:

Q: But, again, has anyone ever said, well, we're now winning?
Mr Lockhart: Everyone has said that to date this has been an effective
air campaign and they're highly confident we'll reach our military
objectives.
Q: So the answer is no?

Accusations and criticisms of the administration can be particularly hard for
the podium to deal with when they are *embedded* within the question, that is,
when they are presented as presuppositions or assertions of a question, part of
its given background information. There are a number of way of embedding a
disputable proposition. One common way is nominalization:

Q: The Senator from Virginia, John Warner, says *the lack of a US exit strategy from Bosnia* puts the US on the brink of disaster right now.

The lack of strategy is firstly *factualized* as a noun phrase and then embedded
both grammatically – in being topicalized – and rhetorically as attributed to
another speaker.

Another way of embedding a contentious proposition is to place it inside a
subordinate clause:

Q: I'm really trying to find out *what hasn't worked* or what are the
factors . . .

If-clauses are especially popular:

Q: *If Gerry Adams can't, in effect, deliver something from the IRA, at least a
commitment to peace*, then what exactly is the US trying to do in
talking with him?
Mr McCurry: We don't accept the premise of that question because he has
been an important contributor . . .

Once again the proposition is presented in the guise of given information. The podium is forced to formally refute the truth of the premise.

A final example is the 'have you stopped beating your wife?' manoeuvre (on a supposed rift between the President and Senator Jackson):

Q: Did the phone call mean that they've kissed and made up?

The presupposition being they were at daggers drawn before the call. If the podium answers either *yes* or *no* he admits there was a tiff at some juncture and the press can launch a 'dissension-in-the-administration-ranks' story.

The last press pursuit technique in our list is *dogged insistence*. The quest for an answer to a particular question can go on for long periods of time, even the whole of a briefing. For example, the session held by Mr McCurry on 21 January 1998, lasting thirty-six minutes, consisted largely of the press attempting to induce the podium to comment, to enlarge upon the President's statement, delivered that morning, that he had not had 'an improper relationship' with Monica Lewinsky. The same question:

Q: Mike, you said this morning the President did not have an improper
    relationship with this former intern. What do you mean by an
    improper relationship?

is asked over and over again in different guises. Eight times the podium repeats that he *will not parse the statement for you*. Five times he has to insist that *it speaks for itself*, three times that he *will not go beyond what was said* and four times that he *cannot amplify* or *interpret* or *characterize* the President's words. In particular, the press want to know why the word *sexual* does not appear:

Q: What is puzzling to many of us is that we've invited you probably two
    dozen times today to say there was no sexual relationship with this
    woman and you have not done so.
Q: Does that mean no sexual relationship? Why not put the word
    'sexual' in? That's the problem.

He is held responsible not only for what his client has said but also what he has not said. Perhaps nowhere else in my corpus of briefings is the podium 'grilled' so hard:

Q: Do you smell anything, a rat or anything?
Mr McCurry: I smell the lights in here cooking furiously everyone who is
    standing under them.

Neutralism under strain

Predictably, given these aggressive rhetorical tactics, the neutralism of the journalists is sometimes questioned by the podium. There is discussion over what a 'fair question' is:

> Q: Joe, I want to go back at something. I think it's a fair question and maybe deserves a thoughtful answer.
>
> *Mr Lockhart*: Do I get to decide whether it's a fair question?

The fairness of the *agent-provocateur* technique is an especially heated debate:

> *Mr Lockhart*: I think what you're trying to do is find a way where *I can set a marker where, at a certain point of time, you can say the policy has failed*, and that's just not how we're doing this.
>
> Q: *It's not bad for us to try to set a marker* upon which to gauge whether or not this is worth it or not.

And the press's seeming obsession with the Clinton–Lewinsky affair places particular strain on the podium's patience:

> Q: You have not provided us a real opportunity . . .
>
> *Mr McCurry*: I dispute that. We come out here every single day. We offer up all kinds of stories – and it's been Monica, Monica, Monica, Monica. And you know that, and I know that. I mean, you can't pretend otherwise. Okay, good. Thanks.

A 'rhetorical' podium

However, it is not in the podium's interest to challenge his interlocutors too often. When in difficulty he will instead often 'retreat' into rhetoric. Probably the single most striking rhetorical device to be found in the podium's language is the use of lexico-syntactic parallelism (or *isocolon* in classical rhetoric). A simple example is:

> I think *everyone agreed to* that; *everyone agreed* that *there must be* a follow-on force, *there must be* US participation, *there must be* participation on the ground in Bosnia.

Parallelism is normally defined as the repetition of a syntactic structure within a short space of text or period of time. When used properly it can convey 'the spontaneous energy of deep feeling or conviction' (Cockcroft and Cockcroft 1992: 129). It creates a rhythmic motion which, as Coleridge remarked, gives the impression of someone striving 'to hold in check the workings of passion' (1956: 206). When overused, however, it 'produces banal and trivializing effects' (Cockcroft and Cockcroft 1992: 129). In these briefings we find abundant examples of both.

The most skilful use of parallelism is the three-part list (or *tricolon*), especially when the third item introduces a degree of modification. Two occurrences of a phrase structure are sufficient to set up the expectation in the hearer/ reader about the third occurrence. The slight change renders the third item emphatic (and, more than incidentally, highlights the speaker's own rhetorical skill). The most successful example from these texts is undoubtedly:

> Mr Lockhart: Well, *you can use words like* 'punishment,' *you can use words like* 'stole,' and *you can be wrong.*

However, this kind of parallelism is quite rare in these texts. More common is three-item parallelism with either no variation:

> Bosnia is a different place today *than it was* a year ago, *than it was* two years ago, certainly *than it was* two and a half years ago . . .

or seemingly random (that is, unordered) change:

> And *those who commit* them, *those who are responsible* for ordering them and *those who are responsible* at the political level will be held accountable in the International War Crimes Tribunal.

Most of the time the podium is thinking and speaking on his feet, whilst the elegance of third-item variation parallelism is a typical feature of pre-prepared rhetoric.

In fact, attempts at 'doing rhetoric' without proper preparation can lead to comic or clumsy effect:

> because we cooperate so *closely* with our *close* ally

> people who have been driven from their homes and *the unseen that we don't see* who have been brutally murdered

And it can be downright dangerous:

Mr McCurry: But personality and who stands here is not a part of it. *That's why* when Joe walks in here and starts on Monday, it will be sort of a seamless transition, because there is only one person that got elected to do the job that we all do here, *and that's* Bill Clinton. *And that's who* you all are covering, *and that's who* we work for. *And that's who* the American people *want to know about* it [*sic*] – they *want to know about* his thinking and his decision-making. *And that's why* you legitimately *want to see* more of him.

Here we see not only a loss of clear-thinking but a slip of judgement. The podium is carried away by the grandiloquence of a series of parallelisms, allied to stock rhetorical expressions such as 'the American people' and fine thoughts about the President. He ends with a disastrous admission that the President is in fact being secretive and that the press's frequent complaints during this period that he is hiding from them are justified ('and that's why you legitimately want to see more of him').

The President's speeches, on the other hand, are generally written in advance. One of the questioners draws attention to his use of the three-part list technique:

Q: The President seemed to indicate yesterday that it was *in the hands of Congress* and *in the hands of the public* and *in the hands of God*.

where 'God', though not syntactically different from the previous two items, is on a rather different semantic plane from Congress and the public. There is also an implied scale from the least to the most important – not uncommon in parallelisms (a technique known as *incrementum*). The journalist, however, adds a fourth item:

But part of it also seems to be *in his hands*.

Not only does this addition supply the syntactic variation which is 'missing' from the earlier parallels but there is an implied ironic question of whether the fourth element – the President – is more important than God. The device is, of course, known as *bathos*, definable as the deliberate deflation of bombast, or fighting rhetoric with anti-rhetoric.

If so dangerous, why does the podium resort so often to this 'rhetorical mode'? Firstly, a certain grandiloquence is normal in US politics. Secondly, it allows him to spend longer responding to questions while (hopefully) giving nothing away. It enables him to provide a 'pseudo answer', i.e. to *appear to answer* while evading the question by generalizing and by raising 'safe topics':

> Q: . . . if the bombing does not work?
>
> *Mr Lockhart:*   Let me address it this way: I think, as the President told the American public last Friday . . . *the price of inaction* here is higher than *the potential price of action*.

There are a couple of linguistic comments to make on these examples. The first is that the repeated expression can be very short. Parallelism is often exemplified with lengthy templates as in the well-known prayer: 'Teach us, Good Lord, to give and not to count the cost, to fight and not to heed the wounds, to toil and not to seek for rest'. But two items are, in fact, sufficient as in the example on page 000 with *that's why*, *that's who*, etc.

The second observation is that most writers on lexical patterning have concentrated on idiomatic expressions. The occurrences of parallelism seen here however show that all sorts of non-idiomatic, 'normal' language can be involved in repeated patterning: *than it was* (example on page 122), *those who* (page 122), *there must be* (page 121).[2] The technique of parallelism is essentially a means to harness even the plainest of language to rhetorical effect.

Conclusions

Much attention is currently paid to the phenomenon of *spin-doctoring*, the tailoring of news and information to cast a favourable light on the institutions of authority. And *spin* and *truth* are often counterposed as mutually exclusive. But, on the evidence of these briefings at least, the term *spin* would appear to be little more than a new name for an old game. It is the art of rhetoric brought up to date and employed by professionals for debate with other professionals. Here, it is one version of the 'truth' put forward by the podium in an adversarial environment and it has to be robust and well-argued or it will not survive. Persuading people to accept your version of events, of the truth, in competition with other versions, has been at the very dialogic heart of rhetoric since classical times. And just as Socrates was alert to the efforts of the doctors of sophistry, in the kind of public dialogue embodied in these briefings, we have our modern defences against the doctors of spin.

Finally, it has been objected, conversely, that the relationship between the press and the political administration in the United States is actually too complicitous, that their interests are too intertwined. This argument is heard from both the left and the far right, though in rather different terms. The former maintain that the realities of press ownership militate against any real independence (see Herman and Chomsky 1999). The latter believe that the Washington establishment and a traditionally left-leaning media are in cahoots to deny middle America a voice to 'talk back' (see Davis and Owen 1998). Be this all as it may, the evidence presented in this chapter shows that this is certainly not how it seems to the protagonists themselves. They perceive the relationship as highly adversarial and comport themselves accordingly. A close analysis of the greater economic and social implications of administration– press relations is beyond my scope here. In the microcosm of briefings the *rhetorical*, the *linguistic* combat is real enough.

Notes

1 'in Goffman's terms, "authorship" is overtly deflected' (Clayman 1992: 173).
2 This fact lends weight to Sinclair's (1992) argument, which extends the notion of phraseology to encompass a great deal more of language than is commonly thought.

References

Clayman, S. (1992) 'Footing in the achievement of neutrality: the case of news-interview discourse', in P. Drew and J. Heritage (eds) *Talk at Work*, Cambridge: Cambridge University Press, 163–98.

CNN-allpolitics (1998) available at <http://www.cnn.com/ALLPOLITICS/stories/1998/10/02/lockhart/index.html>

Cockcroft, R. and Cockcroft, S. (1992) *Persuading People: An Introduction to Rhetoric*, London: Macmillan.

Coleridge, S. (1956) *Biographia Literaria*, ed. G. Watson, London: Dent.

Davis, R. and Owen, D. (1998) *New Media and American Politics*, New York: Oxford University Press.

Herman, E. and Chomsky, N. (1999) 'Manufacturing consent', in H. Tumber (ed.) *News: A Reader*, Oxford: Oxford University Press, 166–79.

Kamiya, G. (1998) available at <http://www. salonmag.com/media/1998/03/cov_27media.html>

Kurtz, H. (1998) *Spin Cycle: How the White House and the Media Manipulate the News*, New York: Touchstone.

Reaves White, S. (1999) available at <http://www.writerswrite.com/journal/apr99/nonf4.htm>

Sinclair, J. (1992) 'Trust the text: the implications are daunting', in M. Davies and L. Ravelli (eds) *Advances in Systemic Linguistics: Recent Theory and Practice*, London: Planter, 5–19.

Warren, J. (1998) available at <http://www.cjr.org/year/98/3/books-kurtz.asp>

13 Politics is marriage and show business

A view from recent Taiwanese political discourse

Jennifer M. Wei

Introduction

In recent years, the use of metaphors has attracted much attention in the field of linguistics (Lakoff and Johnson 1980; Lakoff and Turner 1989; Ortony 1993; Lakoff 1996).[1] In these studies, metaphors are treated not as linguistic embellishments but as fundamental linguistic and cognitive devices that allow speakers to make sense of the world around them. Metaphors are conventional, perceptual and evaluative, and understanding how they structure and influence the way we think and talk about the world has been the focus of many scholarly interests (Quinn, 1991).

Metaphors are also culturally significant: they both limit and prescribe criteria for interpreting expectations (Quinn 1991). For example, war and sports are two of the most common metaphors used in describing politics in the western world, but as we will find in our Taiwanese political discourse data, sports (with baseball and table tennis as exceptions) are not, and have never been, a favourite pastime of the electorate and do not enjoy much circulation in the Taiwanese political scene. People in Taiwan talk about politics in terms of natural phenomena, such as weather, show business (especially primetime TV soap operas) and financial transactions, i.e. stock trading. Thus, sociocultural forces such as the media, recent social events, pressing issues, and voters' attitudes influence the creation and use of metaphors (Wei 2000). This relationship between metaphors and their sociocultural context further suggests the importance of sociocultural-based analysis.

Types of metaphors found in election rhetoric

This discussion of political metaphors will be organized into three topic groups: metaphors of relationships, metaphors of financial transactions and metaphors of costumes. Various aspects of recent Taiwanese politics are depicted and highlighted via these metaphorical expressions. Some of them are quite benign, such as 'marriage', which refers to the inherent compromise and negotiation in politics, and the omnipresent effects of elections, respectively. Others can be malignant, such as 'war' and 'financial transactions', where the metaphorical expressions highlight confrontation and conflict, or the short-term loss and gain of a political proposition. The purpose of such groupings is not to provide an exhaustive taxonomy, but to explain how these metaphors are related to each other, and to provide a more efficient way to contrast and compare the materials in order to present a fuller picture of Taiwanese politics (see also Wei 2001).

Metaphors of relationships

The first metaphor we analyse is 'politics is marriage'. This metaphor was used especially to reflect the relationship between former Taipei Mayor Chen Shui-bian and the Taipei city council. The frictions between them can be attributed to the fact that Chen Shui-bian was the first DPP (Democratic Progressive Party) candidate to be elected Taipei Mayor in 1994, an event which the then dominant party,[2] the KMT (Kuomintang), took as a disgrace. As the election approached, the KMT, which felt threatened by the DPP and its state policies, saw the election as a chance to defend its political resources and maintain power. The DPP, with its increasing political clout, was trying to win more seats in order to challenge the ruling party.

Returning to the marriage metaphor, we found many expressions in which married couples are used to reflect the conflicts and tensions between politicians and their two parties. Some examples follow:

| *Shifu* | *jiu xiang* | *yi dui* | **yuanao** | |
| city-council | like | a | bickering couple | |

| **fenfenhehe** | | *xima* | *buduan* | *shangyan.* |
| separations-and-reunions | plays | constantly | on stage. | |

'The city of Taipei and the council of Taipei are like a *bickering couple*; their *separations and reunions* are constantly brought on stage.'[3]

| *Shifu* | *jiu xiang* | *yi dui* | **yuanao,** | | | |
| city-council | like | a | bickering couple, | | | |

| *qizhong* | *you* | *xuduo* | *bu ke fenli* | *de* | *zeren* | *he* | *yiwu.* |
| between | have | many | inseparable | DE | responsibilities | and | obligations. |

'The city of Taipei and Taipei council are like a *bickering couple*. They have inseparable obligations and responsibilities between them.'

Zai lifayuan	*nian di*	*gaixuan*	*zhiqian*	**lihun**
At Legislative Yuan	year end	re-election	before	divorce

huoshi	**ehua de guanxi**	*shi*	*mian bu liao.*
or	worsening relationship	is	inevitable.

'Actually, if the city of Taipei and Taipei council are a bickering couple, their *divorce*, or at least their *worsening relationship*, is inevitable by the end of next year.'

Xiang	*mei yi zhuang*	**shibai de hunyin**,	*shuang fang*	*dou yinggai*
Like	every-one-piece	failing DE marriage	both sides	both should

dui **ehua de guanxi**	*fuze.*
for worsening relationship	responsible.

'Like every *failing marriage*, both sides should take responsibility for their *worsening relationship*.'

As we see, the above examples use the marriage metaphor to highlight responsibilities and tensions between Taipei and Taipei council. With the mayor from the DPP and the spokesperson of the city council from the KMT, the tension and contention between two parties are also expressed by such a metaphor.

Vocabulary such as *yuanao*, or 'bickering couple', *fenfenhehe*, or 'splitting and reunion', *chongtu*, or 'conflict' and *maoheshenli,* or 'seeming harmony', facilitates the comparison between marriage and politics. Thus, when politicians are in conflict we can think of them as quarrelling couples who sometimes split up.

Unlike the other metaphors used in political discourse, such as war, sports or disease, the marriage metaphor is relationship-oriented; it highlights problems and reflects the public pressure on politicians, as well as the inevitable obstacles that must be endured. It thus evokes a sense of order or an appeal to order, which war and perhaps sports metaphors do not. Therefore, it is more humane and less militant than war, sports and other aggressive, combative, and confrontational metaphors. Furthermore, marriage in Chinese culture, as in most other relationships, does not, compared to the western concept, stress free will or maximization of individual satisfaction. It is not only a holy union of two individuals who commit to each other, but also of two families, which have a lot of interests at stake (Baker 1979). Another striking difference from western practice is that the church and/or state do not witness the ceremony.

Instead, the ceremony is performed in the home of the groom, where food and drinks are offered to the groom's ancestors and elders of his family. Such a difference in practice seems to imply that marriage in Chinese society is secured and witnessed by elders and ancestors of the family who exercise more control and power than the couple's free will. In fact, like deal-making in politics, the primary importance of marriage is the *fulfilment of obligations* to ancestors by ensuring the continuance of the family (Thornton and Lin 1994: 36). Using marriage metaphors to depict political scenarios certainly stresses adaptations, negotiations and obligations in Taiwan's developing democracy.

A campaign is a financial transaction

Once a political competition gets to the final stage, many candidates try various means to attract voters' attention. Making promises, even those that may never be fulfilled, is among the most often used means to gain popularity. The welfare programme became one of the most contested issues during the election. Political promises are likened to writing cheques, and different issues are calculated by politicians and interest groups as profit-taking or loss. The weak and the disadvantaged, especially the seniors and the disabled, are dragged into the political discourse, making headlines and hot topics for potential voters.

Xiguanxing	*de **tiaopiao***		*gou*	*bu qi*	*xuanmin yuqi.*
Habitual	cheque-bouncing		can't	arouse	voters' expectation.

Ruoshi	*youxian xuanpiao*	*budi*		*qiye*	***tozi.***
Weak	limited votes	can't fight		industries'	investment.

'Habitual *cheque bouncing* by politicians can't win the trust of the voters. The votes of the weak are not as significant as the *investment* of the big industries.'

Lee Teng-hui	*si chu*		*wei hoxuanren*	***beishu,***
President Lee	everywhere		for candidates	endorse cheques,

da pi		*DPP*	*de bushi.*
severely criticize		DPP	DE misconduct.

'President Lee Teng-hui is *endorsing cheques* for the [KMT] candidates and [hypocritically] criticizes the misconduct of the DPP.'

Lee Teng-hui	*zai Taipei*	*xian wei Hsieh Shen-shan zhuxuan*
President Lee	in Taipei	first for Hsieh Shen-shan help-campaign

*kaichu delaoren nianjin **zhipiao** zhenjing quan guo.*
write DE   senior welfare cheque shock whole country.

'President Lee Teng-hui campaigning for the Taipei council candidate, Mr Hsieh Shen-shan, by endorsing a *cheque* for "senior welfare" that has shocked the nation.'

In this example, President Lee Teng-hui proposed to give seniors over the age of sixty-five 5,000 NT a month as a token to attract votes for the KMT candidate in his home area, Taipei county. Many politicians copied such strategy, proposing to give more money to attract more voters from interest groups.[4] In this example, we see how the 'senior welfare' issue gained wide circulation and was taken up by many candidates as a useful tactic to attract votes.

*Hoxuanren zai yi   de shi ruhe   **qingsuan** dui-shou de **chennian** laozhang.*
Candidates care   DE is how   clear-out opponent DE 1,000-year-old-debts.

'The candidates aim to *balance the old debts* of their opponents.'

In presenting the campaign as a financial transaction, we see candidates discussing various issues as a kind of investment that brings marketable prospects and profitable returns, though it is not always possible to see exactly how many of these promises are literal and how many metaphorical. Political deals are calculated for the chances of voters being enthusiastic or not. When most voters are excited by the potential 'profits' of an economic, political or social proposition, they may fail to scrutinize the politicians' credentials, intentions and actions.

In the metaphor 'a campaign is a financial transaction', the financial aspect of the campaign is emphasized. As shown by the examples above, the following terms elucidate the nature of this metaphor: *zhipiao*, or 'cheque', *beishu*, or 'endorsement', *kaichu*, or 'write a cheque', *qingsuan*, or 'calculating previous debts', *xiguanxing de tiaopiao*, or 'habitual cheque-bouncing', *tozi*, or 'investment'. We see that making a political promise to voters is likened to writing a cheque to them. How much to write and to whom is weighed by candidates and campaigners, who calculate the returns of votes from a particular interest group such as seniors over sixty-five, the disabled, or women on maternity leave. Since this is more of a symbolic gesture than a real promise, prices can be hiked and haggled, depending on whether there are other candidates making similar political propositions or other interest groups in need of promises in return for votes. However, too many promises fail, resulting in bounced cheques by politicians. Thus, voters are not optimistic about the candidates' financial and political prospects.

Metaphors of costumes

One of the newer metaphors found in recent Taiwan political discourse is 'wearing a particular hat', which refers to the performing of a particular role at a particular time for a particular political purpose. For example, ex-President Lee Teng-hui wore several hats: he was the President of the Republic of China, the party chair of the KMT, and a Christian. However, the Chinese phrase *kou maozi* (dumping a hat on someone else) implies something more than just performing a particular role since it also connotes either accusations or innuendo of scandal. When a journalist reports that a candidate is wearing a particular hat for certain political reasons, and is associating that hat with a certain colour, the metaphor is not only culturally specific, but alerts the voters to the special predicaments of candidates in the campaign. The colour symbolism used in the following examples associates red with political bribery among Chinese and US high officials, gold with financial scandals in property values, black with corruption among KMT high officials, and yellow with sexual misconduct.

| *Jinlai xingqi yigu* | **'kou maozi'** | *fengchao –* | **'hong maozi,** |
| Recently start a | 'dumping hat' | trend | red hat, |

| **huang maozi,** | **hei maozi,** | **jin maozi'** | *mantian* | *feiwu.* |
| yellow hat | black hat | gold hat | whole sky | fly. |

'Recently many of the candidates in the campaign have tended to engage in "hat dumping" [i.e. accusing their opponents of misconduct] – [we see] *red*, *yellow*, *black*, and *gold* *hats* flying over the whole sky.'

| *Qunian* | *daibiao* | *DPP* | *canxuan* | *zongtong de* |
| Last year | represent | DPP | go-into-campaign | presidency |

| *Peng Ming-min* | *shuo* | 'Hsu Hsin-liang | shou le | Tang Shu-bei | wushi wan meijin.' |
| Peng Ming-min | say | 'Hsu Hsin-liang | took | Tang Shu-bei | US$500,000.' |

| **Hong maozi** | *yikou* | *zaocheng* | *zhenghan.* |
| Red hat | dumped-on | cause | shock. |

'Mr Peng Ming-min, one of the DPP candidates nominated for the 1996 Taiwan presidential election, said, "Hsu Hsin-liang has taken the US$500,000 from Tang Shu-bei". The *red hat* [i.e. political bribery, among Chinese and US officials] has created shock waves among the public.'

The colour red has had a very peculiar meaning since the 1950s in Taiwanese political discourse. It was associated with the 'Red China', or Communist China, then in bitter relations with the KMT authorities in Taiwan. However, such peculiarity has lost currency since the 1980s as political authorities have relaxed their tensions and contentions. The colour red used in the current example refers to alleged bribery between KMT high officials and US officials. It is most likely derived from the common practice of *shou hongbao* or 'receiving a red envelope', a practice used to buy favours or to avoid potential harm.

The use of 'candidate hats' to accuse one's opponent of misconduct is quite common, especially towards the end of the election when the stakes are high and strategies to win recognition and support are exhausted. Some of the use of 'hat with colour' is quite new in political discourse, and the examples given here are from a context where certain accusations are made. The association of colours with certain political connotations, such as red with bribery and yellow with sexual misconduct, is deeply entrenched in Chinese culture. Other associations, such as gold with property financial scandals and black with corruption among KMT high officials are more novel in recent political discourse.

Various political events are also incorporated into such usage. Among these are cases of bribery between high US and Chinese officials, manipulation of land values in Nantou county by local financial experts and provincial council members, nepotism among the KMT high officials, and sexual misconduct among the DPP candidates. These activities are referred to as red, gold, black, and yellow hats. Strategically, *luan kou maozi*, or 'dumping a hat on your enemy', implies misconduct by one's enemy. Coincidentally, it was Chinese Communist Party political practice to accuse 'enemies of the people' of all kinds of misconduct and crime including exploitation, capitalism and treason. According to Li Chi (1958), the hat was symbolic of authority and power. The reason seems to be that hats worn by people of authority in the old days were usually large and imposing. Hence to coerce a subordinate to do something through the weight of authority was *da maozi ya xia lai* or 'to press down by the big hat' in figurative language. During the political upheavals in China in the 1950s and 1960s, such phrases were used to symbolize accusations of wrong ideology (ibid.: 48–9). In contrast, the function of such linguistic devices in Taiwanese political discourse seems to be more than 'putting down one's enemy'. It further disgraces and humiliates one's opponents in public while demonstrating one's innocence or superiority. Moreover, instead of combining a hat with various ideologies such as capitalism, officialism or formalism, as during the Cultural Revolution in China, the current use of a hat with colour symbolism adds more specific tones to an insinuation.

Conclusion and suggestions

This chapter has attempted to argue that the pervasiveness and persuasive nature of metaphors have profound influence in the political process in Taiwan, and that popular political discussions are inherently and inevitably metaphorical. It has also examined the sources of some of the new metaphors, and analysed their pragmatic and strategic functions. By using a cognitively and culturally based analytic frame as proposed by Lakoff and Johnson (1980), Quinn (1991) and Lakoff (1996), it has further looked into the specific sociocultural conditions that provide grounds for new and productive metaphors. While providing a sociocultural analysis of a specific political metaphor, it has also found that the pragmatic functions of metaphors are more than just heuristic or cognitive devices. They are also adopted for strategic reasons. Thus, we have seen metaphors that are used to reduce complex political issues to mere bickering between parties and candidates, to authenticate legitimacy for the candidates, to alter the roles of the candidates from those of decision-makers to those of performers, to transform voters into mere spectators, to highlight the financial and combative aspects of the campaign, and to accuse one's enemy of wrongdoing.

One way to discover a more 'dialogic' perspective on metaphor in which the voters, the politicians and the media all take part, is to look into newspapers, commentaries and editorials, and to analyse metaphors in these contexts. For example, the relationship between metaphor and political policy is an interesting one, as we see from the case of *laoren nianjin*, or 'senior welfare', which can refer to either a *caqiangzouhuo*, or 'misfire', or a *kai zhipiao,* or 'the writing of a cheque'. The suggestion for a more dialogic approach in viewing metaphorical usage echoes the suggestion of Pugh, Ovando and Schonemann (1999) that a distinction should be made between weak and strong metaphorical thinking, the former being the use of comparisons to manipulate arguments and rationalize set positions, and the latter an effect to foster dialogue and expand perspectives on complex issues. By identifying not just the politicians' views circulating in the media, but also the opinions of the viewers and other concerned parties, we should be able to engage in a more open forum of how ideas and policies can be voiced and heard via various channels.

We see, then, that the use of a new metaphor breaks up the rigid conceptual framework of an existing political order, and frequently reveals the attitudes of the policy-makers. There is also the question of the extent to which politicians and journalists use or abuse a metaphor and the consequences of such deliberate linguistic manipulation. In the case of *luankou maozi*, or 'dumping a hat at one's enemy', we saw that various social events were presented as stained hats with each colour insinuating an improper behaviour. Regardless of whether any truth or evidence behind such accusations and irrational speculations is ever confirmed, the linguistic device in the media does influence the public's perception of a candidate or an event, so that the ethics of the media and the campaigns do seem to be affected.

Does the public have any means to resist the abuse of a negative metaphor? In the case of 'politics is wearing a particular hat', the same metaphor was also pervasive during the Cultural Revolution in China, and this tells us that such metaphors have again entered Chinese political discourse and regained resonance. Certainly, a comparative and diachronic study of metaphors such as the ones analysed above that are used in Chinese political discourse will reveal their sociocultural evolution and help us understand the dynamic relationship between politics and language.

Notes

1   I am grateful to Professor Sharon Pugh at Indiana University for discussing political metaphors with me and for sharing many of her insights on similar issues.
2   As a result of the Taiwanese presidential and vice-presidential elections in 2000, the KMT lost its dominant position after more than fifty years as the ruling party in Taiwan. The DPP candidate, Chen Shui-bian won the race with a 39.3 per cent vote out of a national turn-out rate of 82.69 per cent.
3   The example is taken from *United Daily*, 10 November 1997.
4   For more details on the story, see *United Daily*, 17 November 1997.

References

Baker, H. (1979) *Chinese Family and Kinship*, New York: Columbia University Press.
Lakoff, G. (1996) *Moral Politics: What Conservatives Know That Liberals Don't*, Chicago: University of Chicago Press.
Lakoff, G. and Johnson, M. (1980) *Metaphors We Live By*, Chicago: University of Chicago Press.
Lakoff, G. and Turner, M. (1989) *More Than Cool Reason: A Field Guide to Poetic Metaphor*, Chicago: University of Chicago Press.
Li, C. (1958) 'The use of figurative language in communist China', *Studies in Chinese Communist Terminology*, 5, Berkeley, CA: Center for Chinese Studies, Institute of International Studies, 48–9.

Ortony, A. (1993) *Metaphor and Thought*, Cambridge: Cambridge University Press.

Pugh, S., Ovando, C. J. and Schonemann, N. (1999) 'The political life of language: metaphors in writings about diversity in education', in C. J. Ovando and P. McLaren (eds) *The Politics of Multiculturalism and Bilingual Education: Students and Teachers Caught in the Crossfire*, Columbus, OH: McGraw-Hill.

Quinn, N. (1991) 'The cultural basis of metaphor', in J. W. Fernandez (ed.) *Beyond Metaphor: The Theory of Tropes in Anthropology*, Stanford, CA: Stanford University Press.

Thornton, A. and Lin, H. (eds) (1994) *Social Change and the Family in Taiwan*, Chicago: University of Chicago Press.

Wei, J. M. (2000) 'An analysis of the metaphorical usage of the 1996 Taiwan Presidential and Vice-presidential Election', *Journal of Asian Pacific Communication* 10: 1–19.

—— (2001) *Virtual Missiles: Allusions and Metaphors in Taiwanese Political Campaigns*, Lanham, MD: Lexington Books.

14 Emotional DIY and proper parenting in *Kilroy*

Nuria Lorenzo-Dus

Introduction

Representations are central to the study of media discourse, especially in talk shows where a gallery of issues and of more or less stereotyped characters are portrayed. Here I examine recurrent representations of parenting in the BBC-hosted *Kilroy* programme and argue that these arise from the show's underlying communication ethos. To encapsulate this, I use the metaphor of 'emotional DIY', which is premised upon the belief that people can (and must) do their best to 'fix' their lives in socially sanctioned ways. In *Kilroy*, 'proper' parenting is conceived of as family structures of the nuclear variety and as a skills-learning process in which children's needs are consistently prioritized. To this end, the host interactionally mediates participants' accounts for the benefit of the overhearing audience. As talk-monitor, he ensures that the accounts of family and parenting generated in the studio produce 'appropriate' representations of parenting.

Kilroy and emotional DIY

Kilroy belongs to the 'audience discussion' (Haarman 1999) subgenre of talk shows. Hosted throughout by ex-Labour Party Member of Parliament Robert Kilroy-Silk, this show has occupied a regular morning television slot over the past two decades. Throughout this time it has marketed itself as a discussion forum on pertinent broad social issues, seeking to 'identify all significant views and test them rigorously and fairly on behalf of the audience'.[1] Concomitantly, the *Kilroy* forum has progressively shifted towards increasing levels of personalization and the kind of 'conversationalization practices' (Fairclough 1989) that pervade tabloid talk shows. *Kilroy*'s discussion format consequently oscillates nowadays between 'civilised intellectual argument' and 'passionate' everyday life dilemmas.[2]

The show's studio space, i.e. a comfortable and intimate amphitheatre, facilitates the combination of personalized and group-oriented discussion. However, most important is the host, who guides the studio talk throughout. He opens the programme by walking down the steps of the amphitheatre and, from centre stage, greeting the studio and home audience and introducing the topic. From then on, he moves amongst the participants, microphone in hand, eliciting their opinions/stories. Kilroy's place within the show's participatory structure is that of a co-participant (he is the 'addressee' of others' stories and contributes at times his own personal experiences) and, predominantly, an 'auditor' or *talk-monitor* (he ensures that the programme's personal but social discussion is promoted and that 'overhearers' are both informed and entertained).

Kilroy shares with other talk shows the presence of socioculturally rooted 'communication rules' (Carbaugh 1990). The analysis of my reference corpus, comprising over fifty episodes during 1997–9, reveals that these encourage private narratives that show participants' efforts to cope with problem scenarios such as marriage failure, bullying, sexual discrimination in the workplace, child abuse and poverty. The host, who often uses these stories to provide specific advice, welcomes participants' experiences of working towards fixing their lives. The ideas of (1) working on improving one's life, characteristic of the 'enterprise culture' (Russell and Abercrombie 1991), and (2) advice-giving in doing so, idiosyncratic of the culture of DIY, are conflated in *Kilroy* to the value attached to verbal sharing as therapy – the so-called 'talking cure' that is typical of the talk show genre.[3] Together, they provide an emotional DIY frame of talk, in which representations of various aspects of society and characters therein are brought into being.

One final point needs to be made in relation to *Kilroy*'s emotional DIY and this is its performed nature. Accounts of parenting need to be examined here in their capacity as performances before overhearers: the viewing audience. Ultimately, it is the latter who, through their loyalty or otherwise, set 'televisuality' (Dahlgren 1995) high on the show's agenda, which in turn influences the performances of both the host and the participants.

Of families, parents and emotional DIY

The family is one of *Kilroy*'s pet discussion topics, even in episodes that do not deal with family-related issues, such as bullying or the welfare system. The discussion of family issues often consists of representations of parenting and evaluations of these in terms of adequate child-raising. The show becomes a kind of DIY manual on the family, notably on the idea of proper parenting as an enterprise upon which to work constantly. Through the figure of its host, it rewards those participants who report proper parenting experiences with full speaking rights and explicit verbal and/or non-verbal support (e.g. hugging them, patting them on the shoulder). Conversely, it chastises those whose reported actions fall outside normative parenting, the host often denying them the speaking floor or overtly challenging their contributions (e.g. 'we don't want to hear you go on about this'). But, above all, the studio talk is structured in such a way that the show appears like a guidance forum providing DIY tips through participants' stories and/or the host's explicit advice.

Representations of proper parenting in *Kilroy* are grounded on the assumption of a loving family relationship, typically within the standard model of the nuclear family. In addition, the show places particular emphasis upon parental self-sacrifice in the interest of raising children. Hence there is an expectation that the work and/or personal lives of parents should be secondary to children's needs. These elements of *Kilroy*'s emotional DIY attitude to parenting are illustrated in the following extracts.

In and through the studio talk, parenting in *Kilroy* is constructed as a skills-learning process with the host as its main facilitator. Extract 1 below is typical of this. It occurs during the final minutes of an episode on father–daughter relationships and is preceded by a series of critical remarks by other participants about those fathers whom they perceive as being overprotective of their teenage daughters:

```
01  Kilroy: Peter ↑
02  Peter:   well (.) I've got a daughter who's coming up to four years soon (.)
03           I don't live with her but it's been very interesting being here with
04           everyone today (.) and listen to (.) how fathers and their daughters
05           who have been through (.) may be most of their teenage years and
06           have coped and what different problems they've come across =
07  Kilroy: = what what sort of effect has it had on YOU (.) what you've
08           heard ↑
09  Peter:   mm (.) well a lot of it I expect to experience but a lot of it (.)
10           HOPEFULLY I'll be able to:: deal with erm with the greatest
11           respect (.) I'll be able to avoid
```

Extract 1. (For transcription conventions, see p. 144)

Extract 1 reveals the elements of the show that can be likened to a DIY manual. First, there is a perceived area of life to be improved/fixed: proper parenting of teenager daughters. Second, there is a potential DIY-er, Peter, who is interested in learning what to avoid (11) and what to expect (03–06; 09). And third, there is a DIY manual, the *Kilroy* show, offering the chance of vicarious experiences that will enable him to 'deal' (10) with similar cases. Within the manual, the host guides DIY-ers like Peter in their acquisition of skills appropriate for their circumstances. It is worth noting that it is Kilroy who asks Peter to take part in the discussion, Peter does not volunteer. It is also Kilroy who encourages personalized discussion (cf. his emphasis on 'YOU' in 07). Experience-based expertise is valued in the show even if, like Peter's, it is yet to be developed. What appears to matter is that Peter's contribution, incidentally during the closing stage of the show, is supportive of the guided skills-learning that *Kilroy's* emotional DIY endorses.

Extracts 2 to 4 below entail three very different parenting contexts but are all representative instances of participants trying to construct their social identities as self-sacrificing parents. Additionally, they all share a recurrent feature of the discourse of *Kilroy*, namely, participants' use of personal narratives as a means to present their views (Lorenzo-Dus 2001). These personal narratives undergo a process of 'narrativization'. Herein the host co-narrates participants' experiences for the benefit of the show's overhearing audience, employing different levels of involvement and performing various narrative roles such as 'dramatizer' and 'problematizer' (Thornborrow 2001).

'I made myself short to help her'

The extract below comes from an episode on child-care institutions. The lexical choice of the verb phrase in the title ('Parents who *walk out on* their children') already predisposes a negative evaluation of those parents whose children are put into care. And this is precisely the context against which, just before extract 2, Jane has presented her story. She put her now-adult daughter Karen into care when the latter was a teenager. To support her claim that she is a proper parent, Jane has used personal experience. Specifically, she has referred to extreme financial pressures and to Karen's drug-addiction and physical attacks on her:

```
01 Karen:  [ . . . ] you DISOWNED me mother =
02 Jane:   = I didn't just disown you (1.0) [to Kilroy] I was always there (.)
03         I made myself short to help her and my grandchildren and I love
04         her and my grandchildren very much (.) I tried to show her then
05         and I'm trying now =
06 Kilroy: = that's good Jane (.) it's trying that counts [moves on to another
07         participant]
```

Extract 2.

After rejecting Karen's challenge in 01 outright with the statement that she 'didn't just disown' her daughter (02), Jane turns to Kilroy for validation of her claim. She warrants it on the grounds that she 'was always there (.) [She] made [her]self short to help her and [her] grandchildren' (02–03). In doing so, she is performing her social identity as a proper parent – an identity based on love, constant care, self-sacrifice and determination. Indeed, Karen's initial challenge does not prevent her mother from expressing her determination to continue with her parental method: 'and I'm trying now' (05). Kilroy's overlapping turn and verbal encouragement in 06 vindicate Jane's representation in a way that brings the norms of emotional DIY back to the forefront of discussion: proper parenting is a learning process, one where 'it's trying that counts' (06).

Monitoring parenting in and through talk

Decisions about which representations count as proper parenting in *Kilroy* are not always in the hands of the participants concerned. Nor are they necessarily made on the grounds of factual evidence (cf. extract 2, where Kilroy is supportive of Jane despite Karen's negative evaluation of her mother's parenting). Instead, they are made principally by the host in his capacity as talk-monitor, an interactional role which is itself shaped by the specific demands of *Kilroy*. These include pandering to its claims of free discussion and communicating emotional DIY-related values, whilst keeping the overhearing audience entertained. Such demands are central in determining which parenting accounts to allot space to in the show and for how long. At the centre of his reasons for doing so are demands for entertainment.

Extracts 3 and 4 below illustrate this well. On both occasions the participants relay personal experiences, the outcomes of which suggest that their self-sacrifices for their children have paid off. In each case, however, the behaviour of the host indicates that the representations of parenting provided do not accord fully with the show's conception of either proper parenting or adequate family structures. Extract 3 is from an episode on the effects of prostitution on families. Its title, 'Coping with prostitution in the family', is representative of the emphasis on applying DIY principles to one's life – the concepts of 'coping with' and 'working on' being recurrent in *Kilroy*. The extract takes place approximately twenty minutes into the episode, after harsh criticisms have been levied against parents whose children have become prostitutes. The participant, Nina, is a mother of seven and formerly a prostitute. She has not yet taken part in the discussion:

```
01  Woman:  [ . . . ] parents have to keep their children away from
02          prostitution =
03  Nina:   = can I can I step in here↑ I've got a sense of responsibility
04          towards my children specifically because they don't see what I
05          do (.) I have seven children and none of my children has become
06          a prostitute nor a rent boy or anything like that (.) now:: for
07          anyone to judge me I have to say that when you've felt
08          STARVATION (.) and when you have CHILDREN (.)
09          YOU DO WHAT YOU HAVE TO [DO [Kilroy places
10          microphone in front of woman]
11  Woman:  [excuse me (.) I have difficulty paying my bills every day of my
12          life
```

Extract 3.

In the above extract, Nina uses personal experience to construct her social
identity as a proper parent. Specifically, she refers to:

1 her conducting her profession without her children's knowledge (03–05).
   This suggests that she disapproves of prostitution, something which may
   help the construction of her social identity as a respectable person, for
   hitherto in the programme prostitution has been unanimously condemned
   as immoral;
2 the positive outcome of her parenting, since she has successfully shielded all
   of her children from prostitution (05–06); and
3 extreme circumstances forcing her into prostitution (06–09). This frames
   Nina's past behaviour beyond normative parenting as an imposition rather
   than a free choice and highlights her self-sacrificing personality.

Surely, then, Nina's claim to be a responsible parent is warranted? She views
parenting as a task to work on, in her case under extremely difficult circumstances, and she is willing to put her children's needs first. Yet, one of the
grounds of her claim, that of starvation pushing her into prostitution, is challenged (11–12). This in turn questions her claim that she has self-sacrificed for
her children. Interestingly, Kilroy seizes upon this to manufacture a negative
evaluation, which is done rather subtly in 09–10 by moving the microphone
away from Nina.

Even though Nina has been using a personal narrative (03–09) to present
her views, she finds herself in mid-utterance having the speaking floor taken
away in favour of the very participant whose previous contribution (01) made

Nina react. In doing so, Kilroy the talk-monitor is killing two birds with one stone, as it were. Firstly, he is providing DIY guidance. There are 'dos' and 'don'ts' in proper parenting and it is just as important to show the benefits of the former as to make the show's studio and home audience aware of the risks of the latter, which Nina represents. Secondly, he is creating the necessary conditions for a sequence of lively confrontation talk (Hutchby 1996) and, hence, televisuality.

Finally, extract 4 below comes from an episode on marriage failure and provides a good example of how close Kilroy's monitoring of specific representations of family issues can at times be. A participant, Nigel, has been describing his marital problems, which he is unable to attribute to any specific reason other than that he and his wife have changed over the past ten years. Another participant has asked him if he would consider getting divorced, since the couple's tense relationship is depriving the children of the harmonious family environment that they deserve:

```
01 Nigel:   I refuse to do that to my children basically (.) THE
02          CHILDREN are my life (.) I (.) you know (.) I'm if anything
03          happens to them (.) I don't know what I'd do to myself (.) I I love
04          the children to death (.) I'd do anything I could for them =
05 Kilroy:  = [soft voice] why don't you make your marriage a happy
06          one (.) ↑
07 Nigel:   pardon↑
08 Kilroy:  why don't you make your marriage (.) why don't you try ↑ why
09          don't you just go ↑ (.) BE AN ACTOR (.) be an actor (.) learn
10          to act (.) learn to come in (.) learn to kind of say (.) how are you
11          Jane ↑ how's your day ↑ (.) learn that kind of thing (.) can't you
12          jus- if you're saying you're doing everything for the kids then
13          YOU'VE GOT TO to put on an act for the kids (.) haven't
14          you ↑ (.) haven't you ↑
```

Extract 4.

Throughout the extract, Kilroy's input involves a dramatization of talk that is highly evaluative and problematizes Nigel's account for the benefit of the overhearing audience. Kilroy's initial remarks resemble those of an interviewer concerned with maintaining a neutralistic stance. For example, in 05 and 08, he uses a question to perform a speech act whose illocutionary force is clearly that of a command. The intonation, the negative interrogative ('why don't you?') and his persistence (three consecutive times) indicate that Kilroy wants Nigel to implement a different DIY method from that reported in 01–04. Basically, Nigel's method consists of focusing on being a good parent but not necessarily a 'proper husband'. This, however, implies a somehow dysfunctional family structure and it is here that we see how Kilroy's monitoring of talk becomes explicit. In 08–12 he gives specific instructions: 'BE AN ACTOR (.) be an actor (.) learn to act' (09–10), 'learn that kind of thing' (11), 'YOU'VE GOT TO to put on an act for the kids' (13). He even adds, as one would expect in any self-respecting DIY manual, practical tips to make the job easier: 'learn to kind of say (.) how are you Jane ↑ how's your day ↑' (10–11).

In extract 4, Kilroy is asking Nigel to apply DIY principles to his marriage life under the pretext that this is the type of self-sacrifice that is expected from him as a good parent. Happy marital relationships are thus represented as subsidiary to the maintenance of nuclear family structures. Forcing marital happiness is simply something that parents have 'GOT TO' do (13) as part of parental self-sacrifice. It is ultimately ironic that, despite being contrary to Nigel's chosen parenting, Kilroy presents it as part of Nigel's own logic: 'if you're saying you're doing everything for the kids' (12), then show it!

Conclusion

In *Kilroy,* representations of parenting as part of the nuclear family structure and as a skills-learning process that involves an element of self-sacrifice are framed within, and frame, the show's overall emotional DIY communication ethos. Similar to other aspects of people's lives, parenting is about acquiring the skills to fix problems that might arise. Herein the programme acts as a kind of DIY manual, using people's experiences to show the 'musts' and 'must-nots' of parenting. Of course, these pre-sanctioned notions of proper parenting need to be presented in a form sufficiently entertaining to maintain the overhearing audience's fidelity, and sufficiently dissembled so as not to belie the show's claims to rigorous and free discussion. Nominally, therefore, representations of parenting need to appear naturally generated from the different characters of the '*Kilroy* drama'. In practice, though, Kilroy the talk-monitor ensures the communication of pre-ordained specific family/parenting values through discursive strategies such as specific questions and leads, re-formulations, evaluations and absolute control of the speaking floor. Participants are aware of this and in some cases they collaborate actively since it is in their interest to go along with the host's performance. Ultimately, representations of proper parenting in this show are subject to the overriding demands of its perceived overhearing audience. It is the latter who, through their loyalty or otherwise, set the agendas that influence the performances of both the host and the participants.

Transcription conventions

[ ]	Non-verbal, paralinguistic, prosodic and contextual information.
CAPITALS	Increased loudness.
[	Simultaneous starting talk.
=	Overlapping talk with no discernible break between utterances.
(.)	Short pause (half a second or under).
(2.0)	Longer pause, in seconds.
[. . .]	Lines omitted from transcript.
↑	Speech act having the illocutionary force of eliciting information; also rising intonation.
an::d	Prolongation ('stretching') of prior syllable.
wor-	Word cut off abruptly.

Notes

1 BBC web site, available at <http://www.bbc.co.uk/info/policy/k-policy.shtml>.
2 Robert Kilroy's words in an interview for the *Evening Standard* (17 February 2000).
3 For further work on the influence of therapy on talk-show discourse see, amongst others, Livingstone and Lunt (1994); Joyner-Priest (1995); Peck (1995) and Shattuc (1997).

References

Carbaugh, D. (1990) 'Communication rules in *Donahue* discourse', in D. Carbaugh (ed.) *Cultural Communication and Intercultural Contact*, London: Lawrence Erlbaum Associates, 119–50.
Dahlgren, P. (1995) *Television and the Public Sphere*, London: Sage.
Fairclough, N. (1989) *Language and Power*, London: Longman.
Haarman, L. (1999) 'Performing talk', in L. Haarman (ed.) *Talk about Shows*, Bologna: CLUEB, 1–52.
Hutchby, I. (1996) *Confrontation Talk: Arguments, Asymmetries and Power in Talk Radio*, Hillsdale, NJ: Erlbaum.
Joyner-Priest, P. (1995) *Public Intimacies: Talk Show Participants and Tell-All TV*, Cresskill, NJ: Hampton Press.
Livingstone, S. and Lunt, P. (1994) *Talk on Television: Audience Participation and Public Debate*, London: Routledge.
Lorenzo-Dus, N. (2001) 'UP CLOSE AND PERSONAL: the narrativization of private experience in media talk', *Studies in English Language and Linguistics* 3: 125–48.
Peck, J. (1995) 'TV talk shows as therapeutic discourse: the ideological labour of the televized talking cure', *Communication Theory* 5: 58–81.
Russell, K. and Abercrombie, N. (eds) (1991) *Enterprise Culture*, London: Routledge.

Shattuc, J. (1997) *The Talking Cure*, London: Routledge.

Thornborrow, J. (2001) '"Has it ever happened to you?": talk show stories as mediated performance', in A. Tolson (ed.) *Television Talk Shows: Discourse, Performance, Spectacle*, Mahwah, NJ: Erlbaum, 117–37.

Tolson, A. (ed.) *Television Talk Shows: Discourse, Performance, Spectacle*, Mahwah, NJ: Erlbaum.

15 Language and American 'good taste'

Martha Stewart as mass-media role model

Catherine Evans Davies

The internationalization of an American lifestyle entrepreneur

In the twenty-first century, the American mass media may impinge more and more on the lives not only of Americans, but also of other English-speaking and English-learning inhabitants of the globe. The focus of this chapter, Martha Stewart, is an example of an American multimedia lifestyle entrepreneur. She is a complex figure who has become a powerful corporate executive through representing the traditional women's role of homemaker and commodifying her vision of gracious living (Didion 2000). Martha Stewart has expanded her American mass-media presence over the past decade as a new symbol of 'good taste' drawn from an idealized traditional upper-middle-class (white, hetero-sexual) lifestyle. Recently, she has moved into the international arena, in Canada, Brazil and Japan (International Alliances), and is contemplating South Korea, Australia and Germany (Herskovitz 2001). In Canada the programme is broadcast in English, as presumably it would be in other countries where English is an official language. In Brazil and Japan, the program is dubbed; whether Martha's communicative style is maintained in the dubbed language is a question to be explored, pursuant to Cameron's analysis (this volume) of American discourse norms being disseminated internationally in the name of 'better' communication.

Media celebrities serve both as a reflection of sociolinguistic patterns and as potential role models for their audiences. The perspective of 'constitutive rhetoric', by which the audience is guided towards becoming a particular sort of subject, is applied by Smith specifically to the Martha Stewart phenomenon: 'In the case of Stewart, audience members are asked to identify with . . . the role model of Stewart herself' (2000: 341). Media celebrities provide examples of ways of speaking and interacting which supplement the face-to-face contacts of our individual daily worlds. While it is clear that the audience is not interacting with Martha Stewart themselves, they are the addressees of a style that is crafted to convey a very personal presence. A media celebrity who could come to represent aspirations within the ideological framework of the 'American Dream' of upward mobility could have a tremendous influence. This influence could potentially apply not only within the United States but also internationally, to the degree that American upper-middle-class standards of living and lifestyle are seen as desirable. Martha Stewart, as arbiter of taste and guide to do-it-yourself gracious living, is modelling behaviour with the express intention of showing people how to do things; it seems a short step for the audience to take her as a linguistic model as well, especially if her presentation of self embodies a coveted social goal. Although sociolinguistics and critical discourse analysts are beginning to turn their attention to media discourse, Scollon, as a rare sociolinguist who has considered how audiences might be incorporating language from sources of public discourse into their English, comments that 'there have been virtually no studies of the social practices by which the discourses of the media are appropriated in face-to-face interaction' (Scollon 1998: vii). Research on Martha Stewart within American Studies appears not to include much attention to her own linguistic performances, apart from commenting on particular words or trademark phrases (cf. Martha Stewart Roundtable 2001).

Ideology, social class and American 'good taste'

Martha Stewart herself is an interesting embodiment of the American ideology of upward mobility, in that she was not born into the social class that she now represents, having earned her status through educational achievement, marriage (which also provided her surname) and entrepreneurial ability. In Bourdieu's terms (1984, 1991), Martha Stewart has acquired this 'cultural capital'. American commentaries on Martha Stewart routinely characterize her as representing the upper middle class and the 'good taste' that goes with it. Gans (1999) observes that the higher taste cultures provide more useful information to their publics, and this seems consistent with Martha Stewart's explicit guidance on lifestyle and aesthetics.

Her show provides information for achieving and maintaining class status, yet a typical American critique of Martha Stewart is that she presents a domestic world that is quite unrealistic and that is far beyond the economic reach of most Americans, including the upper middle class. This might be particularly problematic for an international audience, some of whom would have no way of assessing the economic reality of American life. On the other hand, it is noticeable that she manages to maintain a focus on taste and quality at the same time that she appears to adapt to a wide range of economic levels or financial situations in her audience; for example, on the same show she included both *canard à l'orange* – which she calls 'duck with orange sauce' – and 'spaghetti 101', indicating the most basic information on preparing spaghetti. She appears not on the prototypical upper-middle-class television network, PBS, but rather on regular channels, and on the cable food network. She sells her merchandize through her upscale website, but also at K-Mart, a discount store representing a much lower socioeconomic level of customer than the taste class that she represents. She appears to be democratizing taste, a process which would be consistent with another aspect of American ideology. A powerful message conveyed by her enterprise seems to be that even if you don't have the financial resources, you can still do things with 'good taste', and add a little 'class' to your life. In this sense, 'good taste' is becoming to some extent detached from economic resources.

Analytic framework and data

This chapter uses the analytic framework of interactional sociolinguistics (Goffman 1974, 1981; Hymes 1974; Gumperz 1982, 1992; Tannen 1984; Johnstone 1996) on data from the original television programme that forms part of the multimedia empire. Language is conceptualized as a resource that speakers use to try to project a particular identity.

The data are from observations over a period of about three years of the *Martha Stewart Living* television programme (see also Davies 2002). I have also drawn on my own ethnographic interviews with both fans and detractors, representing white American women of a range of ages and regional and social class backgrounds. In the traditional woman's role of homemaker within her vision of American upper-middle-class domesticity, Martha Stewart's linguistic presentation of self is analysed using a set of three interrelated frames which she must manage appropriately in relation to her audience. The three frames (politeness, credibility and authenticity) (Brown and Levinson 1987; Kotthoff 1997; Bucholtz 1999; Scollon and Scollon 2001) emerged from the totality of the data. They are of course not mutually exclusive, but rather overlapping and synergistic. In effect, the analysis shows how Martha Stewart's American 'good taste' is represented linguistically in relation to an international audience (see also Bell 1984, 2001; Coupland 2001).

The first frame: politeness

Martha Stewart must present a model of appropriate politeness (civility, graciousness), projecting an American upper-middle-class (white, female) combination of 'independence' and 'involvement' politeness strategies (Scollon and Scollon 2001). Her elaborate greeting and thanking rituals would seem to fit within a politeness style oriented towards showing appropriate deference through social distance and the avoidance of impositions ('independence' politeness strategy), a more formal politeness prototypically associated with higher (or dominating) social classes (Brown and Levinson 1987: 245–6). Yet other aspects of her style seem more consistent with a solidarity politeness system (emphasizing involvement and an egalitarian ethos) in which the main principle is to assume similarity and commonality with others. This style is prototypically associated with an American ideology that denies class differences and promotes a fictive equality and solidarity.

Rituals

Formal rituals of politeness surround greeting guests and especially thanking them at the end of their participation. (In the following extracts, tone unit boundaries are marked by /; emphatic stress is indicated by capitalization; ellipsis is indicated by . . .)

> *MS to guest*: well this is VERY fun / thank you VERY much /
> *To audience*: and if you're interested in aprons PLEASE get this book / [title] by [author] / and you'll learn a LOT / more than you EVER knew about aprons /
> *MS to guest*: thanks a lot
> *Guest*: thank you, Martha

Deferential 'involvement'

The segments in which she demonstrates how to do something are presented in a personal way, consistent with a solidarity politeness system. She presents things personally to the audience, using 'I', and addresses the audience as 'you', as illustrated in the following example. Whereas she clearly expresses her personal preferences (especially in the last line), she is also careful to acknowledge the importance of the audience's preferences which might differ from hers.

> you could boil them / but roasting them keeps in all those flavors / . . . / some people put a little olive oil inside / even a little bit of water / but I don't think you need to do any of that

Positive attitudes, passionate enthusiasm and perfectionism

A striking thing about Martha Stewart's linguistic presentation of self is her strongly positive orientation and apparently passionate enthusiasm. These attitudes are expressed linguistically through hyperbolic lexical choice, and through expressive prosody (as illustrated through capitalized letters). This combination of intensifying modifiers and emphatic stress is characteristic of American upper-class speech, and conveys confidence, self-assurance and the expectation of agreement from the interlocutor, as suggested by Nunberg (1980) and Kroch (1996). Optimism and the expectation of agreement are classic strategies of a solidarity politeness system.

One of the few specifically linguistic characteristics of Martha Stewart that receives comment is her constant use of the word *perfect*. It appears at least once in virtually every show. Her trademark expression, 'it's a good thing', which names a typical segment of her show, is also evaluative.

This example is an extraction of all such language use from a brief segment:

> and my mom's recipe is utterly fantastic / . . . / I love borscht / . . . / I LOVE celery leaves / . . . / oh that looks SO GOOD / . . . / um gorgeous / . . . / so that looks good / . . . / so that'll thicken the soup beautifully / . . . / how pretty / . . . / oh I LOVE it with boiled potatoes / . . . / now that is the perfect soup / . . . / it's really good

The second frame: credibility

Martha Stewart must appear to be a credible expert within her domain (Kotthoff 1997). The confidence conveyed by her use of intensifiers and stress is significant. An additional factor in Martha Stewart's speech is its relatively low fundamental frequency; from listening to her mother it appears that this low pitch is inherited rather than a contrived feature, but it still conveys authority in a way that a high pitch would not.

The teacher

One of the ways that Martha Stewart positions herself as a teacher is through the daily preview of the remaining television shows for any given week. The concluding phrase (spoken by a male voice) is 'learn something new . . . on *Martha Stewart Living*'. The audience knows, of course, that this 'something new' will involve yet another aspect of the cultural capital of the upper middle class which she will make explicit for them. Yet, as any good teacher, Martha Stewart is also constantly learning. She is clearly not afraid to position herself as the (albeit precocious) student as well. This example shows her simultaneously positioned as a teacher and a learner.

> the first thing you always have to do / as my mom taught me / is prepare the beets.

Experience

Martha Stewart's extensive experience is typically conveyed linguistically through presuppositions built into discourse: 'I always like to do it this way' and 'My favorite way . . .' both presuppose that she has done whatever it is so many times that she has come up with the best way. She also includes warnings about what not to do, which again imply that she has made all the mistakes and learned from them.

> I like to give a LOT of plant food / TWO packages to a BIG pitcher like this would be sufficient / . . . / now / if possible / make this arrangement where you're going to display it / because if you make it in your kitchen / and then try to carry it to your living room or to your dining room / oftentimes these thorny branches are gonna get stuck on the woodwork / they're gonna get stuck in the chandelier / and I've had just MESSES.

Agency

As a part of American ideology, the whole notion of 'do-it-yourself' is potentially empowering for the audience, towards individual agency in relation to class identification and social mobility. Agency, which goes beyond 'do-it-yourself', is expressed in various ways. Martha Stewart virtually takes her audience by the hand and leads them through a process. In the presence of her audience she also elicits information from her guests, modelling the kinds of questions that a curious, interested and intelligent person might ask.

The third frame: authenticity

The question of authenticity would appear to be different for an international audience, in contrast with an American audience. An international audience, particularly one that had been exposed to unrealistically affluent representations of the lifestyle of Americans, might not be in a position to judge Martha Stewart as 'inauthentic' in the same way that American critics might.

Personal communication

She presents herself as a friend who has figured something out and wants to share it, rather than as an authority. She reveals her enthusiasms, her preferences and her judgements. Even though she is known for her perfectionism, the example below illustrates another dimension of her personal presence; we feel as if we are being taught by someone in her own kitchen in an on-going process of socialization.

> We'll do the chocolate chunks first / you're gonna have to moisten your hands / and – I'll just moisten my hands a little bit / use a one-and-a-half tablespoon scoop / and you want to press the mixture into the scoop / making sure that you get chocolate chunks in it of course / and – these don't rise so you can put them quite close together / and you can also use your hands to give these a slightly pyramidal shape / and I'll show you how to do that /

A successful American who values her immigrant roots and is interested in cultural diversity

Whereas Martha Stewart has achieved a higher social status than she was born into, she clearly acknowledges and values her roots, as indicated by the number of references on her show to her childhood in New Jersey and her Polish background. She frequently includes her mother as a guest expert. She also incorporates many examples of ethnic foods prepared by American representatives of ethnic communities. The example here is from a segment in which her mother is a guest on the show, taking charge of the making of borscht. Bringing her mother on the show, and acknowledging her debt to her mother's culinary skills, clearly situates her as a daughter, as part of a family, and as part of an immigrant tradition. In this segment she even displays her limited knowledge of Polish, indicated within brackets.

> *Martha*:　　now that is the perfect soup
> *Mother*:　　delicious / and I'll tell you in Polish: ['delicious']
> *Martha repeats*: ['delicious']
> *Mother*:　　meaning
> *Martha*:　　very delicious?
> *Mother*:　　delicious

Her variety of American English

For an international audience, Martha Stewart's relative approximation to stereotypes of standard American speech may be a key dimension of her authenticity, especially in parts of the world in which American English has higher prestige than British English. She seems to have a general East Coast upper-middle-class accent, originating from the New York area. Williams (1999) comments that she 'shed her New Jersey accent' in the course of her career. Her vowel system mostly conforms to what is taught in textbooks for 'General American English' (Wolfram and Schilling-Estes 1998).

When she is talking relatively spontaneously, she displays certain typical American speech reductions (*gonna* for 'going to', *kinda* for 'kind of'), but in contrast with another internationally visible American English speaker, President George W. Bush, whose Southern American speech is characterized by frequent 'g-dropping' (*-in* for '-ing'), Martha Stewart has never dropped a 'g' in any of my data. Her usage is consistent with Kroch's (1996: 38) findings about upper- and middle-class speech in Philadelphia. A further characteristic associated with upper-class speech is a creaky or laryngealized voice quality (Nunberg 1980: 170; Kroch 1996: 39) that is very evident in Martha Stewart's speech.

On the other hand, certain characteristics of her speech could be seen as hypercorrections, or as a symbolic concern with 'correctness'. For example, she uses the typically British pronunciation of 'herb', with initial 'h', which she claims always to have pronounced in that way. Martha and her mother also both aspirate intervocalic 't' in 'water' and 'little', but Martha does it apparently differentially, depending on how much attention she's paying to speech. Given that Martha's mother was a teacher, and the daughter of immigrants, it seems quite probable that she was oriented to such British-model pronunciations as the 'correct' way to speak during the era when she was educated. The constellation of characteristics of her spoken language, in conjunction with other aspects of her self-presentation, seem to convey both that she has definite ideas about the right way to speak, and that she is comfortable with herself linguistically across the whole range of her informal standard variety of American English.

Conclusion

Martha Stewart embodies an affluent American lifestyle and models a particular communicative style and set of discourse norms based in the civility of the upper middle class. Such a model might be very attractive internationally in contrast to the 'incivility' of the communication of other American mass media products (cf. Lakoff, this volume). It seems possible that Martha Stewart as mass-media role model could have a tremendous impact on audiences who are able to conceptualize the television show as a resource from which they can pick and choose things that are relevant to their lives, as I found in the American context where women of the lower socioeconomic levels see her as a way of adding a little 'class' to their lives according to their predilections and opportunities. Perhaps in an international context she would be seen as not class-linked but rather as 'affluent American'.

References

Bell, A. (1984) 'Language style as audience design', *Language in Society* 13: 145–204.
— (2001) 'Back in style: reworking audience design', in P. Eckert and J. R. Rickford (eds) *Style and Sociolinguistic Variation*, Cambridge: Cambridge University Press, 139–69.
Bourdieu, P. (1984) *Distinction: A Social Critique of the Judgement of Taste*, trans. R. Nice, Cambridge, MA: Harvard University Press.
— (1991) *Language and Symbolic Power*, trans. G. Raymond and M. Adamson, ed. J. B. Thompson, Cambridge, MA: Harvard University Press.
Brown, P. and Levinson, S. C. (1987) *Politeness: Some Universals of Language Usage*, Cambridge: Cambridge University Press.
Bucholtz, M. (1999) 'Purchasing power: the gender and class imaginary on the shopping channel', in M. Bucholtz, A. C. Liang and L. A. Sutton (eds) *Reinventing Identities: The Gendered Self in Discourse*, New York and Oxford: Oxford University Press, 348–68.
Cameron, D. (this volume) 'Globalizing 'communication''.
Coupland, N. (2001) 'Language, situation, and the relational self: theorizing dialect-style in sociolinguistics', in P. Eckert and J. R. Rickford (eds) *Style and Sociolinguistic Variation*, Cambridge: Cambridge University Press, 185–210.
Davies, C. E. (2002) 'Martha Stewart's linguistic presentation of self', *Texas Linguistic Forum* 44: 73–89.
Didion, J. (2000) 'Everywoman.com: getting out of the house with Martha Stewart', *The New Yorker*, 21 and 28 February 2000, 271–9.
Gans, H. J. (1999) *Popular Culture and High Culture: An Analysis and Evaluation of Taste*, revised and updated edition, New York: Basic Books.
Goffmann, E. (1974) *Frame Analysis: An Essay on the Organization of Experience*, New York: Harper and Row.
— (1981) *Forms of Talk*, Philadelphia, PA: University of Pennsylvania Press.
Gumperz, J. J. (1982) *Discourse Strategies*, Cambridge: Cambridge University Press.
— (1992) 'Contextualization cues and understanding', in A. Duranti and C. Goodwin (eds) *Rethinking Context*, New York: Cambridge University Press, 229–52.
Herskovitz, J. (2001) 'Martha Stewart tries Japan to build business', New York: Reuters, 23 December 2001, available at <http://www.siamfuture.com/Asian News/AsianNewsTxt.asp?aid=2032> (accessed 9 March 2002).

Hymes, D. (1974) 'Ways of speaking', in R. Bauman and J. Sherzer (eds) *Explorations in the Ethnography of Speaking*, Cambridge: Cambridge University Press, 433–51.

International Alliances available at <http://www.marthastewart.com>: Our Company/ International Alliances (accessed 9 March 2002).

Johnstone, B. (1996) *The Linguistic Individual: Self-Expression in Language and Linguistics*, Oxford and New York: Oxford University Press.

Kotthoff, H. (1997) 'The interactional achievement of expert status: creating asymmetries by "teaching conversational lectures" in TV discussions', in H. Kotthoff and R. Wodak (eds) *Communicating Gender in Context*, Amsterdam and Philadelphia: John Benjamins, 139–78.

Kroch. A. (1996) 'Dialect and style in the speech of upper class Philadelphia', in G. R. Guy, C. Feagin, D. Schiffrin, and J. Baugh (eds) *Towards a Social Science of Language: Papers in Honor of William Labov*, vol. 1: *Variation and Change in Language and Society*, Amsterdam and Philadelphia: John Benjamins, 23–45.

Lakoff, R. T. (this volume) 'The new incivility: threat or promise?'

Martha Stewart Roundtable (2001) *American Studies* 42(2): 67–138.

Nunberg, G. (1980) 'The speech of the New York City upper class', in T. Shopen and J. M. Williams (eds) *Standards and Dialects in English*, Cambridge, MA: Winthrop Publishers, 150–73.

Scollon, R. (1998) *Mediated Discourse as Social Interaction: A Study of News Discourse*, London and New York: Longman.

Scollon, R. and Scollon, S. W. (2001) *Intercultural Communication: A Discourse Approach*, 2nd edn, Oxford: Blackwell.

Smith, C. D. (2000) '"Discipline – it's a 'good thing": rhetorical constitution and Martha Stewart Living Omnimedia', *Women's Studies in Communication* 23(3): 337–66.

Tannen, D. (1984) *Conversational Style: Analyzing Talk Among Friends*, Norwood, NJ: Ablex.

Williams, M. E. (1999) 'She's Martha and you're not', Salon Brilliant Careers, available at <http://www.salon.com/bc/1999/02/cov._16bc.html> (accessed 31 March 2002).

Wolfram, W. and Schilling-Estes, N. (1998) *American English: Dialects and Variation*, Oxford: Blackwell.

Part IV

The effect of the media on language

This section looks at ways in which the practices of the media might be affecting our speech or written records.

Ni compares the use of noun phrases in editorials and news reports with those in other linguistic registers. He finds that the structure of noun phrases in media texts falls mid-way between academic writing and conversation.

Biber shows how space constraints within newspapers have led to dense, structurally complex noun phrases which cram in maximum information. This style may be spreading to other areas of English.

Ayto explores English neologisms, and the extent to which they are accepted in modern dictionaries. He finds that blends, such as brunch from 'breakfast' and 'lunch' vary in the extent to which they are accepted by dictionaries. He finds that dictionaries which contain the greatest number are those which have used a large number of newspapers as sources of data.

Simpson discusses linguistic sources of data for the *Oxford English Dictionary* (*OED*). He discusses the extent to which tabloids and emails might be regarded as reliable evidence sources for dictionaries. Printed sources, whatever they may be, are acceptable, he claims, though he points out the difficulties, at present insuperable, of using non-printed sources, such as emails.

Aitchison discusses the descriptions of recent events in New York, as found in newspapers and the web. She finds that numerous different, often polysyllabic words were used in the descriptions, but that these were mostly existing words, rather than neologisms.

16   Noun phrases in media texts

A quantificational approach

Yibin Ni

Introduction

People have intuitions about stylistic differences among different functional registers but such differences had never been seriously tackled with quantitative
approaches until very recently. This study intends to capture the particular
stylistic features of the three types of news media texts, printed editorials,
printed news reports and broadcast news, in terms of a series of linguistic indicators in the noun phrases embedded in the texts. These media texts are
distinguished along parameters such as written vs. spoken and descriptive vs.
argumentative. In doing so, this study examines noun phrases for their syntactic
complexity, e.g. whether they take modifiers and how many modifiers they take
if they do (e.g. *water* vs. *the fresh water in the Scottish highlands*) and the semantically different pre-modifiers they take, e.g. classifiers or descriptors (*wooden box*
vs. *wooden actor*). The indicators chosen for the study are shown to be significant
in distinguishing registers and are able to account for many of the stylistic differences which are intuitively felt but have rarely been pinned down in linguistic
terms.

   With the availability of computers and development of language corpora, the
study of the distributions of linguistic features across different registers of
English has become popular, culminating in the seminal book by Biber *et al.*
(1999). The present project makes use of data collected during the 1990s for
the British component of the International Corpus of English (ICE-GB) (Greenbaum 1996), in particular, the news media texts versus the other three paradigmatic registers: academic writing, fiction and conversations.

The study of the structure of noun phrases and their effects on the style of a register

Noun phrases (NPs) are strings of words with an internal structure centred
around an obligatory head, which may be supplemented by determiners,

pre-modifiers and post-modifiers, such as *a beautiful room with a view* with *room* as the head. A complex noun phrase with various kinds of modifiers can package a relatively large amount of information, which would otherwise have required several clauses with less elaborately modified NPs. Modifiers of a noun phrase serve to elaborate, restrict or attach some personal feelings and attitudes of the speaker to the referent of the head noun. They may make the referent more specific, or make the speaker's feelings and attitudes towards the referent explicit (see below).

Both the syntactic and semantic characteristics of a noun phrase contribute significantly to the style that a certain register assumes. Syntactically, informational content may be packaged more or less densely by the use of different NP heads and the use of noun phrases with different levels of complexity in terms of the number of modifiers they contain. For example, in a register with an interpersonal focus such as private conversation, pronouns are much more frequently used than complex NPs such as the italicized one in a news bulletin:

> Judges are notoriously *their own creatures, disinclined through long exercise of power to heed outside influence*.
>
> (*The Times*, 10 November 1990)

The stylistic characteristics of news media texts

Biber and his colleagues pointed out that a high concentration of nouns, attributive adjectives and prepositional phrases serving as post-modifiers in a text indicates that the text has an 'informational focus', rather than an interpersonal one (Biber 1989: 28; Biber *et al.* 1999: 11; Biber, this volume). In this section, the distribution patterns of the chosen linguistic indicators found in the three types of media texts are compared with those found in the three paradigmatic registers and they are found to be significantly different from each other in terms of the density of the informational content and their communicative functions.

Information packaging in a noun phrase

Among the four paradigmatic registers (academic writing, news, fiction and conversations), academic writing has the highest information density while conversations has the lowest, which can be graphically shown by a series of indicators.

Information density and the pronominal content in a text

The density of noun phrases whose heads are not pronouns, and the percentage of pronoun head NPs against the total NPs in a piece of discourse, usually correlate with the level of information density in the discourse. In tables 16.1 and 16.2, statistically distinctive figures reflect the different levels of information density motivated by the different functions of these registers. The clear distinction, which interestingly cuts across the traditional written/spoken division, shows they are good indicators of different styles in the four registers.

Against the background of the three paradigmatic registers (academic writing, fiction and conversations), tables 16.3 and 16.4 show how the three subcategories of 'news' are different from each other owing to their respective functions.

Between the two extremes (academic writing and fiction/conversation) nestle the three media registers, with written news achieving the highest density of information among them. The information is packaged more densely in the printed news reports than in either editorials or broadcast news. This matches our intuition that printed news bulletins are relatively informationally compact, and require a certain degree of special reading skill. Such a style (illustrated in

Table 16.1 Occurrences of non-pronoun headed NPs per thousand words. The figures are based on the calculation made in Hong (2000).

Registers	Non-pronoun headed NPs
academic writing (40)*	283.8
news (50)	248.5
novels/stories (20)	203.9
face-to-face conversations (90)	118.6

*The number indicates the number of 'texts' in this category.

Table 16.2 Percentage distributions of pronoun head NPs over total NPs occurring in each text category. The figures are based on the calculation made in Hong (2000).

Registers	Percentage of pronoun head NPs over total NPs
academic writing (40)	10.9
news (50)	17.6
novels/stories (20)	38.6
face-to-face conversations (90)	57.7

Table 16.3 Occurrences of non-pronoun headed NPs per thousand words. The figures are based on the calculation made in Hong (2000).

Registers	Non-pronoun headed NPs
press news reports (20)	265.3
press editorials (10)	240.6
broadcast news (20)	239.5

Table 16.4 Percentage distributions of pronoun head NPs over total NPs occurring in each text category. The figures are based on the calculation made in Hong (2000).

Registers	Percentage of pronoun head NPs over total NPs
press news reports (20)	14.5
press editorials (10)	17.4
broadcast news (20)	20.8

the first passage below) is similar to that found in academic writing (in the second passage) (heads are italicized).

> THE *TIMING* of an American television *report* that the United States Drug Enforcement *Agency* is investigating an undercover *operation* that may have been used to smuggle a *bomb* on to Pan Am *flight* 103 destroyed over *Lockerbie*, was described yesterday as very suspicious by a senior American *attorney* at the *inquiry* in *Dumfries*.
>
> (*The Independent*, 1 November 1990)

> The centrally located cell *bodies* maintain the *viability* of an enormous peripheral axon *process* whose *length* may exceed a *metre* in *comparison* to a cell *body* measured in *microns*.
>
> (*British Journal of Anaesthetics*, July 1990)

By contrast, in spoken broadcast news, as in the next passage, more pronouns are used as NP heads. Such a style makes this passage easier to understand, since broadcast news is transient in the air and gives the audience no opportunity to go over it again if the first attempt to process the auditory signals fails.

John is an excellent Chancellor. Douglas a top-class Foreign Secretary. *I* think that perhaps *I* could give *them* the backing to go out and win the election so that *they* can go on doing the jobs that *they* are so obviously succeeding at.

(ITV *News at Ten*, 23 November 1990)

Information density and pre- and post-modification in noun phrases

Those with both pre-and post-modification are the structurally most complex noun phrases, and their higher frequency in a piece of discourse effectively indicates an informational focus. Table 16.5 shows the distinctive value variation of NPs with both pre- and post-modifiers across the six registers.

The results obtained in table 16.5 have confirmed our general intuition about the relative complexity of information packaging among these registers. Editorials as argumentative writing score closely to academic writing in this aspect and distance themselves from news stories, written or spoken. The following short example from an editorial is composed almost entirely of such complex NPs:

It also suggests *gaping holes in auditing procedures and in the systems of regulation; and a disturbing naivety on the part of the big investors.*

(*Sunday Times*, 28 October 1990)

Conversation, with its main function to maintain social contact rather than intense information transfer, comes last on this count. It seems that the style of contemporary fiction is closer to conversation in using fewer both pre- and post-modified complex noun phrases because its writers often assume an informal style. This investigation shows that, in contrast to fiction writers' practice,

Table 16.5 Occurrences of NPs with both pre- and post-modifiers per thousand words, based on the calculation made in Hong (2000).

Registers	NPs with both pre- and post-modifiers
academic writing (40)	24.2
press news reports (20)	17.2
press editorials (10)	22.0
broadcast news (20)	16.1
novels/stories (20)	9.0
face-to-face conversations (90)	3.9

news-story writers used a more formal style to organize information in a more compact way owing to the time limit in broadcasting and space limit in newspapers.

Speakers' attitudes and feelings towards referents of noun phrases

The occurrences of classifying[1] or descriptive pre-modifiers may help create different effects in discourse (Widdowson 1993). For example, the use of classifying modifiers 'contributes to the effect of a bare catalogue' and to the reader such a serial listing in a narrative will give it 'a matter of fact, offhand, almost inconsequential air' (ibid.: 148ff.).

NP pre-modifiers may be divided into several semantically distinctive groups, i.e. relation-qualifier,[2] attitudinal epithet,[3] experiential epithet, and classifier, as illustrated below:

(determiner)	relation-qualifier	attitudinal epithet	experiential epithet	classifier	(head)
a	certain	splendid	old	English	actress

Table 16.6 compares the distribution patterns of four types of semantically different pre-modifiers across the six registers.

The results here again cut across the written/spoken division and the claim made by Chafe and Danielewicz that the high concentration of pre-modifiers in a text indicates its 'writtenness' (1987: 84) needs to be replaced by finer-tuned ones. The higher occurrences of pre-modifiers should be attributed to the degree of information concentration and to the informational focus of the texts. In the light of this new analysis, the prominently lower occurrence of pre-modifiers

Table 16.6 Occurrences of four types of pre-modifiers per thousand words, based on the calculation in Zhou (2001).

Register	Classifier	Relation qualifier	Experiential epithet	Attitudinal epithet	Total number of pre-modifiers
academic writing (40)	40.6	12.0	19.3	3.4	75.3
press news reports (20)	22.7	6.7	16.4	5.2	51.0
press editorial (20)	24.6	8.2	14.0	12.3	59.1
broadcast news (20)	24.2	7.9	11.8	4.8	48.7
novels/stories (20)	7.4	2.8	16.2	5.4	31.8
conversations (90)	3.7	2.7	6.2	3.6	16.2

in creative writing than in spoken broadcast news is accounted for, since creative writing focuses less on information transfer than spoken broadcast news does.

Quirk (1962: 161ff.) commented on the phenomenon of heavily premodified noun phrases in the English of technological or scientific communication and pointed out that 'protagonists of the style will rightly advance its brevity on the credit side'. In spite of sometimes being criticized as a German legacy imported from the United States (Baker 1955), the results here show that this style is still alive and kicking prominently in academic prose thirty-odd years later.

The high concentration of classifiers in the academic texts, and the sharp contrast on this score between them and the texts in registers which have different functions, such as fiction and conversation, prove the role that classifiers play in register formation. In addition, table 16.6 reveals that the proportionally highest frequency of attitudinal epithets lies in fiction. For example, in the first passage quoted below the concentration of classifiers renders academic writing objective, while in the second the concentration of experiential epithets gives literature a personal touch.

> All Freud's early, major works on *normal* psychology reveal that the dynamics of the mind rely on *unconscious* forces rather than intelligence; they show the thoughts, imagery and even vocabulary of the mind to be driven by a process of *visual* and/or *linguistic* association, rather than one of *logical* analysis or deduction.
>
> (Collier and Davies 1990)

> It was midsummer and the evenings were as long as the shadows which elongated the shape of the house in a *jagged* jigsaw across the grass terraces and made the *stumpy* chimney-stacks into *sharp* arrows of doom. The *enormous* tulip tree, a *glowing* blaze in the *dying* sun viewed from the corner of the house which she skirted on emerging from the back yard, arrested Pritchard's attention.
>
> (Lees-Milne 1990)

A concentration of classifiers or experiential epithets may be a discriminating feature of different registers, as shown by these examples, and such different concentrations can also be used in one text of creative writing to create special literary effects, as shown by Widdowson's (1993: 148ff.) analysis of a literary text. However, in news writing, their uses are motivated essentially by topics rather than by consideration of special effects. The following two examples show that the concentrations of different pre-modifiers in different news stories are caused by the particular subject matter that the reporters dealt with, respectively. (In the first, classifiers are italicized; in the second, experiential epithets.)

> In an address to *French* bankers last night Mr Leigh-Pemberton delivered a robust defence of the UK's *evolutionary* approach to EMU and *British* proposals for a 'hard Ecu'. He told his audience that so far the assumption had been that *banking supervision* would be left to *national* regulators – in most cases the *national central* bank.
>
> (The Guardian, 6 November 1990)

> POLICE hunting the killer of a bank manager's '*perfect*' son were last night looking for a mystery jogger. Sports fanatic David Nock, 16, collapsed dying into a policeman's arms after a *frenzied* knife attack. Last night, David's *devastated* family were trying to come to terms with the *apparently motiveless* murder.
>
> (Daily Mail, 22 April 1991)

Noun or NP pre-modifiers and written news bulletins

Nouns or noun phrases used as pre-modifiers in a noun phrase are a prominent feature in written news reports, as is illustrated in table 16.7.

News bulletins score the highest in table 16.7 because such pre-modifiers are very effective space-saving devices, suitable for packaging *ad hoc* combinations of conceptual content, such as:

> *Lockerbie lawyers* say timing of TV report 'suspicious'
> *Interest rate hopes* lift the market
> AFTER the jump in profitability a year ago, Renold, the *chain and gears engineer*, is labouring again.

Such noun–noun combinations as 'Lockerbie lawyers' and 'interest rate hopes' are typically found in printed news, and the exact meaning of many of them is usually context-sensitive and has to be inferred from the particular news report in which they are embedded. For example, 'Lockerbie lawyers' here means 'lawyers representing the American Relative's Group in the Lockerbie bombing case' and 'interest rate hopes' means 'the expectation in interest rate cuts'. However, the same combination can mean radically different things in other contexts: 'Lockerbie lawyers' might also mean 'lawyers from Lockerbie' and 'interest rate hopes' 'the expectation in interest rate rises'.

Table 16.7 Occurrences of noun pre-modifiers per thousand words, based on the calculation in Zhou (2001).

Registers	Noun–noun
academic writing (40)	30.0
press news reports (20)	31.1
press editorials (10)	18.2
broadcast news (20)	21.0
novels/stories (20)	8.7
face-to-face conversations (90)	7.2

Though the frequencies of noun–noun combinations in academic writing and printed news reach almost equally high in table 16.7, there is a difference between them. On one hand, in academic writing many of them are of a much simpler logical relation, expressed with one 'of': e.g. 'grain diameter' = 'the diameter of a grain', 'ozone depletion' = 'the depletion of ozone', 'nerve fibre' = 'the fibre of a nerve', etc. Or these noun–noun combinations are simply conventionalized technical terms, such as 'hydrogen sulphide' and 'Schwann cells'. On the other hand, in news reports most of them are formed *ad hoc*, involving a wide range of semantic relations, such as 'Special Operations Gunship' (*The New York Times*, 16 October 2001: A1) meaning 'gunship operated by the special operations forces'.

Conclusion

This study has attempted to tackle the question of how different kinds of noun phrases contribute to the formation of distinctive styles which different genres assume and shows that the distribution patterns of NPs with different levels of complexity and semantically different modifiers are good indicators of these different styles.

Notes

1 Classifiers are noun phrase pre-modifiers which denote a 'permanent' and intrinsic quality of the referent of the NP and its slot in an NP structure usually lies closest to the head, as are shown by the italicized expressions in the following examples: 'a *wooden* bridge', 'lovely mellow *Dutch* bricks'.
2 I use the term 'relation-qualifier' to refer to expressions such as those italicized in the following examples: 'the *final* red-and-white barrier', '*similar* fanciful ideas', and 'the four *remaining* songs'. This term is the equivalent of what Fries (2000) referred to as 'peculiar adjective'. Since I regard these expressions as occupying a

functional slot in the structure of a noun phrase, I prefer not to use a word-class label such as 'adjective'. Quirk *et al.* (1985: 1338ff.) and Halliday (1994: 183) both have discussed this phenomenon.

3   Attitudinal epithets are noun phrase pre-modifiers that reflect the speaker's subjective attitude towards the referent of the NP in a non-defining manner, as are shown by the italicized expressions in the following examples: 'the *great* names of the past', in which 'great' means 'admirable', and '*Poor* thing', in which 'poor' means 'pitiable' by the speaker (cf. Halliday 1994: 184).

References

Baker, J. R. (1955) 'English style in scientific papers', *Nature* 5: 851–2.

Biber, D. (1988) *Variation across Speech and Writing*, Cambridge: Cambridge University Press.

—— (1989) 'A typology of English texts', *Linguistics* 27: 3–43.

Biber, D. and Finegan, E. (eds) (1994) *Sociolinguistic Perspectives on Register*, Oxford: Oxford University Press.

Biber, D., Johansson, S., Leech, G., Conrad, S. and Finegan, E. (1999) *Longman Grammar of Spoken and Written English*, London: Longman.

Chafe, W. and Danielewicz, J. (1987) 'Properties of spoken and written language', in R. Horowitz and S. J. Samuels (eds) *Comprehending Oral and Written Language*, London: Academic Press.

Collier, P. and Davies, J. (eds) (1990) *Modernism and the European Unconscious*, London: Polity Press.

Fries, P. (2000) 'Some peculiar adjectives in the English nominal group', in D. G. Lockwood, P. H. Fries and J. E. Copeland (eds) *Functional Approaches to Language, Culture, and Cognition*, Amsterdam: John Benjamins.

Greenbaum, S. (ed.) (1996) *Comparing English Worldwide*, Oxford: Clarendon Press.

Halliday, M. A. K. (1994) *An Introduction to Functional Grammar*, London: Arnold.

Hong, H. (2000) 'Distributive analysis of noun phrases: evidence from ICE-GB', MA thesis, National University of Singapore.

Lees-Milne, J. (1990) *The Fool of Love*, London: Robinson Publishing.

Quirk, R. (1962) *The Use of English*, London: Longman.

Quirk, R., Greenbaum, S., Leech, G. and Svartvik, J. (1985) *A Comprehensive Grammar of the English Language*, London: Longman.

Widdowson, H. G. (1993) 'Representations in prose: setting the scene', in J. M. Sinclair, M. Hoey and G. Fox (eds) *Techniques of Description*, London: Routledge.

Zhou, Xuejun (2001) 'Pre-modifiers of English noun phrases as indicators of genres – a corpus-based study', MA thesis, National University of Singapore.

17 Compressed noun-phrase structures in newspaper discourse

The competing demands of popularization vs. economy

Douglas Biber

Introduction

Written registers in English have undergone extensive stylistic change over the past four centuries. Written prose registers in the seventeenth century were already quite different from conversational registers, and those registers evolved to become even more distinct from speech over the course of the eighteenth century (Biber and Finegan 1989; see also Biber 1995).

However, over the course of the nineteenth and twentieth centuries, popular written registers like letters, fiction, and essays have reversed their direction of change and evolved to become more similar to spoken registers, often becoming even more oral in the modern period than in the seventeenth century. These shifts result in a dispreference for certain stereotypically literate features, such as passive verbs, relative clause constructions and elaborated noun phrases generally.

Biber and Finegan (1989: 514ff.) appeal to both conscious and unconscious motivations to explain these historical patterns for essays, fiction and letters. For example, authors like Samuel Johnson and Benjamin Franklin in the eighteenth century argued that writing should be elaborated and 'ornamental' to effectively persuade readers. At the same time, the eighteenth century witnessed the rise of a popular, middle-class literacy, including writers like Defoe and Richardson, who were from the middle class themselves and addressed themselves primarily to middle-class readers. This popularization of literacy in English gained ground in the nineteenth century, reinforced by mass schooling and the demands of a wider reading public for more accessible written prose; thus the linguistic norms for non-expository registers were reversed during this period, and began to shift towards more accessible, oral styles.

In contrast, informational, expository registers like medical prose, science prose and legal opinions have followed a different course (Atkinson 1992, 2001;

Biber 1995; Biber and Finegan 1997/2001). Rather than evolving towards more oral styles, these expository registers have consistently developed towards more literate styles across all periods. The development of literary linguistic features corresponds to the development of a more specialized readership, more special-ized purposes, and a fuller exploitation of the production possibilities of the written mode. That is, in marked contrast to the general societal trends towards a wider lay readership and the corresponding need for popular written regis-ters, readers of medical research prose, science prose and legal prose have become increasingly more specialized in their backgrounds and training, and correspondingly these registers have become more specialized in linguistic form.

The preferred linguistic style of newspaper discourse has also undergone dramatic long-term change, influenced by these same competing forces. Over the course of the eighteenth and nineteenth centuries, newspaper prose was similar to academic prose in developing an increasingly dense use of passive verbs, relative clause constructions and elaborated noun phrases generally. However, the opposing drift towards more oral styles began to influence news-paper prose towards the end of the nineteenth century, followed by more marked change in the twentieth century (see Biber and Finegan 1997/2001).

Over the past few decades, these changes towards more oral styles in news-paper language have accelerated. Thus, Hundt and Mair (1999) track several changes in newspaper prose over the thirty-year period from 1960 to 1990, including a greater use of first and second person pronouns, contractions, sentence-initial conjunctions, phrasal verbs, and progressive aspect. Such changes reflect the continuing popularization of newspapers, adopting more oral features in an effort to appeal to a wider reading audience.

Surprisingly, though, newspaper prose has retained some of its nineteenth-century characteristics associated with dense, informational prose. In particular, newspaper prose continues to rely on a dense use of nouns and integrated noun phrase constructions. Thus, modern-day newspaper prose is very similar to academic prose in certain characteristics (Biber 1988; Biber and Finegan 1997/2001). These linguistic characteristics seem to be a reflection of two major factors: the informational purpose of newspaper prose, coupled with the influence of economy. That is, the 'informational explosion' has resulted in pres-sure to communicate information as efficiently and economically as possible, resulting in compressed styles that depend heavily on tightly integrated noun-phrase constructions.

It might be expected that newspaper prose would exhibit an intermediate style generally: relatively oral in some respects, in response to the demands of popularization, but less oral than registers like fiction or letters; and relatively literate in other respects, in response to the demands of economy and informational compression, but much less so than registers like academic or official prose.

It is in this regard, though, that modern-day newspaper language is especially surprising: in the use of some noun-phrase structures used for compressed expression, newspapers have been innovative in the development of literate styles. In fact, newspaper language is in some ways more extreme than academic prose in the dense integration of information, despite the need to appeal to a broad popular audience. The present chapter documents the use of some of these innovative complex noun-phrase structures in modern-day newspapers.

Methodology: the corpus-based approach

The present study uses corpus-based analysis to investigate the linguistic patterns of use in newspaper prose. The corpus-based approach can be seen as an extension of earlier empirical studies of language use, for example in stylistics (e.g. Carroll 1960) or functional linguistics (e.g. Prince 1978; Schiffrin 1981). More recently, researchers on register/style, discourse and grammar have begun to use the tools and techniques available from corpus linguistics, with its greater emphasis on the representativeness of the database, and its computational tools for investigating distributional patterns in large text collections (see Biber, Conrad and Reppen 1998; Kennedy 1998 for introductions to this analytical approach).

The research findings in the present chapter are mostly adapted from *The Longman Grammar of Spoken and Written English* (*LGSWE*) (Biber *et al.* 1999). The analyses are based on texts from four registers (see table 17.1).

Table 17.1 Composition of the sub-corpora used in the analyses (taken from the LSWE Corpus).

	Number of texts	Number of words
Conversation (BrE)	3,436	3,929,500
Fiction (AmE and BrE)	139	4,980,000
News (BrE)	20,395	5,432,800
Academic prose (AmE and BrE)	408	5,331,800

AmE = American English
BrE = British English

Although conversation, fiction, newspaper language and academic prose are general registers, they differ in important ways from one another (e.g. with respect to mode, interactiveness, production circumstances, purpose and target audience). The analyses were carried out on the Longman Spoken and Written English (LSWE) Corpus, which contains around twenty million words of text from these four major registers. All frequency counts reported below have been normalized to a common basis (a count per one million words of text), so that they are directly comparable across registers.

Only British newspapers are analysed in the present study, sampled from ten different newspapers representing a range of political and regional differences:

National newspapers:	Regional newspapers:
The Independent	*Liverpool Echo*
The Guardian	*The Belfast Telegraph*
Daily Mirror	*The East Anglian Daily Times*
Sunday People	*The Northern Echo*
Today	*The Scotsman*

The national newspapers, mostly published in London, represent different readership levels which are important in the British press: *The Guardian* and *The Independent* represent 'highbrow', broadsheet newspapers; *The Daily Mirror* and *The Sunday People* represent popular, tabloid newspapers; and *Today* represents an in-between category. Texts are also sampled from across the various topics found in most newspapers. The majority of the news texts in this sub-corpus are from three major subject areas: domestic/local/city news, foreign/world news, and sports news. Other major categories are business news (including commerce, economics and finance articles); arts (including cinema, television, fine arts and the media in general, and also some articles on entertainment personalities); and social news (covering everything from reports about society people and events to results of polls concerning social issues) (see Biber *et al.* 1999).

Compressed noun-phrase structures in newspaper prose

Noun phrases occur with roughly the same frequency in spoken and written registers in the LSWE Corpus, as figure 17.1 shows. However, the internal complexity of those noun phrases differs dramatically across registers. In conversation, most noun phrases (85 per cent) have no modifiers at all. Over half of those noun phrases are realized by a simple pronoun. In contrast, around

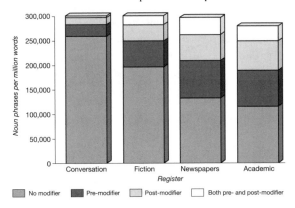

Figure 17.1 Distribution of noun phrases with pre-modifiers and post-modifiers.

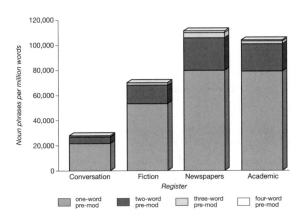

Figure 17.2 Distribution of pre-modification by length.

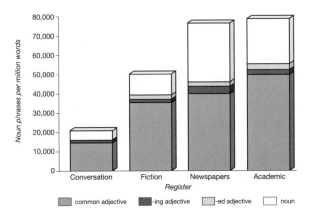

Figure 17.3 Pre-modifier types in noun phrases with single pre-modifiers.

60 per cent of all noun phrases in newspaper language and academic prose have a modifier, with many noun phrases having multiple modifiers.

Even at this level, we see that newspaper prose is in some ways more complex than academic prose, having a somewhat greater use of noun phrases modified by both pre- and post-modifiers. For example:

pre-modifiers	noun	post-modifiers
A Quaker-run training	college	for teachers

Specialized pre-modification patterns in newspaper prose

Pre-modifiers tend to be slightly longer in newspaper prose than academic prose, as figure 17.2 shows.

Thus, noun phrases like the following are not at all uncommon in newspaper prose:

- a Quaker-run training college for teachers
- HP's automatic software distribution system
- the country's biggest state holding company

In examples like these, pre-modifiers are used to compress information into relatively few words, where the alternative would normally require full clauses. (For example, the pre-modifiers in the first example convey the information that the college specializes in training and that it is run by Quakers.)

More detailed analysis shows that a single type of nominal pre-modifer is especially preferred in newspaper prose: nouns. As shown in figure 17.3, nouns account for around 40 per cent of all pre-modifiers in newspapers.

Further, many of these nouns are extremely productive in combining with many different head nouns, usually referring to major institutions like government, business and the media. For example,

- government + action, agencies, approval, bonds, control, decision
- business + administration, cards, community, dealings, empire, ideas
- TV + ads, appearance, cameras, channel, crew, documentary, licence

Even nouns with concrete meanings, like *school* and *water*, are extremely productive as pre-modifiers in news, where they take on institutional meanings:

- school + activities, boards, budget, care, leavers, pupils, work
- water + authorities, bill, companies, industry, levels, privatization

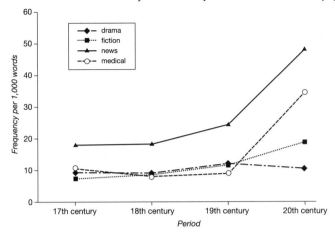

Figure 17.4 Noun–noun sequences across periods.

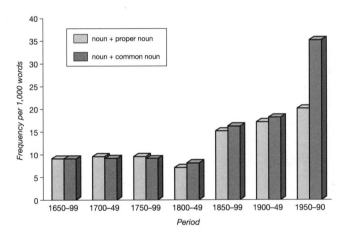

Figure 17.5 Breakdown of noun–noun sequences in news.

From a historical perspective, newspaper prose has consistently used noun–noun sequences to a greater extent than academic prose (see Biber and Clark 2002). Figure 17.4 shows the increase in the use of noun–noun sequences across the past four centuries, based on analysis of four registers from the ARCHER corpus (described in Biber and Finegan 1997/2001).

In the twentieth century, both medical prose and newspaper prose show marked increases in the use of noun–noun sequences, with these features remaining more common in news.

In earlier periods, many pre-modifying nouns functioned as titles (e.g. *Cardinal Corsini*, *Lord Richard Edgcumbe*). Figure 17.5 shows that roughly half of all pre-modifying nouns in older newspaper prose modify a proper noun; these are mostly pre-modifying nouns functioning as titles. It is only in the last fifty years that we see a marked increase in the use of nouns pre-modifying common nouns (e.g. *government approval, business empire*).

The examples below illustrate these patterns of use. The first is from an eighteenth-century news report; the second is from a twentieth-century news report. (Noun–noun sequences are italicized in both texts.)

> At the Court at St James's, the Nineteenth Day of January, 1743.
> PRESENT,
> The King's most Excellent Majesty in Council.

> His Majesty having been graciously pleased to deliver the Custody of the Seals of the Dutchy and *County Palatine* of Lancaster, to the Right Honourable *Lord Richard Edgcumbe*, the Oath of Chancellor of the said Dutchy was this Day, by his Majesty's Command, administred to his Lordship.
> . . .

> Naples, January 4. In the last Week the King performed the Ceremony of investing *Cardinal Corsini* with the *Cardinal Cap*.
> (*The London Gazette*, 17–21, 21–24 January, 18–21 February 1743)

> Thatcher says no to revenge for Lockerbie
> Eye for an eye warning to the United States
> By Philip Webster, Harvey Elliott and Christopher Thomas

> The Prime Minister declared her opposition to avenging the *Lockerbie air disaster* yesterday, as American *intelligence chiefs* admitted failing to link the crash with any *terrorist organization* . . .
> With the incoming *Bush administration* in America certain to face pressure for retaliation, Mrs Thatcher's outspoken rejection of *reprisal raids* could pose the first difficulties in her relationship with the new President
> . . .
> Meanwhile, a further tightening of *baggage inspection procedures* is likely to emerge from a review of Britain's *airline and airport security*. It will be launched this week at a meeting of the national *Aviation Security Committee*, comprising *government, airline, union and safety officials*.
> (*The Times*, 1 December 1989, pp. 1 and 18)

The first example illustrates the primary use of pre-modifying nouns as titles in eighteenth-century newspaper reports (e.g. *County, Lord, Cardinal*). Although this use continues in present-day newspaper prose, there is an even greater increase in the use of nouns modifying common nouns, as illustrated in the second example (e.g. *air disaster, intelligence chiefs, terrorist organization*). In fact, this example also illustrates how multiple nouns can be used in sequence modifying a head noun (e.g. *baggage inspection procedures*).

Overall, the extremely productive use of nouns as pre-modifiers in news results in a very dense, integrated packaging of information. The frequent use of these forms is motivated in part by space-saving considerations, since a single noun + noun sequence typically conveys a complex meaning in compressed form. However, the dense use of these forms places a heavy burden on readers, who must infer the intended logical relationship between the modifying noun and head noun; I return to this point in the conclusion.

Specialized post-modification patterns in newspaper prose

Nominal post-modifiers are also used in newspaper prose as compressed devices to pack extra information into relatively few words. Non-restrictive modifiers are particularly prevalent with this function, especially non-restrictive relative clauses and appositive noun phrases; both of these constructions are considerably more common in newspaper prose than in academic prose (Biber *et al.* 1999).

Non-restrictive relative clauses are typically used to present information that is tangential to the main point, but that might be of interest to some readers. For example:

> Those attending the burial, *which followed a solemn mass in Santiago cathedral*, included Allende's widow Hortensia Bussi, President Patricio Aylwin and his Cabinet.

In other cases, these modifying clauses present tangential information that provides important background for the interpretation of the main story line, as in:

> ASIA – PACIFIC EAST TIMOR. A visit by Portuguese parliamentarians and journalists to the former Portuguese territory, *which Indonesia had de facto incorporated into its territory in 1976*, was scheduled after repeated postponements.

Appositive noun phrases serve similar functions, adding elaborating information about the head noun that provides interesting background but is tangential to the main point. Appositive noun phrases in newspaper prose are especially common with proper nouns as head, as in:

Mr Pyotr Luchinsky, the new first secretary.

As with other compressed structures, appositive noun phrases compress information into a phrasal rather than clausal form of expression. In many cases, the appositive noun phrase can be quite long and complex:

Oliver Gillie, deputy editor of *The Independent Magazine* and formerly medical editor of the newspaper.

Appositive noun phrases are also found commonly in academic prose, but they are less frequent than in newspaper prose, and they tend to serve somewhat different functions. That is, appositive noun phrases in academic prose often provide a technical renaming of the head noun, rather than being used to provide tangential background information. For example:

- IAS (Institute of Advanced Studies)
- hydrogen chloride, HCl
- the various life-history events (i.e., oviposition, hatching and maturation)

Because non-restrictive relative clauses and appositive noun phrases serve similar functions in newspaper prose, they can occur in the same sentence, sometimes with several levels of embedding:

Ariana's board includes Bernard Giroud, who started Intel France in 1971 and left the company last year a corporate vice president to become a venture capitalist, Gerard Yon, formerly sales and marketing manager of Chorus Systemes, the microkernel house, and now president of VST, a French start-up in electronic document management, and Pascal LeVasseur, technical director of Dell France.

Finally, *to*-noun complement clauses are another type of postnominal structure that is especially characteristic of newspaper prose (Biber *et al.* 1999). The common head nouns taking *to*-clauses present human goals, opportunities or actions; for example, *chance, attempt, effort, ability, opportunity, decision, plan, bid*. These meanings fit the typical purposes of news reportage, with a focus on human/institutional goals and actions:

- Regional nerves have been strained by a *plan* to cut off water from Syria and Iraq for a month.
- Meetings on Friday morning also ended without a *decision* to accept the deal which provides for Palestinian self-rule in the Gaza Strip.

• It is increasingly taken for granted that any post-war reordering of the Middle East will include a fresh *bid* to break the Arab–Israeli impasse.

Most of these head nouns are derived from verbs, resulting again in a more compressed style (i.e., an embedded noun phrase instead of a separate clause). An additional motivation for using the nominalized form is that the agent of the plan/decision/bid can be left unspecified.

Summary and conclusion

Several previous studies have documented the ways in which newspaper texts are edited (e.g. van Dijk 1988; Bell 1991). Bell (1991: 76–8) identifes 'cutting' as one of the major goals of copy-editing, to reduce the volume of news to a manageable amount. The main editing device for this purpose discussed by Bell is the simple deletion of text.

The present study suggests that newspaper prose has been linguistically innovative in other ways designed to achieve a compressed style. That is, devices like noun–noun sequences, heavy appositive post-modifiers, and *to*-noun complement clauses are especially characteristic of newspaper prose. These features are all literate devices used to pack information into relatively few words. These devices are also commonly used in academic prose, together with functionally-similar devices like attributive adjectives and prepositional phrases as post-modifiers. However, the features discussed above are noteworthy because they are considerably more common in newspaper prose. That is, at the same time that news has been developing more popular oral styles, it has also been innovative in developing literate styles with extreme reliance on compressed noun-phrase structures.

These increasingly compressed styles of expression are at the same time less explicit in meaning. For example, noun–noun sequences can represent a bewildering array of meaning relationships, with no overt signal of the intended meaning. The following list illustrates only a few of these meaning relationships:

noun–noun sequence	*meaning relationship*
air disaster	N1 expresses the location of N2
reprisal raid	N1 expresses the purpose of N2
baggage inspection	N1 expresses the 'patient' of N2
airline officials	N2 is employed by N1
blood pressure	N2 is caused by N1
glass bottle	N2 is composed of N1

It is probably for this reason that news relies primarily on pre-modifying nouns from those semantic domains most commonly associated with current events such as government, business, education, the media and sports. These are areas where news writers can reasonably expect readers to have well-developed pragmatic knowledge, and so be able to decode noun + noun relationships without too much difficulty. However, it seems clear that the concessions to popular literacy associated with a greater use of oral features, like first and second person pronouns, contractions and phrasal verbs, are surprisingly offset by the increasing use of these compressed noun-phrase structures.

From a historical point of view, these developments are relatively recent, accelerating only in the last fifty to one hundred years. Two functional factors have probably been influential in these developments. First, there has been an increasing awareness of the production possibilities of the written mode, offering almost unlimited opportunities for crafting and revising the final text. The availability of typewriters, and more recently word processors, have been technological developments that facilitate authors' abilities to manipulate the language in written texts. At the same time, we have witnessed an 'informational explosion', resulting in pressure to communicate information as efficiently and economically as possible. Although there may be additional structural and social factors, these two factors can be taken together to explain in part the rapid increase in the use of compressed noun modification devices over the past 100 years.

References

Atkinson, D. (1992) 'The evolution of medical research writing from 1735 to 1985: the case of the *Edinburgh Medical Journal*', *Applied Linguistics* 13: 337–74.

—— (2001) 'Scientific discourse across history: a combined multi-dimensional/rhetorical analysis of the *Philosophical Transactions of the Royal Society of London*', in S. Conrad and D. Biber (eds) *Variation in English: Multidimensional Studies*, London: Longman, 45–65.

Bell, A. (1991) *The Language of News Media*, Oxford: Blackwell.

Biber, D. (1988) *Variation across Speech and Writing*, Cambridge: Cambridge University Press.

—— (1995) *Dimensions of Register Variation: A Cross-Linguistic Comparison*, Cambridge: Cambridge University Press.

Biber, D. and Clark, V. (2002) 'Historical shifts in modification patterns with complex noun phrase structures: how long can you go without a verb?', in T. Fanego, M.-J. López-Couso and J. Pérez-Guerra (eds) *English Historical Syntax and Morphology. Selected Papers from 11 ICEHL, Santiago de Compostela, 7–11 September 2000*, Amsterdam: John Benjamins.

Biber, D. and Finegan, E. (1989), 'Drift and the evolution of English style: a history of three genres', *Language* 65: 487–517.

—— (1997/2001) 'Diachronic relations among speech-based and written registers in English', in T. Nevalainen and L. Kahlas-Tarkka (eds) *To Explain the Present: Studies in the Changing English Language in Honour of Matti Rissanen*, Helsinki: Société Néo-philologique, 253–75. Reprinted in S. Conrad and D. Biber (eds) *Variation in English: Multidimensional Studies*, London: Longman, 66–83.

Biber, D., Conrad, S. and Reppen, R. (1998) *Corpus Linguistics: Investigating Language Structure and Use*, Cambridge: Cambridge University Press.

Biber, D., Johansson, S., Leech, G., Conrad, S. and Finegan, E. (1999) *The Longman Grammar of Spoken and Written English*, London: Longman.

Carroll, J. B. (1960) 'Vectors of prose style', in T. A. Sebeok (ed.) *Style in Language*, Cambridge, MA: MIT Press, 283–92.

Conrad, S. and Biber, D. (eds) (2001) *Variation in English: Multidimensional Studies*, London: Longman.

Hundt, M. and Mair, C. (1999) '"Agile" and "uptight" genres: the corpus-based approach to language change in progress', *International Journal of Corpus Linguistics* 4: 221–42.

Kennedy, G. (1998) *An Introduction to Corpus Linguistics*, London: Longman.

Prince, E. F. (1978) 'A comparison of Wh-clefts and It-clefts in discourse', *Language* 54: 883–906.

Schiffrin, D. (1981) 'Tense variation in narrative', *Language* 57: 45–62.

van Dijk, T. A. (1988) *News as Discourse*, Hillsdale, NJ: Lawrence Erlbaum.

18 Newspapers and neologisms

John Ayto

Introduction

Picture the situation. It is November 2000. The leadership of the most power-ful nation on earth is in the process of being usurped in a bloodless coup. The world's second largest democracy is telling electors who want their votes counted to shut up and go away. And what are British journalists getting excited about? One little word, of four letters: *chad*, denoting the small bits of waste paper produced by punching cards. It is not new, though in 2000 it evi-dently was new to most British journalists. It goes back to the 1940s. But it is kind of odd, quirky – the sort of word to catch a journo's eye as a piece of shiny paper catches a magpie's eye. And so, when a row blew up during the US presidential election over whether punched ballot papers had been correctly identified and counted, we had the column inches on *chad* – where the word came from, what it meant, what different sorts there are, and so on. Euan Fer-guson in the *Observer*, for example, enlarged on *chad* subspecies:

> A *dimple chad* is a simple indentation. A *pregnant chad* or *nipple chad* bulges
> out but has not been punched through at any point. A *hanging-door chad* has
> one corner hanging off slightly; a *swing-door chad* has two corners hanging,
> and a *tri-chad* is one with three corners hanging off. So now you know.
>
> (Ferguson 2000)

A particular favourite was *chadless*, which gave the suffix *-less* probably its finest hour since *zipless* in the 1970s. So *chad* was the media buzzword in Britain in November. One moment I particularly treasure was the British TV commenta-tor who referred to it as *chaad* – presumably on the basis that you say *bæth* and we say *baath*.

All of which leads to the theme of this chapter: the role, or perceived role of newspaper writers in disseminating and even creating English neologisms. The general perception, well established over, at the very least, the last seventy years, but based largely on impressionistic evidence, is of journalists desperate to enliven jejune copy, taking final refuge in the coinage of outlandish lexemes, 99 per cent of which will never leave the wastepaper basket in which they're deposited at the end of the day.

Is this true, or is it all terribly unfair? Certainly the compiler of a fairly recent, light-hearted collection of 1990s vocabulary (Rowan 1998) has identi-fied large numbers of new coinages as having been popularized (in some cases a brief or dubious popularity) by their coverage in newspapers, and in some cases having been dreamt up by a particular newspaper or periodical (e.g. *autopathography* in *Time Out*, *giro gypsy* in the *Daily Express*, *middle youth* in the older woman's magazine *Red*). And of course journalists are uniquely well placed, if they so wish, to stake a claim for themselves or a colleague which will solidify over time, even if closer examination invalidates it (the modern use of the term *the establishment* is a case in point: the legend that it was coined in the mid-1950s by the journalist Henry Fairlie has hardened into general acceptance, but in fact it has been around since at least the 1920s).

Blends

Maybe the reputation is exaggerated. In order to try to see if some less impres-sionistic evidence can be found in this area, this chapter will concentrate on a particular section of it – but a section which by repute holds a special fascina-tion for journalists: the blend. For the purpose of this investigation, the fairly broad characterization formulated by John Algeo will be followed: a blend is 'any combination of two (or more) etyma with omission of part of at least one etymon' (Algeo 1998: 76). A frequent paradigm is *motel*, formed from *motor* and *hotel*.

Of course the phenomenon of blending is by no means brand-new. As Garland Cannon points out in his key study (Cannon 1986), it was at work as long ago as the Old English period; and the now familiar *brunch* (*breakfast* + *lunch*) is pre-1900. Nor is it by any means solely the preserve of those seeking to make a verbal splash with an amusing or arresting coinage. It is now a perfectly respectable method of creating new scientific or technical terminology, for example *quasar* (*quasi-* + *stellar*) and *formaldehyde* (*formic* + *aldehyde*). And what is apparently the latest buzzword in the fashionable field of biotechnology is a blend: *proteomics* (*protein* + *genomics*). Nevertheless, it is quite clear that instances of blending multiplied exponentially in the twentieth century. And there is anecdotal evidence that an important contribution to this increase was made by writers of journalism. Specifically, a period of fashionability is identified in US newspapers and magazines extending from the late 1920s to well into the 1940s (with *Time* magazine well to the fore). In particular, writers of syndicated columns are credited with instigating and perpetuating the fad. More particularly still, the sharp-penned columnist Walter Winchell is fingered as the arch-blender. In a survey of the phenomenon published in 1939, Lester Berrey printed a list of selections from one year's output of blends perpetrated by Winchell (Berrey 1939: 3–10). There were fifty-one of them, only six of which Berrey felt the need to explain to his readership. Many of them have the same groan-inducing quality as the so-called puns in *Sun* headlines: *nincompetitor* (*nincompoop* + *competitor*), *ohmigoddess* (*oh my god* + *goddess*), *sinfant* (*sin* + *infant*), *spontaneous combust-up* (*combustion* + *bust-up*), *storkestra* (*stork* + *orchestra*), *weddiversary* (*wedding* + *anniversary*), etc. The majority are ad-hoc formations, with an eye more to an immediate effect than to long-term survival, and only two of them – *infanticipate* (*infant* + *anticipate*) and *revusical* (*revue* + *musical*) – seem to have caught on sufficiently to come to the attention of contemporary lexicographers. *Infanticipate*, incidentally, soon died out – probably because it was dangerously close to *infanticide*; *revusical* was still around at the end of the 1960s, but it's possible that these more recent examples represent a recoinage rather than continuous unbroken usage since the 1930s.

Journalists find blended names for hybrid animals and plants particularly irresistible, and that trend seems to have got up steam in the 1920s and 1930s too. Those are the decades of the *swoose* (*swan* + *goose*), of the *liger* (*lion* + *tiger*) and the *tigon* (*tiger* + *lion*) (not to mention the *lygon* and the *tyron*), of the *pheasen* (*pheasant* + *hen*), the *catalo* (*cattle* + *buffalo*) and the *topato* (*tomato* + *potato*).

The hypothesis to be tested is: that the 1930s, for whatever reason (journalistic fad or other), were *the* twentieth-century decade of the blend. To find an answer, I have analysed material I assembled for a book called *Twentieth Century Words* (Ayto 1999). This was a decade-by-decade record of new vocabulary in English in the twentieth century. Each decade is represented by a selection of about 500 lexical items and usages first recorded in that ten-year period. Figure 18.1 is a graphic representation of the number of blends in each decade-section of that book.

The profile is quite revealing: after a fairly fallow first twenty years, a considerable post-World War I cranking up, building up to a peak in the 1930s, which then levels off to a certain extent, but never drops back to pre-World War I figures. So the 1930s perhaps truly warrant the title 'decade of the blend', but not so much because they hugely outnumber any other decade in blend production, as because they set a trend whose effects are still very much in evidence.

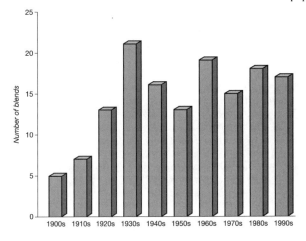

Figure 18.1 Number of blends by decade.

The role of the journalist

But this does not answer the question whether journalists should be taking all or part of the credit or blame for these developments. The circumstances of any given coinage are more often than not lost, and those that survive may be distorted by accretions of myth. And it goes without saying that the earliest written record we have of any coinage does not necessarily reflect its origins. Nevertheless, examination of the first known occurrences of twentieth-century blends may provide some information. One hundred blends recorded by *OED* (*Oxford English Dictionary*) from 1900 onwards were investigated. For fifty-four of them, the earliest citation given is from a newspaper or some other form of periodical publication. For comparison, a parallel, randomly selected sample of 100 non-blended post-1900 neologisms from *OED* were examined. Of them, only forty-five are first cited in newspapers or periodicals. This may suggest (though not of course prove) a tendency for blends to get their initial printed airing in newspapers and similar texts.

Corroboration for this can be found elsewhere. Table 18.1 contains figures for the percentage of blends in various general corpora of English words. Cannon is by some distance the largest of these six corpora, and therefore perhaps the one most to be relied on for an accurate estimate of the prevalence of blending in the second half of the twentieth century as a source of stable long-term vocabulary. Clearly, *Longman* is a long way ahead of any of the other corpora in the percentage of blends it includes. Algeo tentatively puts this down to its tendency to 'include a good many voguish and nonce forms, which favour the process of blending'. Perhaps, as editor of *Longman*, I might be allowed to

Table 18.1 Percentage of blends in different corpora of English words.

Barnhart	Longman	OED2	NEWS	BDC	Cannon
4.8	9.8	3.3	1.1	0.5	1.0

Barnhart: a sample of 1,000 words from the *Barnhart Dictionary of New English 1962–1973* (Barnhart, Steinmetz and Barnhart 1973)
Longman: volume 1 of the *Longman Register of New Words* (Ayto 1989)
OED2: a sample of 393 words from *OED2* made by John Algeo (Algeo 1998: 84)
NEWS: a sample of words from the *OED*'s *New English Word Series*, as analysed by John Simpson (Simpson 1988: 143–52)
BDC: a sample of around 2,700 words from the *Barnhart Dictionary Companion* (Barnhart 1987)
Cannon: a corpus of 16,500 words assembled by Garland Cannon from two *Barnhart* dictionaries and the 1981 addendum to *Webster's Third International Dictionary* (Cannon 1987)

amend that assessment slightly, and suggest that the main reason is that the evidence on which *Longman* was based was gathered almost exclusively from newspapers. A good 99 per cent of the citations it includes are from newspapers and other nonspecialist periodicals, a far higher concentration than is (or would have been) the case in any of these other corpora, whose data is much more evenly spread over all print sources.

This adds weight to the findings from the *OED* citation sources. It will probably always be a matter of chance whether the conception of any one blend, or any new coinage, can be pinned on one particular person, journalist or otherwise, but we can I think suggest with some confidence that as far as delivery is concerned, it very often is 'the press what done it'.

References

Algeo, J. (1998) 'Vocabulary', in S. Romaine (ed.) *Cambridge History of the English Language*, vol. IV, Cambridge: Cambridge University Press.
Ayto, J. (1989) *Longman Register of New Words*, vol. 1, London: Longman.
—— (1999) *Twentieth Century Words*, Oxford: Oxford University Press.
Barnhart, C. L., Steinmetz, S. and Barnhart, R. K. (1973) *A Dictionary of New English 1963–1972*, London: Longman.
Barnhart, D. K. (1987) *The Barnhart Dictionary Companion Index (1982–1985)*, Cold Spring, NY: Lexik House.
Berrey, L. V. (1939) 'Newly-wedded words', *American Speech* 14: 3–10.
Cannon, G. (1986) 'Blends in English word formation', *Linguistics* 24: 724–53.
—— (1987) *Historical Change and English Word-Formation*, New York: Peter Lang.
Ferguson, E. (2000) 'Whoops, there's a chad in my lunchbucket', *Observer*, 19 November.
Rowan, D. (1998) *A Glossary for the 90s*, London: Prion Books.
Simpson, J. (1988) 'The new vocabulary of English', in E. G. Stanley and T. F. Hoad (eds) *Words for Robert Burchfield's Sixty-Fifth Birthday*, Cambridge: D. S. Brewer.

19 Reliable authority

Tabloids, film, email and speech
as sources for dictionaries

John Simpson

Introduction: Johnson's 'best writers'

Dictionaries tell us, amongst other things, what words mean. We consult dictionaries for reliable information about the language and its usage. Some English dictionaries specialize in modern usage, and others, such as the *Oxford English Dictionary* (*OED*), record both modern usage and the history of English. But whatever the dictionary, much of its authority lies in the wealth of data available to the editor or editors, on which the dictionary's lexical analysis is based.

Since before the time of Dr Johnson's great dictionary of 1755, most reliable lexicographers have sought to base their analysis of the language upon authoritative data. Until the advent of computers, this has typically involved amassing card files which record lexical data from texts illustrating the variety of the language which the lexicographer wishes to address.

Johnson's method well illustrates the situation in the mid-eighteenth century. He read texts illustrative of what he called 'the wells of English undefiled' – the best literature of the two hundred years or so before his day. He would obtain books from wherever he could – often from his friends – and while reading them he would mark words which he felt might be good examples of the use of the language. He would then have his assistants copy these out under the relevant headwords of his draft. Unfortunately, his friends often received their books back rather the worse for wear. Some of these heavily underlined texts are now archived in research libraries, allowing scholars to study Johnson's data-collection methods in some detail.

Authority for Johnson (1755) meant the authority of the 'best' writers – those that were regarded by him as the appropriate models to follow in framing his own record of the language. When Johnson started planning his dictionary in the 1740s, he imagined that he would be able to produce a dictionary which 'fixed' the meaning of the vocabulary of English for the foreseeable future. It was a common eighteenth-century view. Pope, Swift and others had lobbied earlier in the century for an Academy of English to supervise English, after the model of other European countries. But as Johnson settled down to the work of compiling his dictionary, he realized that language would not submit to this legislative tyranny. As soon as language seemed to be fixed and captured in a dictionary, it moved on. Johnson's authoritative models were predominantly literary writers. Since Johnson's day, views of what can constitute reliable authority have developed considerably, and this chapter addresses issues which are confronting lexicographers today.

Newspapers as 'witnesses'

Recently the *OED* received a letter from a member of the public asking 'what exactly constitutes a printed record. If newspapers count for the purposes of the *OED*, then that is good news to begin with.' The writer wanted to know what the *OED* regards as a reliable authority for the purposes of compiling an authoritative description of English. He apparently did not think of 'authority' in the way Johnson did: as a source which represents the model of English which the dictionary seeks to describe. Rather, an 'authority' here was a valid 'witness' to lexical usage, a source which a dictionary might cite not as a model, but simply by way of descriptive example. It is perhaps surprising that the appropriateness of newspapers as 'witnesses' to the language should still be in question.

However, the issue of whether newspapers are appropriate authorities goes back many years. In the 1880s, when the first edition of *The Oxford English Dictionary* had just embarked on its fifty-year publication cycle, Benjamin Jowett, Master of Balliol and Chairman of the Delegates of the University Press (the body of academics that oversees scholarly publishing decisions at the Oxford University Press) presented the founding editor of the *OED*, James Murray, with a document entitled *Suggestions for Guidance in Preparing Copy for the Press*. In this document, the Delegates raised objections to the use of illustrative quotations from newspapers. Murray called this criticism 'by far the silliest that the Dictionary has elicited'. He went on to say that 'I am certain posterity will agree with me, and that the time will come when this criticism will be pointed out as a most remarkable instance of the inability of men to acknowledge contemporary facts and read the signs of the times.' As Murray (1977) has pointed out in her biography of her grandfather:

> By the time the Dictionary was completed in 1928 the earlier policy of the
> Delegacy had been long forgotten and in describing the unique characteris-

tics of the work, the [University] Press boasted that quotations had always been up to date, citing *The Times* in praise of this feature: 'It is not the document so much as the use of it that counts; and to illustrate the general acceptance of a word . . . any respectable and recognized publication – book or newspaper – may very likely be more apt for the lexicographer's purpose than a literary masterpiece.'

(Murray 1977: 221–4)

What is a 'witness'?

Nowadays, the question has moved on. One of the key issues confronting lexicographers today is precisely what is acceptable at the start of the twenty-first century as a lexical authority. The question is not quite as simple as it may sound. The obvious answer is that nothing is an 'authority' but that anything may act as a 'witness'. Everything is grist to the lexicographer's mill.

On the rare occasions when Murray did not have a printed example to hand in order to illustrate a word or meaning, he took the unusual course of inventing one – relying upon his own 'native' knowledge of the language to achieve something representative. Nowadays this is generally regarded as unscholarly practice. Since Murray's day it has not been employed in compiling the *OED*. Here are some of the examples which Murray apparently invented to complement the written record:

abomination	to regard smoking with *abomination*
about	Better to earn a little than hang *about* doing nothing
	The idlers hanging *about* the door of the public house
abuse	It is characteristic of the English drunkard to *abuse* his wife and family (Murray was of course a Scot)
abusiveness	The *abusiveness* of their language passes description.

In fact, these examples demonstrate more about Murray's code of ethics than the language of his time. Invented quotations are still a feature of some dictionaries, and considerable attempts are made at ensuring their objectivity, but nevertheless the process of inventing authority is as fraught with problems now as it was in Murray's day.

If we should not invent evidence, then we should perhaps seek it more widely. A principal concern for the *OED* in choosing citable texts is that the data should be available for reverification by others in the future. In this way, the procedure can be regarded as something akin to a scientific experiment which must be reproducible by a second and subsequent research team. On this basis, illustrative quotations from printed texts do not usually present problems as they will typically remain available in research archives.

Oral evidence is an enormous body of material that is not covered to any significant degree by any archiving method, and as a result the *OED* has not in the past cited such evidence for the use of language. Clearly it is not possible to cite oral evidence collected to today's standards with regard to the language of the past, but nowadays – if resources were available – it would be prudent to amass an oral archive alongside a written one. Archives do exist, as at the Survey of English Usage and, rather ironically, printed evidence of this is sometimes used by the *OED*; similarly, the British National Corpus includes about fifteen million words of spoken language, available in transcribed form. Other oral sources are also accessible, but at present the comprehensive analysis of the spoken language lags behind that of the written language and different transcription methods produce different results (e.g. the standardization of colloquial *could of* (etc.) to *could have* on some broadly transcribed corpora).

Similarly, different newspapers have different claims to authority. In 1928 the broadsheet *Times* was happy to regard itself as a reliable authority. More recently, the tabloids (presenting news in a 'compressed' form like the original proprietary 'tabloid' tablets or pills of the late nineteenth century, and nowadays often in an informal and sensationalist style) are widely regarded as opinion formers and, by implication, as influences on everyday style. It would be unusual for a dictionary which attempted to represent a comprehensive picture of the language to refuse to address the lexical and stylistic commonplaces of the tabloid press, and indeed they are cited in dictionaries such as the *OED*.

But what of film, music, radio and television? If the tabloids present news and opinion in an approachable and entertaining style, can the lexicographer look to entertainment generally to furnish evidence for usage? Again the *OED* is predominantly citing archived records, and so this presents some problems. Nevertheless, film and broadcasting scripts are widely available and often the copyright holders will provide the original typescripts. So the first recorded evidence for the expression 'magic!' (meaning 'great!' or 'fantastic!') in the *OED* comes from the unpublished typescript of the film *The Long Arm*, dated from 1956 – considerably earlier than the first examples from a regular printed source. 'Don't call us, we'll call you' is similarly first attested in the script of Billy Wilder's *Some Like It Hot* of 1959.

For a dictionary of contemporary English, this historical documentation is unnecessary. It is enough that modern records of a term are found – or maybe even known to the editorial staff – but for the *OED* the concept of 'authority' is slightly different. In weighing whether it is necessary to rely on archived occurrences of a word, it is necessary to consider the alternative. Hearsay or remembered evidence is problematic: how reliable is a correspondent who recalls using 'magic!' to mean 'great!' at school fifty years ago? If one such example is accepted, what of the next? Lexical analysis would be built like a house of cards, awaiting any one of these correspondents to retract their evidence and consider that they may have been mistaken. The most that it is possible to do is what Murray did at 'canard', first recorded in print in 1864: 'I saw the word in print before 1850', or to note tentatively – if the evidence seems to be reliable – that a word is said to have been used at some time prior to the first attested record.

The problem of the web

Much the same applies to musical lyrics, although these are more comprehensively archived than film scripts. The first recorded evidence for the verb 'to conga' in the *OED* dates from the sheet music of the song 'I came, I saw, I conga'd' in 1941; and the first record of the expression 'what's (something) all about?' dates from a popular song *The Love Bug Will Bite You* of 1937. Album sleeve-notes are also good citable and archived sources of song material.

One area which is presenting problems to lexicographers today is the reliability of data posted or published on the world-wide web as citable source material. Print sources provide an index documenting when a word may first have been used – though almost all will have been used earlier in speech. But nowadays some usages originate in email and other electronic forms of communication. Is the transient medium of the web a reliable source for historical dictionaries? If it is disallowed, then lexicographers will be missing the opportunity to record early usages of terms and syntactic patterns which may become central to the language in the future.

In the mid-1980s the *OED* was informed on a number of occasions that 'flaming' (or sending hostile email messages – similar to the later 'spamming', or sending out junk mail electronically) was widely used on the internet – but at the time there were no traditional records of the expression in the *Dictionary*'s card or computer files. Copies of contemporaneous emails were produced to substantiate the term's longevity, and we were challenged to consider it for inclusion in the *Dictionary*.

In this and similar cases we determined that we could cite our first archived record of the term, and note the date at which the usage was said to originate. But doubts remained about whether this was the ideal solution. The internet is still a new medium of communication and of information dissemination, and it does not yet have a reliable method of archiving itself. Some texts may appear more established, and better archived, than others. Amongst these are online versions of printed texts published by traditional book and journal publishers (indeed, the *OED* itself has been available in this format since March 2000). At present, this variety of text is accepted by the *OED* as citable – though not in preference to more traditional sources if the option is available.

Email is more difficult still. There is no doubt that email sources provide evidence for lexical items which are difficult to find elsewhere, but a correspondent who supplies a file copy of an earlier email has the opportunity to edit it in advance, in order to manufacture a historical record. In the conservative world of historical lexicography, there is always the chance that by this means the linguistic record could be corrupted.

Similarly, text on a personal web page can be a very useful source of information about the language, but the question of reliability remains. Web pages come and go. The scholar wishing to reverify information provided by a historical dictionary may not have access in the future to web pages referred to as 'authorities' today.

These are difficult issues, and ones for which there is as yet no final answer. At present the *OED* is prepared to cite evidence from the date at which that evidence became available to the *Dictionary*, and to regard earlier claims in much the same light as hearsay oral evidence. This is regarded by some as a policy which is too conservative. But it is also a view shared by traditional archivists and librarians. In order to maintain a knowledge framework within which information is datable and (as far as possible) accurate, it seems that at present it is not possible to be less circumspect. As time passes, the web will perhaps offer a more regulated archive, or lexicographers may develop alternative methods of recording material of this nature, but in the meantime reliable authority today is a much broader concept than it was one hundred years ago – in keeping with general notions of what is acceptable as a record of the language – but there are still areas of dispute which have yet to be resolved. At present the *OED* is actively assessing the problem in the hope that in future the gates of reliability can be pushed further open, but until then they remain only guardedly ajar.

References

Johnson, S. (1755) *A Dictionary of the English Language*, London.

Murray, K. M. E. (1977) *Caught in the Web of Words: James A. H. Murray and the Oxford English Dictionary*, New Haven, CT, and London: Yale University Press.

Oxford English Dictionary (1989) 2nd edn, vols 1–20, prepared by J. A. Simpson and E. S. C. Weiner, Oxford: Clarendon Press.

20   From Armageddon to war

The vocabulary of terrorism

Jean Aitchison

Introduction

On 11 September 2001, two planes intentionally crashed into the New York World Trade Center, whose twin towers burst into flames and collapsed, resulting in multiple deaths. Ever since, onlookers – both those present, and those who watched film and television representations – have struggled to describe these events, and their aftermath.

Several linguistic questions arise. First, how were these unprecedented events described by politicians and the media? Second, did 11 September trigger exceptional language, produced in an exceptional way, or does/did the language used reflect normal reportage, and ordinary linguistic processes? Finally, are the descriptions likely to have a permanent effect on the language? These points will be discussed below.

Reports and comments on the attacks were voluminous. It was impossible to keep track of every one published or broadcast. This chapter is based on a *Guardian Special* which reprinted over twenty separate accounts and comments, published in *The Guardian* soon after the attacks (Guardian 2001); a BBC book *The Day that Shook the World* (Baxter and Downing 2001) which contains fifteen papers assessing and analysing the situation pre- and post-11 September; and miscellaneous other reports, culled from various newspapers and the internet in the days and weeks following 11 September.

Descriptions of the attacks

Language loomed large as a topic following the terrorist attacks. The response of the American President George Bush made headline news. He swiftly made some 'off-the-cuff', unconsidered comments, which were later replaced by more thoughtful, presumably scripted, responses.

As a first reaction, Bush spoke of a 'national *tragedy*', and of his determination to hunt down 'those *folks* responsible', a word which to him meant presumably 'people'. Unfortunately, to many of his listeners, the term had a somewhat friendly, non-serious feel. This was presumably explained to Bush, and the word *folks* was not repeated.

On the evening of the attacks, Bush spoke of *evil*: 'Thousands of lives were suddenly ended by *evil*', 'Today our nation saw *evil*'. As one commentator noted: 'Mr Bush, with help from his writers, was beginning to find a voice. From "folks" to "evil" in one day was an important semantic step' (Paul Reynolds in Baxter and Downing 2001: 88).

Early on, Bush used the label *war*: 'We're at *war*. There's been a *war* declared'. This term met with criticism:

> A fundamental mistake was made . . . when President George W. Bush was persuaded by his advisers to declare that his country was at war. Language is important. If a nation is at war, everything is changed. Talk of war creates a ready-made set of expectations that may not be met . . . It tells us that the solution is military.
>
> (John Humphrys, *Sunday Times*, 28 March 2002)

The word *war* was retained, but was amended to *war against terrorism*, on the grounds that in a war, an enemy is required. Bush asserted that this was a *real war*, not just another version of 'the war on drugs' or 'the war on crime'. At an early stage, he described it as a *crusade*, a term which he did not repeat after the likelihood of it offending the Arab world was pointed out to him.

America then placed itself at the helm of an 'international coalition against terror'. *Justice* rather than *punishment* was called for, and the campaign was at first named 'Operation Infinite Justice' by Bush. But this label could be seen as an insult to Muslims, who believe that only Allah can mete out infinite justice, it was pointed out. The campaign was therefore renamed 'Operation Enduring Freedom', with Bush stating that the enemies of America were the 'enemies of freedom'.

Bush's language therefore illustrates the linguistic confusion which surrounded such an unprecedented event. His condemnation was clear, though the terminology required to describe it took time to evolve.

Numerous non-Americans also condemned the attacks. A spokesperson from Egypt described them as *heinous and unimaginable*; one from Jordan spoke of *horrible terrorist attacks*; one from Saudi Arabia said they were *inhuman*, and against all religious values; one from Syria denounced the *appalling attacks* on innocent civilians; Colonel Gaddafi of Libya spoke of *horrific attacks*; and President Muhammed Khatami of Iran spoke of his deep regret at the *terrorist killing* of large numbers of defenceless people (Barnaby Mason, in Baxter and Downing 2001: 129–30).

Similarly, journalists and other commentators flailed around seeking for adequate language to cope with the situation:

> Oddly, for all the media coverage . . . the events in New York, Washington and Pennsylvania have not yet found a name. Atrocity, outrage, terrorist attack: nothing quite conveys the enormity of it all, and 'apocalypse' is overdoing it a little in the absence of four horsemen. The French vision of 'megacatastrophe' comes close.
>
>   (Douglas Fraser, *Sunday Herald*, 30 September 2001)

Almost all of the words used were well known. Only one apparent neologism occurred, *deathscape*, presumably formed by analogy after *landscape*:

> Fire escapes were gnarled and twisted . . . Through this *deathscape*, firemen and medics now worked with crazed zeal.
>
>   (Michael Ellison and Ed Vulliamy, *The Guardian*, 12 September 2001)

Nouns and adjectives predominated in the descriptions. In the data examined, over forty different nouns relating to shock, horror, death and violence were found:

> abomination(-s), anguish, apocalypse, Armageddon, assault, atrocity(ies), attack(s), barbarism, calamity, carnage, cataclysm, catastrophe, crime, crisis, cruelty, death, deathscape, destruction, devastation, disaster, evil, fanaticism, hatred, horror, inferno, massacre, murder, nightmare, nihilism, obscenity, onslaught, outrage, rage, savagery, shocks, slaughter, suicide, terror, terrorism, tragedy, violence, war.

These nouns sometimes occurred unqualified, for example:

> It was an *apocalypse*
>   (unnamed survivor, quoted by Michael Ellison and Ed Vulliamy,
>   *The Guardian*, 12 September 2001)

> The pedestrians seemed to be realising that they had survived a *catastrophe*.
>   (Jay McInerney, *The Guardian*, 15 September 2001)

More usually, one or more of over thirty adjectives accompanied these and other nouns (such as the unemotive *event*), some of them derived from the nouns. The adjectives mostly expressed horror and suprise:

> amazing, apocalyptic, appalling, atrocious, barbaric, brutal, cataclysmic, deadly, dehumanising, demented, devastating, evil, explosive, heinous, horrible, horrific, immense, inexplicable, insane, malignant, monstrous, murderous, searing, shocking, spectacular, terrible, terrorist, traumatic,

unbelievable, unconscionable, ungraspable, unimaginable, unprecedented, unspeakable, vast

For example:

This has been an ungraspable tragedy.

> (Matthew Engel, *The Guardian*, 13 September 2001)

Who could blame the Americans for demanding some type of recompense . . . for the hitherto *unimaginable crime* that had been committed against them?

> (Hugo Young, *The Guardian*, 13 September 2001)

The following three dozen or so qualifier-noun sequences occurred (in alphabetical order of the qualifiers), some of them as two-word descriptions, others as part of longer sequences:

apocalyptic atrocity, apocalyptic nihilism, appalling attacks, atrocious ingenuity, barbaric terrorism, bloody act, cataclysmic abominations, catastrophic morning, deadly accomplices, deadly sequence, dehumanising hatred, demented sophistication, devastating attack, devastating toll, evil fanatics, explosive destruction, fanatical assault, frenzied fanaticism, hate crime, immense catastrophe, insane courage, kamikaze attacks, kamikaze planes, malignant rage, mass murder, monstrous calling-card, murderous martyrdom, murderous violence, searing experience, shocking act, terrible act, terrible atrocity, terrible thing, terror attacks, terrorism crisis, terrorist atrocity, terrorist attack, terrorists' rage, terrorist tragedy, Tuesday's terror, ungraspable tragedy, unimaginable crime, unspeakable evil, vast horror.

A number of longer descriptions (three or more words) were found, for example:

We were watching *death on an unbelievable scale*

> (Ian McEwan, *The Guardian*, 12 September 2001)

brutal indiscriminate mass murder

> (A. C. Grayling, *The Guardian*, 15 September 2001)

the largest ever massacre on US soil

> (Seumas Milne, *The Guardian*, 13 September 2001)

the most terrible atrocity the world has witnessed

> (*The Observer*, 14 October 2001)

an evil, bloody act that left thousands dead
> (Rebecca McClelland, *Sunday Times*, 11 November 2001)

Other longish descriptive phrases were:

> appalling homicidal stunt, big terrible event, carnage and sudden death, cult of murderous martyrdom, day of mass murder, deadly sequence of hijackings, east coast carnage, great human disaster, hatred-fuelled fanaticism, horrific suicide attacks, inexplicable assault on freedom and democracy, most searing experience in American life in modern times, orgy of fresh developments, spectacular terrorist attack, spectacular terrorist exploit, suicide hijacker attacks on America, terrible thing that has been done to America, unconscionable suicide attacks, unprecedented and devastating attacks of Sepember 11th, worst terrorist atrocity ever on American soil.

Many of the phrases found were polysyllabic. Of the two-word sequences listed on page 196, over thirty contained at least one word of three or more syllables. In over ten of them, both words had three or more syllables:

> apocalyptic atrocity (5–4), apocalyptic nihilism (5–3), atrocious ingenuity (3–5), barbaric terrorism (3–3), cataclysmic abominations (4–5), demented sophistication (3–5), explosive destruction (3–3), murderous martyrdom (3–3), murderous violence (3–3), terrorist tragedy (3–3), ungraspable tragedy (4–3).

The words used were mostly well-established ones. What characterized them was their variety and accumulation.

Figurative language was rare. Metaphor was not a prominent feature, unless 'dead' metaphors such as *nightmare*, *apocalypse* were included in the count.

An exception was an article by Fergal Keane, discussing 'The mind of the terrorist' (in Baxter and Downing 2001). He referred to 'the dark corridor of the terrorist mind' (ibid.: 62), and quoted a line from W. B. Yeats:

> The heart fed on fantasy, grown brutal from the fare
>
> (ibid.: 55)

Similes also were sparse: 'We . . . watched the Twin Towers being smashed, like a child's toy', said Orla Guerin (Baxter and Downing 2001: 144), but this was an exceptional description.

Alliteration (adjacent words beginning with similar sounds) was found intermittently:

> apocalyptic atrocity, appalling attacks, frenzied fanaticism, murderous

martyrdom, synchronized slaughter, terrorist tragedy, the twin-towers tragedy, Tuesday's terror.

Fewer verbs were used to describe the events, though some indicating harm and death occurred:

The aim was to *torture* tens of thousands and to *terrify* hundreds of millions.
(Martin Amis, *The Guardian*, 18 September 2001)

People we don't know *massacred* people who we do
(Arundhati Roy, *The Guardian*, 29 September 2001)

Other verbs referred to the suddenness of the event, and to shock and breakage:

The crisis that *burst* on the world on September 11th
(Mike Wooldridge, in Baxter and Downing 2001: 128)

the explosive destruction that *shattered* the world we thought we had known before
(Stephen Evans, in Baxter and Downing 2001: 34)

Two books were published with titles containing the word *shook*: *The Day that Shook the World* (Baxter and Downing 2001); *Two Hours that Shook the World* (Halliday 2002).

From the beginning, words for the attack were more prevalent than labels for the attackers. The perpetrators were at first a mystery. They were referred to as:

enemies of freedom, evil fanatics, extremists, a handful of madmen, hijackers, suicide attackers, suicide bombers, suicide terrorists, terrorists, Tuesday's attackers.

When their identity was revealed, the descriptions became more specific:

the September 11th terrorist Mohammed Atta and his deadly accomplices, the suicide terrorist Mohammed Atta.

Reference to the event itself homed in almost immediately on the date, 11 September:

shocks such as September 11th, the attacks of September 11th, the catastrophe of September 11th, the crisis of September 11th, the crisis that burst on the world on September 11th, the events of September 11th, the September 11th attacks, the September 11th atrocities, the synchronized slaughter of September 11th.

Occasionally, the word *Tuesday* was used: 'Bloody Tuesday', 'Tuesday's apocalypse', 'Tuesday's terror. But several months later, it was the date which was
still fixated upon:

> 9/11 has become international shorthand for a catastrophic morning in
> the United States . . . The two numbers have entered the vocabulary of
> horror.
>
> (Siri Hustvedt, *The Observer*, 10 March 2002)

The immediate location of the attacks, the cordoned-off area where the towers
once stood, was christened *Ground Zero*, reportedly by the rescue services:
'Ground Zero, the epicentre of the disaster that struck New York' (Sarah
Baxter, *Sunday Times*, 23 September 2001). The term *Ground Zero* dates from
1946, and is 'that part of the ground situated immediately under an exploding
bomb, especially a nuclear one (for maximum effect, nuclear bombs are deton-
ated before they actually hit the ground)' (Ayto 1999: 279) – though the
phrase is sometimes used more widely to describe an area devastated by a
bomb or other explosion.

Some reports referred to the attacks on the 'Towers' or the 'Twin Towers':
'Terror at the Towers' ran a *Sunday Times* headline (16 September 2001). Further
location of the attacks was only sometimes specified, as, for example: 'the
horror brought down on Washington and New York' (Olga Guerin, in Baxter
and Downing 2001: 145). Sometimes the event was referred to in even broader
terms, as: 'America's tragedy', 'last week's American tragedy', and 'the attacks
on the US'.

A further characteristic of the language used was its attempt to appear
'factual'. 'Factoids' (pseudo-facts) can be defined as 'facts which have no existence before appearing in a magazine or newspaper' (Norman Mailer, 1973,
quoted in Ayto 1999: 473). The death toll was at first the focus of absurdly pessimistic guesswork, which gradually became more realistic:

> 6,818 are feared to have died (Deutsche Presse-Agentur and *Sunday Times*,
> 23 September 2001)
> Dead and missing in US reach 5,350 (*Sunday Times*, 16 September 2001)
> Over 4,000 fatalities (Jack Straw, BBC Radio Four *Today* Programme,
> January 2002)
> 2,672 death certificates have been issued. A further 158 people are unac-
> counted for (*The Observer*, 10 March 2002)

In the early stages also, a number of unsubstantiated superlatives were bandied
about:

largest ever massacre on US soil; most searing experience in American life in modern times; most spectacular terrorist attack on the United States; most terrible atrocity the world has witnessed; worst terrorist atrocity ever on American soil

To summarize this section, the language used was composed of mostly everyday words. A significant characteristic was the large number of different lexical items involved, all relating to disaster and tragedy. These were often polysyllabic, and were frequently combined into longer sequences. Neologisms and figurative language were rare, and gruesome 'facts' were exaggerated.

The next section discusses the extent to which this language is normal, or abnormal.

Normal or abnormal?

Newspapers prioritize shock-horror stories: 'Real honest-to goodness life, with murders and catastrophes . . . happens almost exclusively in newspapers', the French playwright Jean Anouilh once wrote.[1] So the topic of the Twin Towers was newspaper fodder of the highest order.

The 'weightiness' (polysyllabicity) of the words used to describe the events of 11 September was noticeable. This reflected the gravity of the event. It illustrates a well-known iconic tendency in language: 'heavy' acts or large numbers tend to be represented by 'heavy' words, the most obvious example being that in almost all languages, plurals are longer than singulars (Haiman 1985; Nänny and Fischer 1999). So an established tendency towards iconicity was exploited, rather than invented.

Traumatic events may trigger new vocabulary items. Yet new words are not normally necessary, except in the case of new technology. Of the multiple new words spawned in the two World Wars (1914–18 and 1939–45), those that have survived mostly relate to novel technology: *air-raid, anti-aircraft, bomber, camouflage, chemical warfare, depth charge, dogfight, gas mask, incendiary bomb, mustard gas, U-boat*, are among those which are still heard today from World War I. *Air-lift, blitz, bomb-site, doodlebug, flying bomb, heliport, jeep, paratroops, radar, Sten gun, strafe*, are among those still around from World War II (Ayto 1999). General, non-technical terms dating from these wars are far fewer in number.

The 11 September attacks did not involve any new technology, they represented use (or misuse) of existing resources, so this may be why new words were so rare.

Murders and disasters do not need to be dramatized, they are already dramatic. A glance at any newspaper shows that the more dramatic the story, the fewer literary devices are needed to gild it. The highest count of metaphors, and the largest proportion of 'disaster' words tend to be found in the least dramatic sections of the newspaper, for example, finance and sports, which are felt to need 'pepping up':

> In a history of *disasters* stretching across 30 years, Scotland has been plagued by *calamity*, lapses in concentration and self-induced *tragedy*. The goalkeeper is always to blame, and always will be.
>
> (Cosgrove 1991)

The lexical item *disaster*, as with other disaster words such as *catastrophe*, *calamity*, *tragedy*, is sometimes thought to have 'weakened', since it can also be used for a lost sports match, a wet hat or an unappetizing meal (examples from the British National Corpus):

> To get a panama hat wet is to court *disaster*. The hat becomes limp and shapeless.

> The gravy's a *disaster*. It's got too much fat in it.

Yet a more recent viewpoint is that a word such as *disaster* has not so much weakened as 'layered', that is, developed multiple layers of meaning and become polysemous (Hopper and Traugott 1993).

The *disaster* words used in descriptions of 11 September represented their main, and older, dictionary meanings, where a *disaster* is 'a sudden event such as an accident or natural catastrophe that causes great damage or loss of life' (*New Oxford Dictionary of English* 1998). No evidence exists that 11 September has in any sense hastened the layering, it possibly simply reminded some people of the older, serious usage.

Words that have layered usually leave some subtle linguistic clues as to which meaning is intended. In the past few years, major disasters have mostly been identified by the geographical location of the incident: *the Bradford football disaster*, *the Hillsborough disaster*, *the Lockerbie disaster*, *the Warrington IRA atrocity*, *the Zeebrugge ferry disaster* (Aitchison 2001; Aitchison 2003; Aitchison and Lewis in press).

Occasionally the date has been added to the place, as: *the 1986 Chernobyl nuclear disaster*. Even more occasionally, a date only has been used as identification: *The 'Bloody Friday' atrocity of 21st July 1972*.

The events of 11 September are therefore not unique in being labeled primarily by the date, but they are one of only a few single day disasters which have been given a date description – though major wars, such as the 1914–18 war, are often identified by their date. So date labelling exploits a possibility readily available in the language. Because it is a not-often used possibility, it serves to mark out 11 September as notable.

Another word which has remained associated with 11 September is *terrorist*. The term *terrorist* (from French *terroriste*) re-emerged into general use in 1947 to mean a member of a clandestine or expatriate organization aiming to coerce an established government by acts of violence against it or its subjects (Ayto 1999: 310). It is now generally used to mean 'someone who spreads terror', alongside the noun *terrorism*.

Terrorist and *terrorism* were labels given by politicians from the earliest official reports of 11 September. Mayor Giuliani commented on the afternoon of the attacks:

> the people of New York are much stronger than *barbaric terrorism*.
> (quoted by Michael Ellison and Ed Vulliamy, *The Guardian*,
> 12 September 2001)

The terms *terror*, *terrorism* and *terrorist* have remained widely used on both sides of the Atlantic. Six months on, the BBC (British Broadcasting Corporation) was remembering 'the biggest *terrorist* attack ever seen', and Bush also was stressing that *terrorism* can never win.

Conclusion

Overall, the events of 11 September are unlikely to have a major effect on the English language. A general observation on language change is that a language tends to throw out numerous different variants, in a 'multiple births' situation (Aitchison 2001). Then these get whittled down. This is normal, linguistic behaviour. The multiple descriptions spawned by the terrorists' attacks have now been narrowed down to an agreed way of talking about them, which has only slightly shifted the language from what it was.

The events may have reminded readers of some 'catastrophe' words which were rarely used, such as *apocalypse*, *cataclysm*. The word *outrage* figured prominently, partly because it was used in two senses: the attack itself was an *outrage*, and people felt *outrage* (anger) at what had happened. The phrase *Ground Zero* is likely to have become more widely known, though with the label attached to a particular location. And the description of major catastrophic events by the date may become more likely. These are minor alterations.

The overwhelming final feeling of many is that words are unable to do justice to the emotions aroused by the events. As the nineteenth-century writer Samuel Butler once wrote:

We want words to do more than they can . . . we expect them to help us to grip and dissect that which in ultimate essence is ungrippable as shadow. Nevertheless there they are; we have got to live with them.

(Butler, quoted in Crystal and Crystal 2000: 188)

Note

1   Anouilh (1950, Act III).

References

Aitchison, J. (2001) *Language Change: Progress or Decay?* 3rd edn, Cambridge: Cambridge University Press.

—— (2003) *Words in the Mind: An Introduction to the Mental Lexicon*, 3rd edn, Oxford: Blackwell.

—— and Lewis, D. M. (in press) 'Polysemy and bleaching', in B. Nerlich *et al.* (eds) *Polysemy: Patterns of Meaning in Mind and Language*, Berlin: Mouton de Gruyter.

Anouilh, J. (1950) *La répétition*, Geneva: La Palatine.

Ayto, J. (1999) *Twentieth Century Words*, Oxford: Oxford University Press.

Baxter, J. and Downing, M. (2001) *The Day that Shook the World: Understanding September 11th*, London: BBC Worldwide Ltd.

Cosgrove, S. (1991) *Hampden Babylon*, Edinburgh: Canongate Press.

Crystal, D. and Crystal, H. (2000) *Words on Words: Quotations about Language and Languages*, London: Penguin.

The Guardian (2001) *September 11: A* Guardian *Special*, London: Guardian Newspapers.

Haiman, J. (1985) *Natural Syntax: Iconicity and Erosion*, Cambridge: Cambridge University Press.

Halliday, F. (2002) *Two Hours that Shook the World. September 11, 2001: Causes and Consequences*, London: Saqi Books.

Hopper, P. and Traugott, E. C. (1993) *Grammaticalization*, Cambridge: Cambridge University Press.

Nänny, M. and Fischer, O. (eds) (1999) *Form Miming Meaning: Iconicity in Language and Literature*, Amsterdam: John Benjamins.

Index